The Sea and Man

THE SEA

Jorma Pohjanpalo

AND MAN

translated by Diana Tullberg

5D
STEIN AND DAY/*Publishers*/New York

Translation subsidized from the funds
for the promotion of Finnish literature

Translation copyright © 1970 by Stein and Day, Incorporated
Copyright © by Jorma Pohjanpalo as *Meri ja ihminen*
Library of Congress Catalog Card No. 79-104633
All rights reserved
Published simultaneously in Canada by Saunders of Toronto, Ltd.
Printed in Finland by the Otava Publishing Co., Helsinki 1970
Stein and Day/Publishers/7 East 48 Street, New York, N.Y. 10017
SBN 8128-1303-0

Contents

- 7 Foreword
- 9 The seas: the salty cradle of life
- 23 Man learns to move around on the water
- 34 From native haunts to wider horizons
- 76 The conquest of the seas
- 102 From sail to steam
- 158 Passenger ships in ocean service
- 181 Cargo ships in world shipping
- 199 The birth of a modern ship
- 219 Harbors: links between land and sea
- 246 Merchant shipping: its forms and cargoes
- 256 The outlook for world shipping
- 270 The underwater world and its exploration
- 285 The fruits and treasures of the sea
- 303 Bibliography
- 305 Index

Foreword

Ever since the beginning of time the sea has been of vital importance to our tiny planet as it spins through the vastness of the universe. Water covers almost three-quarters of the entire surface of the globe, so that even our greatest continents are in fact but islands in the world sea.

The ancient sea, several billion years old, is the cradle of mankind's eventful process of evolution. Adapting himself as best he could to his land environment, man gradually learned to make tools and various necessities, among them forms of water transport. From tree trunks, rafts, dugouts, and other primitive vessels, he eventually learned how to build real craft, and thus sea-going ships.

Seafaring is an ancient art, and the utilization of waterways—specifically the seas—has throughout time been a vital prerequisite for interaction between nations. The great voyages of discovery at the beginning of the modern age opened up world-wide horizons to navigation and offered exciting opportunities for men fearless, resourceful, and enterprising enough to seize them. The world economy would never have developed to its present level without the potential provided by shipping. In spite of the rapid advances made by land and air transport recently, the seas have still preserved their significance as essential traffic routes, particularly for the transportation of bulk goods. Fast, modern, mammoth craft ply the world seas; nuclear energy is making rapid progress as a source of marine power; before long more and more shipping will be submarine.

Ships have often changed the course of history, and they have molded the economic growth of nations and continents. Sea battles have been of vital significance for the fates of peoples ever since the pre-Christian era. It is rarely recognized how great a role mastery of the sea has played in political and military history. Still less is there general awareness of the steady work quietly done by shipping over the centuries, work whose value can hardly be overestimated.

With their vast and multitudinous natural resources the seas also comprise a reserve of raw materials which has unimagined potential. As other raw material sources begin to dry up and production costs soar, the intelligent utilization of these resources will become more vital. If we wish to provide enough food for the world's booming population, we must resort on a far wider scale to intelligent farming of the sea and its fruits.

The subject matter of this book is

of universal interest, yet, like the history of mankind, so broad and complex that any attempt to treat of it must perforce be perfunctory and unbalanced in many respects. Even so, this work aims at providing a comprehensive survey of the importance of the sea, and specifically of peaceful shipping, to mankind — yesterday, today and tomorrow. Our lives and our prosperity still depend on the sea. It is a fact that we would all do well to keep in mind.

The Finnish original of this book appeared in spring 1969. The English translation is practically identical, though some local matters connected mainly with Finland or the other Scandinavian countries have been excluded as of insufficient interest to foreign readers. As far as has proved possible, certain changes and additions have also been made to ensure that the information given is as up-to-date as possible.

Helsinki, January 1970

Jorma Pohjanpalo

The seas — the salty cradle of life

The mystery of the origin of the world has fascinated speculative minds since the beginning of time. All kinds of hypotheses and theories have been put forward. A quarter of a century ago, it began to be generally accepted that everything is constituted of hydrogen, which accounts for two-thirds of the composition of water. In the end, we know, there is only one entity — the "universum," composed as it is of innumerable separate atoms.

In the antique world, it was the Greeks who learned most about the world itself. For a long time educated Greeks believed that the world was a flat plate surrounded by an ocean, with a semispherical firmament above. Even Thales (c. 600 B.C.), who is said to be the first real Western philosopher and the father of the natural sciences, thought that water was the basic element of the cosmos, the universal substance. He believed that everything was made of water and that to water everything would in time return. In his *History of Western Philosophy* Bertrand Russell says that this supposition must by no means be considered foolish as a scientific hypothesis. Right up to the sixteenth century men believed that the earth was the center of a small and relatively straightforward universe.

The watery face of our planet

Our planet, circling the sun in the cosmos, is highly water-dominated. A mere glance at a globe or a map of the world is enough to show how very surrounded we are by sea. Water in fact covers almost three-quarters of the total surface of the earth; even the bigger continents are just islands in the embrace of the world sea. The continents are grouped on the globe so as to give the southern hemisphere much more sea than the northern — 81 per cent of its surface area. Not that the northern hemisphere — with over 60 per cent water — is exactly dry. If the surface of the earth were smooth, it would be covered all over with water to a depth of about 8 feet.

The vast waters of the earth are divided mainly into oceans. These oceans (modern geographers say there are only three: the Atlantic, the Indian Ocean, and the Pacific) are in fact the great "open waters" of the world sea. In round figures, and including the lakes, the seas of the world are estimated to hold almost 336 million cubic miles of water. The total volume of the continents and islands above sea level is comparatively rather slight,

Don Quixote and Sancho Panza riding through the universe.
Woodcut by Gustave Doré (1832–1883). Musée des Beaux-Arts, Strasbourg.

only about 1/11 of the volume of water in the sea. Compared with the other members of the solar system, Earth can with good reason be called the sea water planet. As far as is known at present, no other planet has this coating of water. Geologically, the sea is the most important cause and instrument of the earth's internal and external mutations.

What do we know about the genesis of water and oceans on our planet back in the dawn of time? Four basic hypotheses accounting for the origin of the universe have been formulated. Though they differ, all contain so many points of contact with the Genesis story of the creation that this can be taken as an allegorical account of the beginning of the world.

To get some idea of how the seas were formed means going back to the very early days of our planet. According to present scientific opinion, our section of space (our Milky Way, to which the sun and its circling planets belong) came into existence some five to seven billion years ago.

The world and the formation of the seas

Astronomers, geologists, and chemists, in particular, have put in a lot of work trying to give a rough age for the earth. The salinity of ocean water, the moon's annual 5-inch withdrawal from earth, the gradual cooling of our globe and the slow breaking-down of radioactive substances in rocks and meteorites are all factors indicating that the earth is several thousand million years old. Each scientist has his own time system, but their final figures seem to agree fairly well. With the aid of a great deal of geological evidence, especially the properties of a group of three radioactive substances found in meteorites, the general estimate now widely accepted is that the earth's solid crust is four and a half to five billion years old. The world sea must be roughly the same age.

There are many possible explanations for the origin of Earth—it could, for instance, be a cast-off from Mother Sun—but most theories share the belief that the earth first started as a vast circular concentration of cold gas and cosmic dust which gradually took shape by centrifugal force. Fairly soon, under the influence of pressure and radioactive forces, it began to get hot. At one time the earth was so hot right through that all the water now in the oceans hovered in the atmosphere in the form of a thick cloud. Gradually, as the globe cooled down again, the gases condensed into liquid, and the matter separated into various layers. The outermost layer formed the earth's crust, which is only some 18 miles thick on the average. Centuries of heavy rain probably produced rivers, lakes, and seas on its surface, thus giving the earth's crust its covering of water, the hydrosphere, which includes not only the actual surface water, but also the moisture in the ground and rocks.

There have been other hypotheses about the early stages of water condensation. It has, for instance, been suggested that a "boundary line surface" was produced, with a layer of water below ("the ocean") and a layer of gas above ("the atmosphere"). Ever since, there has been a continuous condensation process, with the waters of the ocean increasing and the pressure of the atmosphere decreasing.

Map of the world from Homer's time, 1000 B.C.

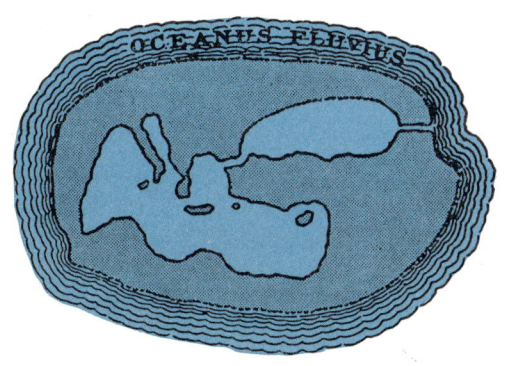

Some scientists claim that the first seas were only slightly saline and that the salinity of the seas has risen over countless ages, as the original source of the seas' salinity was probably the base rock of the continents. When the first great rainfalls began, they started a long process of crumbling, dissolving, and wearing down the crust of the newly formed earth, washing myriads of mineral particles into the water. Another scientific hypothesis is that the salts produced during volcanic activity passed into the sea just as it was beginning to form on the slowly cooling earth's surface and that the sea has been fairly salty right from the start.

Another fascinating theory relates the origin of the seas to that of the moon, Earth's child. Some geophysicists believe that due to the pull of the sun, two tremendous tidal waves circled the semi-solid surface of the earth. The one on the sun side eventually built up to such a height that the equilibrium was shattered, and the sun's attraction tore a great lump of the earth's thin crust away, probably where the Pacific is now; by the laws of gravity, this lump started to circle the earth in its own orbit. The fair-sized depression where the moon had been wrenched away gradually filled in and formed the Pacific trough. According to some hypotheses, the remaining earth's crust slowly moved

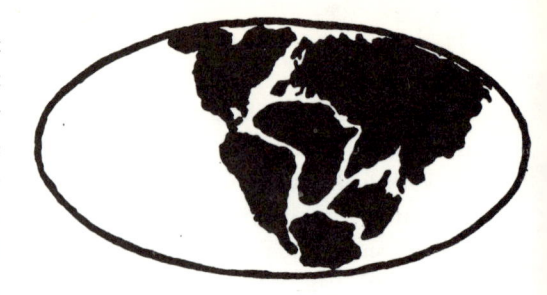

The rough outlines of the breaking-up process that took place in the earth's crust after the separation of the moon.

to fill in this depression and as it shifted around in various directions split to form the Atlantic.

The rock bed of the floor of the Pacific is basalt, the characteristic material of the middle layer of the earth's crust, whereas the floor of the other oceans is granite, the rock typical of the surface of the globe. This fact, too, supports the view that it was the granite floor of the Pacific that tore away to form the moon. If the moon really originated this way, there must be a significant connection between this fact and the formation of troughs and land shelves in our present oceans.

Many geologists believe that in the distant past all the continents formed one great land mass and that forces inside the earth made this gigantic continent split up into several parts. Over half a century ago the German meteorologist and geophysicist Alfred Wegener put forward his famous continental drift theory.

If we examine an atlas we soon notice that the west coast of Africa and the east coast of South America are the same shape. This fact has given scientists food for thought for centuries, but Alfred Wegener was the first properly trained researcher to tackle the problem from many sides. After studying the ancient flora and fauna of West Africa and South America and their bed rock, Wegener published his continental drift theory in 1912. This proposes that originally all the continents were one great continent — Pangaia — which then broke up, the various pieces drifting away to their present positions. Numerous facts support this hypothesis. Paleomagnetism has recently produced some very convincing evidence of continent movement. At the moment many scientists agree that South America, Africa, Australia, and Antarctica were originally one continent — which they call Gondwana — and that North Europe, Europe, and most of Asia formed another, called Laurasia.

According to modern measurement the movement of the continents, and thus the formation of the Atlantic, did not begin until some two hundred million years ago. This theory is not unanimously accepted, however. A few years ago the Finnish Professor Aarno Niini put forward his own cosmogonic theory about continental drift. This suggests that the continents were originally one homogeneous conglomeration, but that they have separated under the influence of violent upheavals on one side of the globe.

The beginnings of life

All through the ages philosophers and naturalists, especially, have pondered the origin of life, "spontaneous generation." The chemical basis of life is protoplasm, the composition of which may vary greatly from one form of life to another. Half of it is, however, water, whose unique properties as a nearly universal solvent and almost immutable substance were apparently the main reason for its being the first

---

THE BEGINNING AND END OF EVERYTHING. The very winds that move over the lands have been cradled on the sea's broad expanse and seek ever to return to it. The continents themselves dissolve and pass to the sea, in grain after grain of eroded land. So the rains that rose from it return again in rivers. In its mysterious past it encompasses all the dim origins of life and receives in the end, after, it may be, many transmutations, the dead husks of that same life. For all at last return to the sea — to Oceanus, the ocean river, like the ever-flowing stream of time, the beginning and the end.

Rachel L. Carson

EROSION. This group of phenomena comprises the exogenic forces working on the earth's surface: weathering, water dissolution, and the wearing action of running water, ice, surf, and wind. All these create new forms of what already existed and result in lower relative altitudes. Running water is not only an important shaper of the earth's surface; it also plays a central part in human life. Rivers have formed excellent traffic channels throughout the ages. They have also been widely used as sources of power and for irrigation.

great cradle of life. To begin with, there were perhaps only single-celled forms, each cell consisting of a minute quantity of protoplasm with a small dense center, the nucleus.

Perhaps life began in the slime or clay that gathered long, long ago in shallow bays and the estuaries of rivers. Possibly it originated from large molecules made up of carbon atoms. The English biologist Julian Huxley compares the warm, shallow waters of the primeval world to distilling bottles, swarming with various carbon chains. Some of these carbon chains then became capable of reproduction and thus set off the eventful course of development toward ever larger and more complex forms of life. Very early in the history of the world, life was multicellular, highly progressive, and to some extent differentiated. The advance toward a vast range of plant and animal species has continued unremittingly.

Until recently photosynthesis and thus autotrophic, i.e. independent, plant life was thought to have begun about two billion years ago, on the basis of the Finnish Professor J. J. Sederhom's discovery of clay shale fossils at Aitolahti, Näsijärvi, in Finland at the end of the nineteenth century. These fossils were of plants, probably leaves, which were the product of photosynthesis. But in 1965, Professor Hans Dieter Pflug, a paleontologist at Giessen University, made a scientifically vital microfossil find in the Swaziland stone formation in East Transvaal, South Africa. Geochronological research has given these fossilized organisms, so far the oldest found, a minimum age of 3.1 billion years. The new discoveries thus date the beginnings of organic life even nearer the time that the earth itself was formed. Algae, fiber structures, and bacilli could be detected in the fossils. The algae, probably one form of primordial organism, are like all other organisms made up of molecules containing carbon and hydrogen.

Over vast periods small plants and other minor organisms developed from these simple micro-organisms. As millions of years went by, the stream of life flowed stronger and ever more complex: beings appeared which had organs for taking in and digesting food, for breathing, and for reproducing. "Sponges grew on the rocky bottom of the sea's edge and coral animals built their habitations in warm, clear waters. Jellyfish swam and drifted in the sea. Worms evolved and starfish, and hard-shelled creatures with many-jointed legs. The plants, too, progressed, from the microscopic algae to branched and curiously fruiting seaweeds that swayed with the tides and were plucked from the coastal rocks by the surf and cast adrift." This is how the American writer Rachel L. Carson, in her book *The Sea Around Us*, describes the complicated course followed by the developing organic world, a path that led to ever higher and more numerous forms of life.

Life on earth develops

Geological strata and the fossils in them reveal the main lines of plant and animal development. They also tell us how the oceans and continents were formed, how the mountains and valleys took shape as the earth's crust flexed itself, and how the climate has changed.

For three-quarters of geological time the continents were probably empty and bare, whereas the seas in that time developed simple, drifting forms of life that later left the water and lived on dry land. The earliest vertebrates, primitive species like fish, made their appearance about 500 million years ago. Plants began to spread over the ground from the water's edge, presumably somewhat over 400 million years ago. One after another they adapted

---

THE TRANSLUCENCY OF SEA WATER and its color have been given an increasing amount of attention in research. The degree of translucency depends on the amount of solid particles and surface plankton organisms in sea water. Its color ranges from blue to various shades of green. The blue appears because daylight reflects from water molecules or from tiny particles floating in the water. All the red rays and most of the yellow rays in the spectrum are absorbed from the light ray on its way to the water and back to the eye, so that our visual sense perceives mainly a cold blue light. Particles of slime and plankton floating in the water change the blue to green. For this reason coastal waters and inland seas are usually greenish, and open stretches of warm oceans a bright blue. There may be very many shades in coastal waters; milky white, yellowish, brown, red, and gray are caused by algae and large amounts of other micro-organisms.

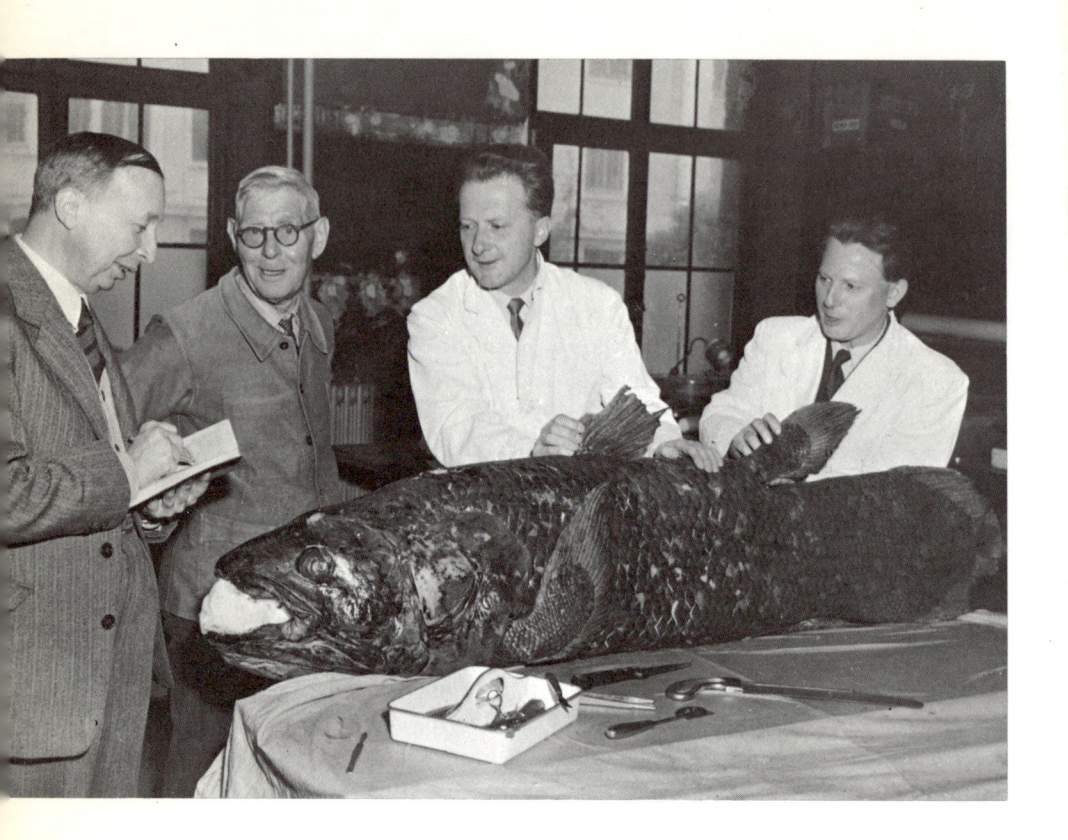

This coelacanth, *Latimeria chalumnae*, was caught near Grand Comore Island, off the East African coast, on May 4th, 1967, at a depth of 1300 feet. The sensational fish, claimed to be the oldest living vertebrate, was injected with formol to keep it intact. It was then flown to Paris, where it is shown being inspected by Professor Jacques Millot and his assistants. Scientists believe the creature to be a link in the evolution of land animals from the earlier age of fishes.

to the bleak conditions the land then offered, and thus began the process of animal evolution in this new world. The first animals to move around on land, amphibians developed from crossopterygians ("fringe-finned fish"), did so about 300 to 350 million years ago. They were followed by the first reptiles, about 100 million years later. Some reptile groups, however, like the ichthyosaurus and the plesiosaurus, were not happy on dry land and returned to the sea. The same kind of readoption of sea life has since taken place in many other animal groups. The first mammals returned to their home element—the sea—fifty to seventy million years back. Their descendants in modern times are the sea lions, seals, sea elephants, and whales. There may well be "sea monsters" larger than whales living in the ocean depths.

On December 22, 1938, African fishermen netted a rare, strange-looking fish, some five feet long and weighing over 100 pounds, at a depth of about 230 feet in the Mozambique Channel off Madagascar. Scientists identified it as a crossopterygian of the Coelacanthidae family, which fossil finds had led then to believe extinct for some sixty million years. The next individual was not caught until 1952, off the island of Anjouan in the French Comoro Archipelago in the Indian Ocean. So far some twenty-five of these living relics of the Cretaceous period have been caught in East African waters. This crossopterygian, named *Latimeria chalumnae*, is considered the closest living relation to the fish from which we believe all land vertebrates are descended. This most important zoological find of the century has also added conviction to the theory that after a long and eventful evolution, man developed from a land-adapted fish.

"When they went ashore," writes Carson, "the animals that took up a land life carried with them a part of the sea in their bodies, a heritage which they passed on to their children and which even today links each land animal with its origin in the ancient sea." The change to a life on land meant a whole series of revolutionary mutations in the fish, but on the other hand this created new potential for the evolution of vertebrates. After all, this type has progressed a great deal farther on land, both physically and mentally, than in the water. Just think of achievements like bird song and the human brain.

The development of man

All organisms evolve in order to adapt to their environment as best they can. Only the fittest emerge triumphant from the struggle for existence. The number of fossil finds throwing light on human development grows every year. Remains of primeval men, or hominids, have been found at various times since the latter part of the last century, and other surprising finds may be made in the future, too, as anthropologists search purposefully for clues that will tell us more about man's prehistory.

At the moment most scientists believe that all organisms are related and have developed from perhaps only one or two common, basic, primitive forms.

The development of man is the most recent stage in the gradual evolution of life on earth and is a unique phenomenon in its history. Several types and species in the chain of development that leads to man have disappeared in the last million years. The forefathers of man must be considered human from the time that they first learned to exercise their brains. One proof of brain activity is the use of tools. Our species—man in the widest sense of the word—has succeeded in surviving, increasing, and winning pre-eminence, thanks to constant self-improvement and amazing adaptability. Man's most recent and important improvement is the accumulation of experiences, the basic requirement of any culture.

The English scientist Sir Alister Hardy has put forward the interesting theory that primeval man once lived mainly in the water. Our distant forefathers could well have dived for shellfish and worms, caught crabs and perhaps some fish for food. They were relatively safe from terrifying predatory beasts in inshore waters or a cave on the beach. The consequences of leading this aquatic life in tropical seas, says Hardy, are still visible: it is easy to stand up in the water, so man may have learned to walk on two legs almost without noticing it as he waded along the shore; he would not need fur in the water except on top to protect him from the sun, as his head was more often above the surface of the water than under it; while he was walking or wading along, his hands were free, and gradually he learned to put them to various uses.

One indication that the human species is much older than is usually assumed is the remains of a skeleton found in 1958 in a Miocene stratum in Tuscany, Italy. The find endorses the theory of professor J. Hürzeler, the Swiss paleontologist, that there were beings reminiscent of man as well as manlike apes at least ten million years ago. Gradual environmental adjustments led from the primitive Ramapithecus man of that period to the apeman of the Australopithecus family who lived in Africa a good million years ago. The later descendants of this apeman, the Pithecanthropi, learned to use fire and to make the first tools an estimated half a million years later.[1] Anthropologists assume that Pithecanthropus, who walked upright, developed in Africa and spread into the Far East in the early Pleistocene era (Peking man).

The next recognized stage of human

---

[1] In 1967 the English anthropologist Louis Leakey found evidence east of Lake Victoria, Kenya, to show that the African forefathers of man *(Kenyapithecus wickeri)* used primitive stone axes to break up animal bones as long as twelve million years ago.

THE ICE AGE. The last Great Ice Age means that period of world history, very much colder than now, which may have begun some million years ago, in the first half of the quarternary period (Pleistocene Epoch). While this Ice Age lasted, most of Europe and North America were covered with a single great layer of ice, as Greenland and Antarctica are today. In Fenno-Scandinavia the continental ice field stretched out in all directions from the fells of Scandinavia until it covered the whole of northern Europe and a large part of central and eastern Europe, and met up with the ice fields stretching from Scotland in the west and the Urals in the east. The non-ice-covered areas of central Europe, to the north shores of the Mediterranean, were treeless tundra; southern Europe was covered with coniferous forest. During this tremendously long Ice Age there were, however, several fluctuations in climate, and geologists have distinguished three or four different glacial periods between which the climate was something like it is now. At its height the ice field covered a good half (about 9,400,000 square miles) of the continent, and in the final period the whole of Fenno-Scandinavia and large areas south of the Baltic. As it moved over the land the continental ice field rounded and smoothed the face of the rock and drew channels in it, carrying away great quantities of stone which piled up in the farthest parts of the ice field either under it (ground moraine) or at its edge (terminal moraine). There are many coastal moraine zones and related wide glacifluvial sandy heaths in North Germany and Denmark, and Finland has its Salpausselkä ridge. The continental ice field eventually started to melt around 16,000 B.C. and the edge of the ice gradually withdrew northward. Even today ice covers about 10 per cent of our land surface. The present day is thus in fact closer to the Ice Ages than to really ice-free eras. The far-reaching significance of this fact is rarely fully recognized.

evolution was Neanderthal man, who takes his name from the discovery made in a cave in the Neander Valley, near Düsseldorf, in 1856: the crown of the skull and two legs of a prehistoric man. This race, whose individuals already knew how to make an axe, a spear, and simple jewelry, spread all over Europe, from seventy to fifty thousand years ago. Finds have also been made in Siberia.

During the Great Ice Age, roughly thirty thousand years ago, a new and more advanced human race appeared in southern Europe, probably from Asia. It has been given the name Cro-Magnon after the skeleton find made in 1868 in the village of the same name in southwest France. These men, like the modern European in mental powers, were capable of extremely high achievements. It is thought that as the

Great Ice Age passed, Cro-Magnon man followed the wandering herds of reindeer toward the north.

There have, in fact, been few changes in man's appearance since the end of the Paleolithic stone age. Anthropologists are generally of the opinion that the two main human types—Neanderthal man and modern man—have developed from Pithecanthropus.

This brings us up to modern man. *Homo sapiens*, "wise man," has made some drastic changes in conditions on our planet, particularly in the last five hundred years. Changes in our ways of life, technical developments, and a rise in our lust for authority and power faster than the moral standard of our various cultures has been able to bear have led to the surprisingly shortsighted examples of despoilment and pillage, dictated by ephemeral goals, which characterize modern history.

Recent statements by some of our leading astronomers show that we are beginning to abandon the old unquestioned belief that rational, human life is not possible on any other planet. As Sir Bernard Lovell, Director of England's Jodrell Bank radioastronomy station, and many other scientists see it, innumerable observations indicate that there are millions or billions of planets that could have the basic substances needed for life—hydrogen and carbon. And where life is at all possible, life also in time develops. Meteorites show evidence of the sort of organic changes or evolution elsewhere in the cosmos that would be the prerequisite for life on other planets. Lovell is also sure that there are innumerable "old planets" where life is much more highly developed than on earth, i.e., where some kind of "super-men" have achieved a fantastically high level of intelligence, culture, and technology; compared with them, we are apemen. Lovell believes, however, that there is nothing in our own solar system similar to the human life on earth.

Man has several proofs in his own body of his earlier form and original aquatic life. In a sense the ocean still flows in his veins, a billion-year heritage from the ancient sea. Like all the other vertebrates, man's blood cells contain a solution of sodium, calcium, potassium, and magnesium in roughly the same proportion as in ocean water, though at only about half the strength. Even the protoplasm that fills all our cells has the same chemical composition as the first single-celled forms of life in the primeval sea. Perhaps our blood temperature is the same as that of the prehistoric sea from which our forefathers once emerged and gradually, slowly, evolved.

"And as life itself began in the sea," writes Carson, "so each of us begins his individual life in a miniature ocean within his mother's womb, and in the stages of his embryonic development repeats the steps by which his race evolved, from gill-breathing inhabitants of a water world to creatures able to live on land." The amniotic fluid that surrounds the sensitive tissues of the human embryo replaces the water surrounding embryonic fish; it has been called "the last relic of the sea."

Water is an essential condition of life on earth. It is vital in all our activities, breathing, digestion, blood-circulation, and glandular functions. In normal conditions plants and animals carry 60 to 90 per cent of the individual's overall weight in water. Water shares in the eternal and complex round of life by handling the transmission of the nutrients needed by organic nature both in the organism

The stormy North Sea. Photo: P. Kinnari.

and outside it. The organism gets the nutrients it needs through water. Similarly the waste products of the organism's metabolism are carried away by water.

Although over 70 per cent of man's weight is water, his daily biological water requirement is not large compared with his other water needs. Biologically, man needs only about two to three quarts of water a day — depending on the climate and what he is doing — to keep his cellular metabolism and body temperature constant. Yet he may use many hundred times that, especially if he has a high standard of living, in washing and in keeping his surroundings clean, for his work and other purposes. Our growing need for water is one of the fundamental features of modern society, and how much water we use can rightly be considered one yardstick of our living standards.

Water is one of the earth's most important natural resources, an unmatched source of power. The existence of water, or more specifically of the oceans, has permitted the great advances of world shipping. To industry, water is a vital raw material. So close is the link between water and life that the story of man's evolution could be described as his struggle for water, as Bernard Frank has put it.

Man learns to move around on the water

Immeasurably long ago, our vertebrate forefathers had already become so estranged from the water element that it took a long time and much effort before man managed to overcome the obstacle that water constituted for him. Whatever our idea of primitive man and his way of life, he in any case had to move around in his native region at an early stage. He then found himself faced with rivers, straits, pools, lakes, and seashores. If he could not cross these natural barriers by wading, he was confronted with a real problem. To begin with, man could only stand helpless on the brink.

But life means curiosity, motion, and a spirit of enterprise. The barbarians covered completely unknown regions on their hunting expeditions, using their own brute force to get their spoils from place to place. Primitive man searched for contacts outside his own restricted circle partly because he felt a need to meet his fellows, partly to exchange vital goods and experiences.

To begin with, man's only sphere of movement was dry land. If conditions were good, he could work up a fair speed and preferred to overcome obstacles by climbing rather than jumping. But the primitive peoples did not have much success adapting the vagaries of their terrain to the requirements of traffic, whereas water proved a convenient means of transport—though to begin with it limited man's freedom of movement. It obviously took man a long time to get used to water, but his ability to overcome various kinds of water barriers was one of the basic conditions for the spread of the human race. Primitive aquatic craft, weapons, the use of animal skins for clothes, and the wheel are the basic cultural achievements that pointed man's way to mastery of the globe.

Originally, the nomads probably only had to cross some minor water barrier which separated them from better pastures. Perhaps they just followed their animals' example and learned to swim.

Hand in hand with man's conquest of natural forces has been his development of tools. When he first seized a stick or stone to increase his striking power, far back in the distant past, man was using a tool for the first time as an aid in his everyday life, or as a hunting weapon, or in battle against his own kind. Later generations in turn fashioned devices to simplify the manufacture of tools.

With time, and expressly when he had to transport some necessary equipment, man's thoughts turned to the invention of a means of transportation.

24 The sea and man

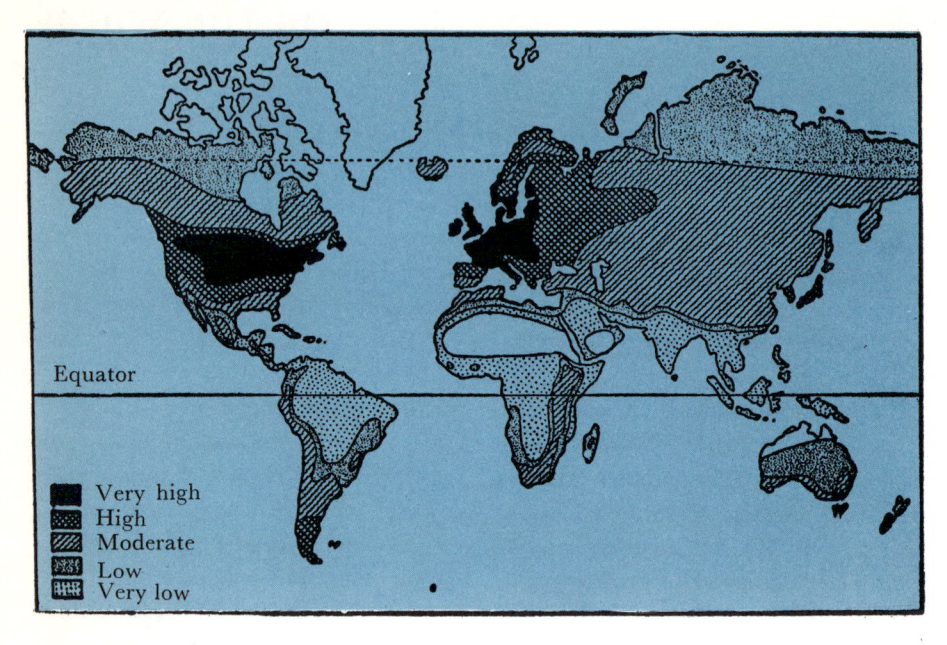

Legend:
- Very high
- High
- Moderate
- Low
- Very low

The American geographer Ellsworth Huntington has developed a theory in many books that climate decides man's working strength and health (see map), and thus the rise and fall of his cultures.

All through the ages, in fact, the constant desire to improve his implements has been a leading human characteristic.

Wood as the basis for movement on the water

The fact that the necessary raw material — timber — was ready to hand both prescribed and simplified the course of man's movement on the water. It may have been a tree trunk felled in a storm or ripped from the bank in a flood and borne along by the water — perhaps carrying some animal — that gave man his first idea for a primitive craft. He must have learned to move on the water on a log or thick branch. If the branches were lopped off, he found it was easier to navigate but at the same time likely to capsize. This discovery may have been made hundreds of thousands of years ago. In very primitive conditions, for instance in the remote waters of the Australasian archipelago, the same kind of transportation is probably still used today, the native using his arms as oars and rudder, and perhaps his legs, too, as motive power.

Man learns to move around on the water 25

An Australian aborigine rides out of the past on a mangrove raft, one of man's earliest forms of water transport.

We will never know how long it took from man's first, cautious trip astride or lying face down on a floating piece of wood to the time that he first hollowed out a tree trunk. The dugout technique helped man stay on top of the floating wood, thus speeding up the development of water transportation. Gradually gaining experience and coming to terms with the water element, man was emboldened to try his powers in the unknown; every age and every region has independently developed its own seafaring and acquired its own sea territories.

Some historians believe that the first brave attempts at crossing the water barrier were made as early as twenty-five to thirty thousand years ago. In any case, more practicable means of transportation than the tree trunk came into use quite early on, particularly when man realized how easily and with what little effort even heavy loads could be moved from one place to another by water. With time, man also realized that many other substances float easily and can up to a limit be made to bear objects heavier than themselves.

Primitive means of water transportation

The discovery that a tree trunk floats led man to tie two or more together with creepers, reeds, etc., thus producing rafts and floats. Rafts are to be found here and there all over the globe. Vessels of bamboo or logs are widely used even today in many coastal areas and on rivers in tropical zones. They are usually paddled, rarely equipped with a sail. The hollow, light bamboo cane is a popular raft material in the tropics. In the Fiji Islands, for instance, a long raft with two layers of bamboo

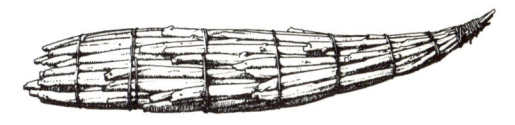

The oldest raft structures known are at least 8,000 years old.

and a side structure is used on the lagoons and inland waters.

In the 1880's the German ethnologist Otto Finsch found the most primitive form of raft conceivable in use on the north coast of New Guinea near the mouth of the river Sechstroh. It was a thick tree root with a strong bamboo cane tied to each side, buoyant enough to carry the natives through the surge to Finsch's steamship, anchored out in the open sea.

The catamaran, a primitive vessel like a raft, is still used in coastal areas in the tropics. On the Coromandel Coast in India it consists of four or five strong and slender tree trunks, the middle one being the longest, and the front of the raft curves upward into some kind of bow. This craft has very little in common with the modern vessel called a catamaran. The outrigger canoe is also thought to have originated in parts of the Pacific and the Indian Ocean.

The most easily available raw material has of course decided the form and type of man's most simple craft. Egypt had very little timber, but a luxuriant grass, papyrus, grew lushly along the Nile, from which boatlike rafts could be made. The Babylonians, who also had little timber of their own, used semispherical craft made of plaited grass, covered with hides (the *quppu*, or guffa). Even today these round vessels, nowadays made watertight with

The ethnologist Otto Finsch came across an extremely primitive form of raft in the 1880's on the north coast of New Guinea—a thick tree root, surrounded by strong bamboos.

bitumen and carrying up to twelwe tons, can be seen in Iraq river traffic. The remote regions of Ireland and Wales still use primitive coracles plaited of willow twigs and covered with hides, particularly for fishing. Some of them are shaped like ordinary boats; others are round like the Mesopotamian guffas. Iraq river traffic also uses age-old kelek rafts, which consist of two or three tree trunks supported by inflated lambskin sacks. The Indians, on the other hand, made rafts out of empty, stoppered, clay pots, fitted into special frames.

Writing of the method employed by the soldiers of Chyros the Younger to cross the river Euphrates 2,400 years ago, the Greek historian Xenophon describes how they used animal hides: "They filled the hides of their tents with light hay, fastened them at the edges and

A guffa being built near Baghdad.

The leather boat, or coracle, used for fishing on the rivers and lakes of Ireland and Wales, complete with seat boards and paddles.

The balsa, a primitive raft made of bundles of reeds, is used by local natives on Titicaca, the largest lake in South America. This 125-mile lake lies on the boundary of Peru and Bolivia, about 13,000 feet above sea level.

sewed them up so that the water did not get inside." A relief from the eighth century B.C. has been found in ancient Nineva showing people crossing the Tigris on a "swimming mattress" made from animal hides. The same method is still used in some Asian countries, for instance Tibet. The nomads there carry sewn-up animal skins around with them which are then inflated when needed.

There have been many forms of primitive craft, ranging in shape from circular to long and narrow. Most of these primitive forms of water transportation, some of which date back to prehistoric times, are still used today in various parts of the world, particularly in remote areas. Far back in the past, man got used to moving around on the water in various kinds of primitive vessels, using branches or sticks to help him, and later paddles and oars with shafts. Long ago, too, man learned to use fire and water, beasts of burden and draft animals; all these helped him free his energies for tasks calling for intelligence. After he discovered the use of metals and learned how to make steel tools, he was able to make boats

On the Sutlej river in the Himalayas, pig or cow skins are inflated and lashed together to form rafts.

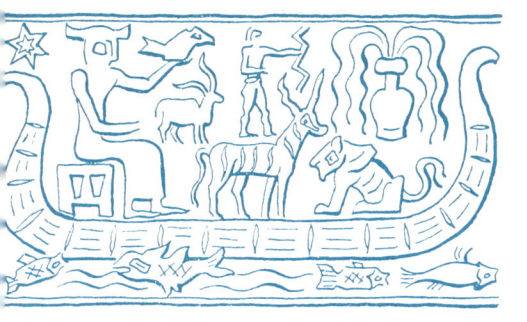

Ziusudra of the Sumerians' ark, shown in this picture, was the forerunner of Ut-napishtim's ark and Noah's ark of the Bible. The ark holds Ziusudra, with a raven in his hand, animals, and the jar of the water of life. Above shines the pendant of the Goddess Ishtar, a heavenly sign that men will no longer drown.

from more than one piece, using boards and planks fastened together with wooden plugs, leather straps, tough tree roots, and so on, in default of nails and bolts. In consequence of the discovery of the rudder, he could start building bigger vessels, as right from the start this proved a much more effective navigational device than a paddle.

The development of dugouts and boats

The craft of civilized nations can be classified in many ways: by building material, type, motive power, and purpose. For a discussion the earliest two groups are enough: one includes vessels made by hollowing out a single piece of wood; the other, hollow vessels put together from boardlike pieces. The vessels in the former group are dugouts; those in the latter are boats made and assembled from tree bark and animal skins.

The impractical nature of rafts, and in particular the difficulty of steering them, set man thinking of a better form of water transport at quite an early stage. We can feel sure that primitive man often saw a hollow tree being carried along by the waters after a storm or flood; in fact such trees were probably used as vessels in this form for some time. Finally man hit on the idea of felling a growing tree and making a dugout. Felling thick trees and hollowing them out, mainly using fire as an aid, was a difficult and time-consuming task. But it was an undertaking which did much to develop man's endurance and strength; and this vital invention, which allowed the

WONDERFUL THINGS. There be three things which are too wonderful for me, yea, four which I know not: the way of an eagle in the air; the way of a serpent upon a rock; the way of a ship in the midst of the sea; and the way of a man with a maid.

Proverbs 30:18-19

vessel to carry more and made it easier to steer, formed the basis for all man's later feats in putting the world's seas to his service.

The dugout, made from one large tree, is known all over the world, wherever suitable trees grow. In Scandinavia, Iceland, Switzerland, and Hungary dugouts have been used right up to our own times. In Asia, Africa, South America, and Australia, the natives of many regions still make dugouts from strong tree trunks, hollowing them out with fire and tools. The dugout does not need much of a channel —a foot or so of water is enough—and you can land a dugout almost anywhere.

This cultural achievement was attained in Europe as long ago as the Stone Age. In 1955 a ten-foot-long oak dugout, estimated at close to nine thousand years old, was found in a peat bog in the province of Drenthe, Holland, the oldest dugout so far found in Europe.

Other ancient dugouts excavated in Central Europe are often extremely large: oak vessels are up to 60 feet long, five feet wide, and almost four feet high. It has been proved that the Indians of the southwest coast of America used vessels like this up to 65 feet long, taking about sixty oarsmen. The tremendous teak dugouts of the rivers of India are even longer, reaching some 98 feet.

We know of some thousand ancient single-timber dugouts in Finland. These average about thirteen feet long and 20 inches wide. Compared with the

A stonecut by the Eskimo artist Pitseolak of Cape Dorset: "The dangers of seafaring."

SEA CITY. There will soon not be enough dry land, and we will have to build our towns in the sea. This is a view being taken with full seriousness by a group of Englishmen. There are plans to build a Sea City about 15 miles off Yarmouth sometime at the beginning of the twenty-first century. The city will have room for 30,000 people. The scheme is being led by Sir Harry Pilkington, who has founded a special "Glass Age Committee" for the purpose. The planned city, of which a model has already been made, would be anchored to the sea floor on piles, and would also have pontoons.

MAN AND THE SEA. He cannot control or change the ocean as, in his brief tenancy of earth, he has subdued and plundered the continents. In the artificial world of his cities and towns, he often forgets the true nature of his planet and the long vistas of its history, in which the existence of the race of men has occupied a mere moment of time. The sense of all these things comes to him most clearly in the course of a long ocean voyage, when he watches day after day the receding rim of the horizon, ridged and furrowed by waves; when at night he becomes aware of the earth's rotation as the stars pass overhead; or when, alone in this world of water and sky, he feels the loneliness of his earth in space. And then, as never on land, he knows the truth that his world is a water world, a planet dominated by its covering mantle of ocean, in which the continents are but transient intrusions of land above the surface of the all-encircling sea.

Rachel L. Carson.

---

dugouts of Central Europe, Finnish dugouts are rather simple both in wood (mainly pine) and size. A thinly hollowed pine dugout found while digging the foundations of a house in Helsinki in 1950 is believed to be the oldest of Finland's Stone Age dugouts, probably about four thousand years. Its central section, found in clayed mud about 35 feet below sea level, was 16 feet long.

Dugout development did not stop with the single-timber trough, but advanced by joining two dugouts together side by side. When the adjoining sides were removed, the result was a two-timber dugout. Even five-timber dugouts have been found in swamps.

Aside from dugouts, boatbuilding certainly did not start with heavy tree trunks; lighter material was used to begin with. Boats were made of sewn hides before man learned to make them out of wood. The simplest forms of hide and bark boats are made in one piece, like the dugout. The birch-bark boats of the Indian tribes in the northern areas of North America, made from bark removed from the tree in one piece, called for the greatest skill. The Eskimo's open umiak ("women's boat") and enclosed kayak, made of skins, are very similar to the birch-bark boat. Hide boats used to be very common over widespread areas in both hemispheres.

There have been many guesses at how the boat form of transport was first invented. The ancient poets, for instance, eulogized the paper nautilus *(Argonauta argo)*, one of the cuttlefish, as the sea beast whose appearance first

The Finnish boys Leevi and Lauri Hytönen, who discovered a boatbuilding center on the shores of Saittalampi, part of Lake Konnevesi, in summer 1962. The boys are pictured standing next to some ancient dugouts.

gave man the idea of boat design. It was earlier thought that the paper nautilus preferred to swim on the surface with its great tentacles spread as sails. But the paper nautilus is found only in Mediterranean coastal waters. Early man more likely imitated such naturally hollow objects as shells and bark fragments.

In any case, from the dugout and the hide boat, developments gradually led to the boat proper. Even rather early primitive dugouts may have been made with detachable sides. Soon boat-

Man learns to move around on the water 33

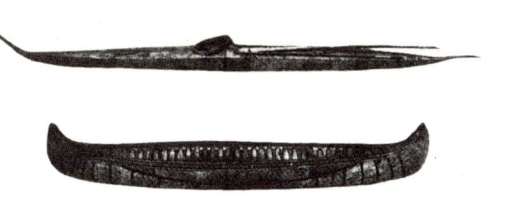

An Eskimo kayak from arctic Canada (above) and a canoe made of pieces of birch bark by the Canadian Algonquin Indians.

builders started to raise the height of the dugout with side boards and strengthen it with ribs. As the number of boards grew, the dugout itself became narrower and narrower, eventually shrinking to form a keel. It was the board-built boat that permitted the increase in size and seaworthiness that led eventually to the development of the ship.

MODERN EXPEDITIONS.

In summer 1947 the Norwegian scientist Thor Heyerdahl and five comrades sailed some 5000 miles in 101 days, from Peru to Polynesia, on the primitive raft Kon-Tiki, built of balsa logs, bamboo, and reeds. Heyerdahl wanted to prove his theory that the islands of the south Pacific could have been settled some 1,500 years ago by people from South America — from the east, rather than from the west, as had been the theory until then.

Since this splendid achievement, which attracted world-wide interest, Heyerdahl has devoted himself to the problem of the large number of similarities between the cultures of the eastern Mediterranean countries (such as Egypt) some 3,000 years ago, and of Mexico. Heyerdahl believes that the ancient Egyptians and Phoenicians could have sailed from Africa to the New World thousands of years ago by reed raft. It had to be proved in practice, and so a 43-foot 10-ton papyrus raft, the *Ra*, was built under Heyerdahl's direction near Cairo. In May 1969, the 54-year-old explorer and his crew of six left from the port of Saf in Morocco on this perilous transatlantic crossing. Though *Ra* sailed over 2500 miles, only some 430 miles from the South American coast, the raft had to be abandoned in August because it had been badly damaged in storms and was a threat to the safety of the crew. Heyerdahl still considers that the expedition provided adequate proof of the validity of his theories.

3 The sea and man

From native haunts to wider horizons

When the craft of boatbuilding and the art of sailing had developed far enough in prehistoric times, coastal and inland sea navigation began. The main stimulus was certainly fishing and the exchange of goods, i.e. trade. The importance of maritime connections grew, parallel with the development of means of water transport. It was, after all, often much easier to carry both people and goods by sea than overland: there were either no roads at all, or such as there were were very primitive, for bridges did not exist and the primeval forests formed a great barrier.

The first ship to circumnavigate the earth.

An important and far-reaching invention came when man learned how to make the disk and from it the wheel and axle. Another tremendous step forward was the discovery that the power of the wind could be caught in a sail, that the wind could be leashed to make a vessel move. In inventing the wheel and the sail, symbols of his conquest of the physical world, man gradually made himself master of both land and sea, and later, too, of the air.

Ocean travel and seafaring in general were of course impossible by raft, hollowed-out tree trunk, hide boat, or bark canoe, which could be powered only by paddling; learning the art of sailing was of absolutely vital significance for the development of seafaring. One central problem was how to make the vessel stable; two primitive solutions were the double and the outrigger canoe.

A boat with water under it is the central motif of this reddish-brown ceramic pot (about 16 inches high). Found in Upper Egypt, the pot is from the pre-Dynastic era (before 3000 B.C.). This pot is in the Cairo Museum's great collection of ancient treasures. (Top left.)

The oldest known picture of a sailing ship is on the side of this amphora, or clay pot, which is almost 3,500 years old. The mast with its squaresail is near the tall, curving bows. The pot is 23 inches high and the base color a brownish-yellow with the design in dark purple. British Museum collection, London.

From the time true ships were first developed, man has used them for two main purposes: the exchange of goods (trade) and war. In the pre-Christian era voyages of discovery were only side products. There are many gaps and deficiencies in our knowledge about the earliest sea-going vessels, and most of what we know concerns those used in the eastern parts of the Mediterranean. The pictures we have of these, too, are generally so stylized that it is difficult to interpret the detail.

The appearance and importance of sailing ships

The use of a sail on a vessel is a relatively new development everywhere in the world apparently, although cultures that have disappeared leaving no trace might well have used sailing craft thousands of years before what we now believe to have been the earliest examples. The earliest types of sail were probably made of animal hides or woven matting; they seem to have been developed independently in many different regions.

The earliest known pictures of a sailing ship are over five thousand years old. The British Museum collection contains a late prehistoric clay pot made in Upper Egypt, the side of which shows a boat with a sail. This find is from the Nekade II, or Gerza, culture, which most experts date between 3500 and 3100 B.C. A seal cylinder depicting a sailing ship was found in a Sumerian Eridun al'Ubaid culture grave. It dates from the Dšemdet Nasr era, around 3100 B.C. These, then, were forerunners in the use of the "ship-pulling cloth." Like the oar and rudder, the mast is a vital feature of a ship and plays an important part in the cosmology and mythology of the Babylonians, writes Professor Armas Salonen, the Finnish orientalist.

The oldest known sail, apparently the only type used for thousands of years, was a simple, square affair. At the fall of the Roman Empire in 476 A.D., all ships had square sails. For several centuries after this, sources tell us almost nothing about shipping on the Mediterranean. It is not until the end of the ninth century that two Greek manuscripts give us our first pictures of medieval craft on this sea. From their appearance these small ves-

A Sumerian seal cylinder, about five thousand years old, depicting a sailing boat.

THE PORTOLANO AND PE-RIPLUS guided ancient mariners on the Mediterranean and Black Sea. The *portolano* was a chart showing the harbor channels and was intended to supplement the coastal sailors' guide, the *periplus*. The Scylacis periplus is the oldest and most complete of these coastal route descriptions and the only one to have been preserved. The chart that apparently supplemented it no longer exists, but together they formed the Mediterranean seafarer's most important guide in the fourth and fifth centuries B.C.

A periplus called Stadiasmus, or "Circumnavigation of the Great Sea," originates from roughly the fifth century A.D., but is surprisingly like modern sailing directions. It gives the distances of the various headlands from each other, the prevailing winds for approaching various islands, anchorage facilities and supplies of fresh water. For example: "From Hermaea to Leuce Acte 20 degrees; nearby a small island two degrees from land; this is a suitable anchorage for cargo ships; but on the coast by the high headland is an open anchorage suitable for all kinds of craft. Temple of Apollo, the famous oracle: water available in the temple."

sels seem to be designed like the trading ships of antiquity, but feature something new in the history of navigation —the lateen sail, a three-cornered sail attached to a diagonal yard.

The name *lateen* stems from the word Latin, probably because north Europeans first came across it in the Latin countries, when they started to sail as far as the eastern Mediterranean in the Middle Ages. The lateen, a halfway stage between the square sail and the jib, is of Arabian or possibly Polynesian origin. It reached the Mediterranean via the Arabs and is still widely used there, on the Red Sea and the Persian Gulf, the west coast of India, the east coast of Africa, etc. The jib, on the other hand, is a considerably more recent invention, which really comes into its own for tacking.

The peoples of the Aegean Sea used only rowed vessels right up to around 2000 B.C. It is claimed that the Cretans learned about the sail from the Egyptians, among whom sails were in common use as early as the Old Kingdom (c. 2500 B.C.). The first sailor of immortal fame was Odysseus, who came from the island of Ithaca and spent years sailing around the islands of the Aegean Sea and nearby waters.

The peoples of the south first met those from farther away with the aid of the sail. With the aid of the sail Europe raised its flag on strange shores all over the world and spread western culture in all directions of the compass. The outcome was fruitful interaction between different peoples, for the sea, which had once divided peoples and races, now linked them. Seafaring created the conditions for rapid material and intellectual advance of overseas nations. Knowledge, skill, and better tools reached many lands by means of the sea. Right up to the present time, dominion of the sea has always been decisive in conflicts between great powers.

"Not until we have conquered the sea can we really say we have brought the globe under our sway. It represents everything valuable and fresh in a culture," says the Danish ethnologist Kaj Birket-Smith, "for the land is often too cramped and stale." Thus man's conquest of the sea is a deed to which only the very greatest of his other achievements are comparable.

The sail, then, seems to have come from cultural regions between the Mediterranean and India. From there its use spread along the coasts of the continents—north to Scandinavia and east across the whole of Oceania and along the east coast of Asia up to the Eskimos. It was not universal by any means. It is not to be found in the Bismarck Archipelago in New Guinea, for in-

Ancient Egyptian rowing boat in the tomb of Ti bei Sakkara, (c. 2650 B.C.).

Ancient Syrian ships (reliefs in the palace of King Salmanasar, 722–705 B.C.).

Relief showing the stern of a sailing vessel, carved in the rock wall of the road to the old acropolis of Lindos by Pythocritos of Rhodes around 180 B.C. The relief formed the basis for a sculpture intended as a mark of respect to Agesandros, son of Nikion, for his great services to the towns of Lindos and Nike. Photograph by the author.

stance, though it was widely known in the rest of Melanesia and Polynesia. It is obvious that the Malaysian-Polynesian race managed to spread throughout the farflung islands of the Pacific only because they knew how to use the sail.

The necessary conditions for seafaring

Coastal waters and inland seas, with land more or less near at hand, provided the best setting for primitive seafaring. These geographical conditions existed in the Mediterranean, the North Sea, the Baltic, the Red Sea and the Persian Gulf, the South East Asian archipelago, the coastal waters of East Asia and the islands of the West Indies. The oldest centers of advanced culture lay on waterways: Egypt, enriched by the floods of the Nile; Mesopotamia on the rivers Tigris and Euphrates, the upper reaches of the river Indus in northwest India; and the loess lands of the Hwang Ho river region in north China.

But other factors also played their part. The existence of islands and high mountains suitable as landmarks was a great advantage from the seafarer's point of view, as were favorable climatic conditions, reliable winds, and clear air.

A historical study must not devote attention merely to geographical and material conditions, of course. Any study related to man means taking into account many complex psychological factors which are impossible to analyze fully. Nevertheless it has been shown that a tropical climate has an enervating effect on man; on the other hand it was more difficult for seafaring to make progress in very cold regions than in milder climes.

Most of the resources which modern man has to thank for his material

OKEANOS, to the people of the antique world, meant the mysterious and dangerous sea surrounding the world they knew. The Atlantic Ocean on the other side of the Pillars of Hercules, or Straits of Gibraltar, was the great unknown, full of fast, terrible currents and strange, awesome monsters. Since those days the searching, inquiring human mind has to some extent succeeded in explaining the secrets of sea currents and tides and in studying the great stream of marine life that began so long ago and that now contains a huge range of flora and fauna. We have good cause for thinking of the Atlantic as the world's greatest "stream": it carries about 75 million tons of water a second clockwise round the gigantic trough of the Sargasso sea in its center.

ARISTOTELES

When Aristotle (384–322 B.C.) was going to Corinth by ship, a severe storm blew up.

"We ignorant wretches are not afraid, but you, the great philosopher Aristotle, are trembling."

"Yes, but I have a different kind of soul to guard!"

affluence and high level of culture come from a zone in the central latitudes of the earth.

In the early days of human history, however, those parts of Europe and Asia were uncivilized wastes, across which poured wave after wave of intrepid barbarians. The first cultures developed farther south, along the great rivers of Mesopotamia, on the banks of the Indus, and in the valley of the Nile.

As the focal point of civilization moved westward in the course of time, culture also began to spread north. The energy and strength of Western nations is thought to be largely due to their environment and their capricious climate, but other factors were also influential, among them religion. The Christian religion is extrovert, whereas most of the other great religions are largely introspective.

A glance at an atlas is enough to show which regions of the world provided good conditions for primitive navigation. The Mediterranean and the waters of East Asia had some obvious advantages; their proximity to the old river valley cultures obviously played some part, too. The waters of north Europe and Arabia form another group, obviously under the spreading influence of the older civilizations. The Sunda islands and the West Indies were very far away from the centers of European civilization. The Malaysians reached by far the highest standard of primitive seafaring. One branch of this race spread over most of the scattered islands of the Pacific probably as early as the beginning of the Christian era. The Polynesians used double boats and outriggers in their fearless and skillful ocean sailing.

Navigation on the Mediterranean

The real heart of the *oikoumenē*, the Greek word for the inhabited world, was the ancient world, primarily southwest Asia; from here the centers of culture later moved gradually west and east. To the ancient Greeks the Mediterranean and its vicinity was the *oikoumenē*; it was the only sea they knew, stretching for some 2400 miles from the shores of the Near East to the Straits of Gibraltar. Although they knew nothing for sure about what lay outside their own limited horizons, they nonetheless guessed that the land continued to the south. They conjectured that the regions beyond were not inhabited by man and were even unfit for human habitation. Nowadays our *oikoumenē* includes some 9/10 of the surface of the globe, if seas with regular traffic are included.

All around the eastern Mediterranean, cultures dependent on the sea made their appearance quite early, and the industrial specialization and commerce of civilization began to find a place in the barbarian self-supporting economy. New traditions of navigation were created, geographical knowledge gathered, and information about new lands, raw materials, and technical methods passed on to eastern cultures.

Navigation was just beginning in the Mediterranean when the first walls of Jericho fell, an estimated nine thousand years ago. The shores of the Mediterranean have been the cradle of seafaring, as they have of the whole of European culture. This spacious inland sea provided a means of communication for the nations around it, and the inhabitants of its shores thus became good sailors even in prehistory. For centuries seafaring meant coastal traffic, with the craft always trying to keep within sight of land, and the human eye being the main instrument of navigation.

We are used to considering the islands of the Aegean Sea, the gulf between Asia Minor and the Balkan peninsula, as the birthplace of navigation: this area, with its innumerable natural harbors, provided almost ideal conditions for seafaring. Traveling from island to island by various simple craft was no great feat. The high mountains and headlands of the coast made easily recognizable landmarks; even long ago local sailors ventured well out into open waters. Dawn came from the east, from the interior of Asia Minor, and in the west lay Greece, where the sun set. The word Asia, by which the Greeks meant Asia Minor, perhaps originates from the Assyrian loan word *aszu*, meaning sunrise. On the other hand, the word Europe is thought to have come from the Semite word *ereb*, meaning sunset.

On the Aegean Sea, as throughout the whole Mediterranean area, the air is very clear and limpid, particularly in summer, and at night the stars shine out brightly to guide mariners. The Aegean Sea is one of the most impor-

MERMAIDS were first mentioned by Alexander the Alexandrian, an educated Greek, in the first century B.C. A wave once cast up on the shore a sea maiden with a fish tail. She was a graceful girl with a lovely face, but below the waist as scaley as a fish. The mermaid was so afraid that she burst into tears when a crowd of people gathered to stare at her. King Gaza, who ruled the region, ordered the people away, and the mermaid dived back into the sea. The Roman historian Pliny tells of the mermen whose song tempted ships to their doom. He was unable to give a description of these mermen, however, as anyone who set eyes on them disappeared. In Pliny's day people had already begun to believe that the "mermaids" were seals, which were said to cry like man and suckle their young.

---

tant crossroads of culture, lying as it does between Asia Minor, the Balkan peninsula, and the island of Crete. It was thus the main training school of navigation in the Mediterranean cultural area and the best starting point for an art of navigation which was in time to conquer the world's seas. Piracy has also been an important means of livelihood for the people of these regions since olden times. It was not thought shameful, because it brought a successful exponent riches and fame.

The estuaries of the rivers flowing into the innumerable gulfs of the Mediterranean became centers of trade and seafaring because of their ports. They offered ships spacious anchorage and loading facilities in their islands and harbors. Maritime trade in turn helped to spread culture from one nation to another.

Water traffic in Egypt and on the Nile

The oldest water craft that deserve the name of "boat" probably went up and down the Nile. In the first century A. D. the Roman writer Pliny mentions the traditional belief of his own time that the first ship was invented in Egypt. Papyrus reed rafts were used very early along the Nile; the fellaheen of the middle and upper Nile use them today as their fathers did six thousand years ago. From these, the Egyptians eventually learned how to bind bundles of reeds together to form slender boats, low, spoonshaped craft, about four times as long as they were wide. This explains the oldest Egyptian name for boat—"bound one." An old grave painting shows three Egyptian workmen binding reeds into a very elegant canoe. Moses' mother probably put her infant in a vessel of this kind: "she took for him an ark of bulrushes, and daubed it with slime and with pitch, and put the child therein" (Exodus 2:3). Through many intermediary stages this primitive vessel very likely developed into a seagoing ship, built in the same way as the river boats.

Besides paintings, sculptures, and a number of model boats, the wonderful ancient tombs of Egypt contain inscriptions which throw a great deal of light on the origins and development of boatbuilding in the practically treeless land of the Pharaohs.

During the last few decades several valuable archaeological excavations have taught us more about ancient Egyptian vessels and how they were built. One important find in 1954 was the first of two burial ships, both walled up in solid rock on the south side of the Great Pyramid. This magnificent discovery shows how advanced both shipbuilding and stonemasonry were at that period. The mastless ship is 140 feet long, 18 feet wide, and 25 feet tall. The deck structure included three roofed shelters, and twelve oars were found.

This giant, relatively well-preserved ship was dismantled carefully into 651 parts. When restored it will be placed in a specially built museum on the site where it was found. So far it is not known for sure whether this handsome ship, built entirely of foreign wood, was used during the king's funeral ceremonies or whether it was intended for the king's use in the other world: on his travels to Buto, Sais, and other holy places.

The obelisks which still stand defying time in Paris, London, and New York were once raised in front of the temples at Luxor and Heliopolis. They were carried there long ago from the south, from Aswan near the first cataract of the Nile, a good 125 miles away, where they had been hacked out of the granite cliff in one great piece. The barges on which such great chunks of stone, weighing up to 350 tons, were brought down the river were the most incredible of all the vessels built in Egypt because of their vast size. Allowing for two colossi lying side by side, the estimated dimensions of the transportation craft must have been: weight without load 800 tons and with load 1,500 tons, length over 200 feet, width over 80 feet, and depth over 6 feet. These barges, built about 3,500 years ago, were presumably made in the

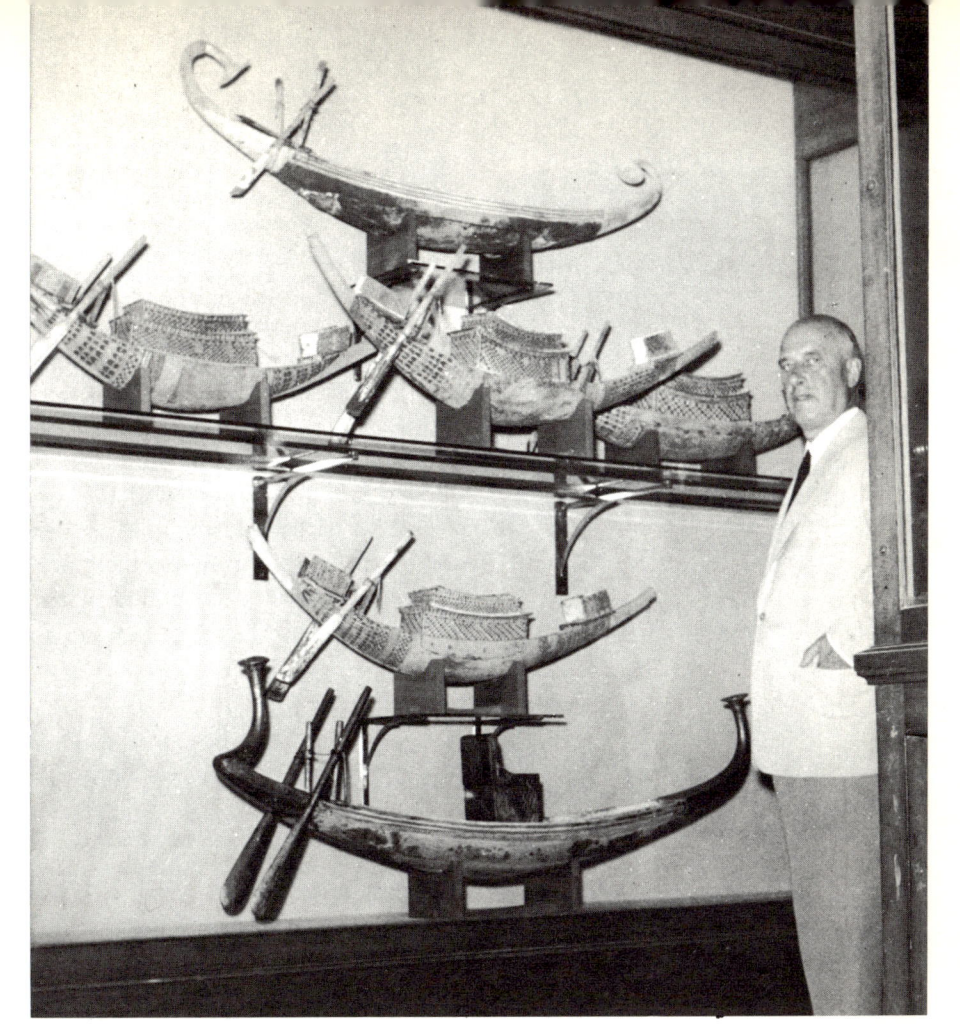

The treasures of Pharaoh Tutankhamen's 3,300-year-old tomb included miniature ships fitted out for the ruler's needs in the afterlife, here being studied by the writer in the Cairo Museum.

traditional way from small pieces of wood, perhaps some 12 inches thick, carefully plugged together. The huge barge was towed by twenty-seven smaller rowing boats in three lines. Each towing vessel had thirty rowers as well as a helmsman and taskmaster.

A 3,400-year-old Egyptian grave inscription tells us the following about a man called Ineri: "I, the supervisor, observed the installation of two large granite obelisks at the double doors of the god's stone chamber. I directed the construction of the fine vessel, 120 cubits long and 40 cubits wide, on which these obelisks were conveyed. The vessel successfully reached the vicinity of the Karnak area."

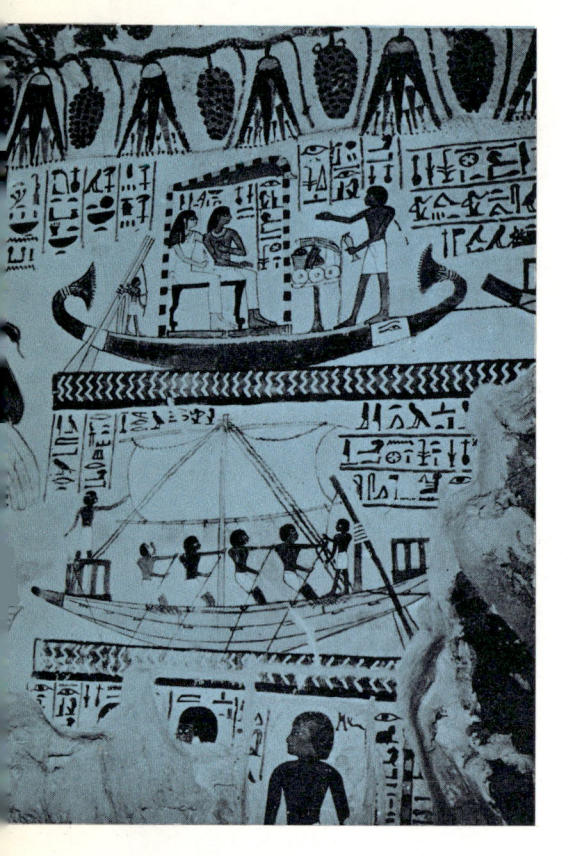

During the Middle Kingdom (c. 2000 B.C.) the Egyptians already knew how to build ships 210 feet long and 65 feet wide, taking 120 men. The technique they used to build their wooden ships, which followed the papyrus boat pattern closely, used neither keel nor ribs. On stormy seas there was thus a perpetual danger that when the ship rode the crest of a wave it

Well-preserved, colorful sepulchre frescoes in Thebes (now Luxor), Upper Egypt.

Frescoes in the sepulchre of Menena, an official in charge of the treasury, in Karnak, Thebes (now Luxor), 18th Dynasty (c. 1400 B.C.). A convoy is carrying the deceased's body to the Temple of Osiris, chief judge of the underworld, in Abydos (Upper Egypt).

would break up across the middle, made up as it was of small sections. To prevent this, the Egyptians stretched a strong hawser brace from bow to stern, supported by sturdy pillars in the middle. The Greeks and Romans used the same technique.

Presumably river traffic developed into seafaring proper as early as the latter half of the fourth millennium B.C. One pressing reason for this development was the great shortage of timber. The early voyages of the Egyptians beyond their own country took them to the coast of Phoenicia-Palestine and to Cyprus and Crete. The Bible describes how Joseph sent corn by sea from Egypt to his father in the land of Judah. At the right time of year it was possible to sail from the Nile estuary to Byblos, the best harbor for the Lebanon timber trade and already a city by the beginning of the third millennium, in four days — a distance of 300 nautical miles. The return trip, when rowers had to be used, took eight to ten days.

The timber needed for shipbuilding and other purposes came from Lebanon, brought to Egypt by ship or on rafts. Egypt's first real boats were also carved out of these tree trunks. The earliest text describing timber transportation, from the reign of King Snofru (c. 2630 B.C.) tells of a ship which carried forty "ash" trees (either fir or cedar). In Lower Nubia ships were built from the local material, tough acasia wood, from which only short planks can be cut.

In the Red Sea, the Egyptians sailed as far as the mysterious, miraculous land of Punt, which probably meant the shores of Africa around the Somali headland. From there they brought myrrh resin for medicine and embalming, incense for their religious ceremonies, slaves, apes, and above all, gold, as the gold deposits of Upper Egypt had been used up as early as the Twelfth Dynasty, around 2000 B.C. In the last decade of the fifteenth century B.C. Queen Hatshepsut sent a large trade expedition to Punt, whose inhabitants, villages, plants, and animals she then used as decorative themes for the large terraced rock temple she was having built in Deir al-Bahar. When we think of the Egyptians' weakly constructed, keelless ships and the dangerous waters of the Red Sea, the voyage to Punt must be considered a very fine achievement. Probably Punt exchanged goods with both India and Egypt, as South Arabia was an early center for Indian goods.

The Sumerians as master shipbuilders

Until quite recently it was thought that Egypt was the source of our oldest information about shipbuilders and their craft. Scientific circles long held the view that the leading shipbuilders of the ancient world were the nations of the eastern Mediterranean, especially the Phoenicians. Professor Armas Salonen, the Finnish Orientalist, rebutted this theory in 1937, however, with his research into cuneiform characters. He has proved that the leading shipbuilders of the ancient world and the real founders of shipbuilding technique were the Sumerians, the ancient Babylonian civilization. It is a historical fact that this "Land of the Twin Rivers" was the first to build vessels that braved and withstood the many terrors of the deep.

A good thousand years before the Phoenicians made their name as a seafaring race, the Sumerians had created the techniques on which shipbuilding even today is fundamentally based. Shipyard documents written in Sumerian and cuneiform characters from the second and third millennium B.C. reveal that the Sumerians knew the art of building ships with a keel and ribs. This art did not reach the Mediterranean peoples until hundreds of years later, through the Semites; even today wooden shipbuilding uses the same techniques all over the world. If suitable wood was not to be found locally, the Sumerians and Babylonians took their timber from elsewhere, mainly Syria.

Using a keel and ribs, the ship's sides could be made from very thin planks and boards. The width to length ratio was 1 to 3, a proportion that experience has proved the most suitable for cargo ships. The faster rowing boats and warships were much narrower, up to a ratio of 1 to 8. Cargo ships were usually as high as they were broad.

The ships were usually owned by the highest crown officials, the temples, and the financiers, who hired out their ships at a high price to merchants and others who needed them.

In the earlier *makurru* vessels that preceded wooden boats, those made of reeds, grass, etc., and intended for long-term use, both ends were finished off to form a kind of point. In appearance they thus looked very like the moon sailing through the sky in its first quarter. These boat-type vessels were the pattern for the wooden ships built later in that these, too, were built with high bows and high stern.

The biggest cargo ships built in the Land of the Twin Rivers, where the Egyptians said "the water runs backwards" (i.e. in the opposite direction to the Nile), had a volume of over 1000 cubic feet, or almost eleven modern registered tons. They were some 45 feet long, 15 feet wide, with bows and stern that could be up to 20 feet high.

In the neo-Babylonian period in the sixth century B.C., even bigger ships were built. The normal type was, however, a vessel of eight modern re-

Noah's ark, if it had been built in the fifteenth century.
Woodcut in a Bible printed in Lübeck, 1494.

gistered tons produced serially. If these are compared with the ships of other later nations, the earlier type corresponded roughly to the cogs of the east Frisian islands in the sixteenth century A.D. The erroneous claims of Herodotus about the tremendous tonnage of the Babylonian ships stems from the fact that the two types of vessel were confused and highly exaggerated.

The standard example of exaggeration is the Old Testament story of Noah's ark, which in reality was no ship, but rather a huge boxlike construction. The proportions given for Noah's ark convert to about 450 by 75 by 45 feet, for a volume which would correspond to 19,876 modern registered tons. "It must have been a miracle indeed," writes Professor Salonen, "if the men who could only build vessels of a bare eleven tons at the height of their capacities, suddenly found themselves able to build arks of 19,876 registered tons, like Noah's ark of the Bible, or even 76,300 registered tons, like its model, the Ut-napishtim ark."

Malaysian-Polynesian seafaring

In the field of primitive seafaring the Malaysians reached an extremely

4 The sea and man

high standard and won mastery of the sea long before any other nation at a corresponding cultural level. On the other side of the world, too, the Eskimos and some coastal tribes in northwest America were not far behind. Their seafaring, to be sure, flourished only at certain seasons, when the harsh natural conditions allowed them to set off on long voyages.

One branch of the Malaysian race spread into Oceania, the vast island labyrinth of the Pacific, probably around the beginning of the Christian calendar. If we can believe the stories, their ancestors set off east from the East Indies around 200 A.D. According to one estimate the first people reached the Samoan islands around the year 450, and these then became a kind of base for further expeditions.

The ancient Polynesians were splendid sailors and conquerors, and sailed all over the world's largest ocean in well-built ships long before Columbus, even getting as far as America. These audacious seafarers discovered and conquered more of the earth's surface than any other primitive people. According to recent Indian research, their ancestors sailed the Pacific as far as Mexico and Peru even in prehistoric times, as settlers, traders, and adventurers, and were thus the first to discover the western parts of the New World. Some settled permanently in the new country they had found; hence the high level of the Aztec and Inca cultures.

The Norwegian Thor Heyerdahl, on the other hand, whose crew made the famous journey on the raft Kon-Tiki from Peru to Polynesia in 1947, believes that the islands were first settled by people from the eastern shores of the Pacific. Heyerdahl has published a comprehensive study to back up his theory, called *American Indians in the Pacific*.

These "sunrise Vikings" powered their canoes, fitted with supporting timbers at the sides, by paddling, and used sails plaited from pandanus fiber. On their later voyages they used boats up to 65 feet long. To make them steadier in rough seas they sometimes joined two boats together side by side with a cross beam.

We can assume that a considerable proportion of the inhabitants of Madagascar came across the Indian Ocean from Java in primitive vessels over a thousand years or so, around the beginning of our calendar. The history of this island, if any, is convincing proof of the movements that took place across vast oceans in various parts of the world.

From the point of view of world history as a whole, however, Malaysian-Polynesian seafaring is insignificant. This is also the case with Chinese and Indian navigation, both of which must go back a very long way. We

The lavishly decorated Thot Kath boat on the Menam river, Bangkok. The King of Siam used this once a year during the ceremonial presentation of new gowns to the Buddhist monks. Danish National Museum, picture archive, Copenhagen.

know very little of the early seafaring of these two ancient civilizations. In spite of long and lively trade connections with the southern lands of the East, they remain a mysterious area hidden behind the curtain of antiquity. For this reason the descriptions given in *Periplous maris Erythraei*, a navigation handbook in India and China compiled around 80 A.D. by a merchant from Berenice, on the Red Sea, held good in spite of their vagueness up to the time of Marco Polo at the end of the Middle Ages.

The Cretans and Phoenicians as sailors

The first center of European culture was Crete. As long as 5,000 years ago a seafaring nation developed there with a civilization rooted in ancient Egypt. Knowledge and skills spread from this tiny island to the shores of the Aegean and the Greek mainland. Around this time, for instance, we are told that certain Greeks traveled from Crete right across the sea to the eastern Mediterranean on trading expeditions. As far as we know the Cretans were the first real seafarers, in the sense that they traveled long distances on the open seas in their little craft without assistance from the mainland. Around 1250 B.C., when Crete was overrun by the Achaeans, its former power and glory soon faded, and eventually the island became a mere hideout for pirates.

The role of leading Mediterranean seafaring and trading nation now passed to the Phoenicians, a people related to the Semites, who had come from the south shore of the Persian Gulf and settled in a long, narrow strip of land between the mountains of Lebanon and the Mediterranean, the coastal regions of the land later called Palestine. As this coastal plain was better suited to fruit and wine culture than to corn, its growing population had to rely on the sea for subsistence.

The Phoenicians traversed the seas mainly as traders and were the first to venture really long distances, setting up trading posts and trade colonies nearly everywhere they traveled. In their cedarwood craft, many with long rows of rowers in several tiers for windless weather, they sailed along the Mediterranean coasts carrying silver and iron, sheep and goats, cotton cloth, works in bronze, and slaves. Before long the Phoenicians ventured west of Gibraltar, which speaks of a quite highly developed navigational skill. They discovered the rich minerals and other resources of the coastal regions of southern Spain, a place mentioned as Tarshish, which probably referred to the region around the Guadalquivir river estuary. The Phoenicians traded regularly with wealthy Tarshish and whispered not a word about their discovery to other nations. On their return home their high-bowed, clumsily built, decked ships were full of gold. Gold became so cheap that the Phoenicians are said to have made their ships' anchors out of it to save room. The Second Book of Chronicles (9:20–21) says: "And all the drinking vessels of king Solomon were of gold, and all the vessels of the house of the forest of Lebanon were of pure gold: none were of silver; it was not any thing accounted of in the days of Solomon. For the king's ships went to Tarshish with the servants of Huram [king of Phoenicia]: every three years once came the ships of Tarshish bringing gold, and silver, ivory, and apes, and peacocks."

The Phoenicians shipped all kinds of goods from various countries, copper from Spain and tin from as far away as Cornwall, England. Probably between 900 and 600 B.C., they began to reach even more distant waters. To begin with they sailed to the south end of the Red Sea and traded with the people of Aden, then ventured into the Indian Ocean and made

THE OLDEST KNOWN FISH-ING TACKLE dates from the early European Stone Age (20,000–8000 B.C.). It consisted of small fish spears, or harpoons, cast by hand. The same kind of harpoons are still found today in the tropics; they are not cast by hand, however, but shot from a blowpipe. Here and there in tropical areas, too, there are natives who fish with bow and arrow, another age-old fishing method. Fishing with bait goes back a very long way; stone fishhooks have been found in strata attributed to the middle of the New Stone Age (8000–3000 B.C.). The fishing rod has over the ages developed a huge range of different models and sizes. Economically important line fishing has been practiced ever since the seventeenth century on the sand banks of Newfoundland. Nets were used as long ago as the Stone Age: Egyptian reliefs (4th Dynasty, 3430–3160 B.C.) show nets being used.

---

contact with the riches of India. Some of the few existing references to these early voyages are found in Chapter 27 of the Book of the Prophet Ezekiel, which throws a great deal of light on navigation. It mentions that the masts of the vessels in the Phoenicians' ancient port of Tyre were made from the cedars of Lebanon, the sails of "fine linen with broidered work from Egypt," and "blue and purple [cloth] from the isles of Elishah was that [awning] which covered" them.

One of the earliest maritime exploits of the Phoenicians was a voyage carried out in the service of the Pharaoh Necho around 500 B.C. The expedition started from the Red Sea, circled the whole of Africa, and returned to Egypt, three years later, via Gibraltar. Herodotus writes of this in his history: "And they say, something which I certainly cannot believe though some other might, that while they were sailing round Libya the sun was on their right hand." This speaks in favor of the voyage's authenticity.

The expedition of the Carthaginian leader Hanno, around 460 B.C., is an exceptional example of the many

The Colossus of Rhodes, a bronze statue of the sun god Helios, was erected around 290 B.C. This gigantic figure, 100 to 130 feet tall by all accounts, was one of the Seven Wonders of the ancient world.

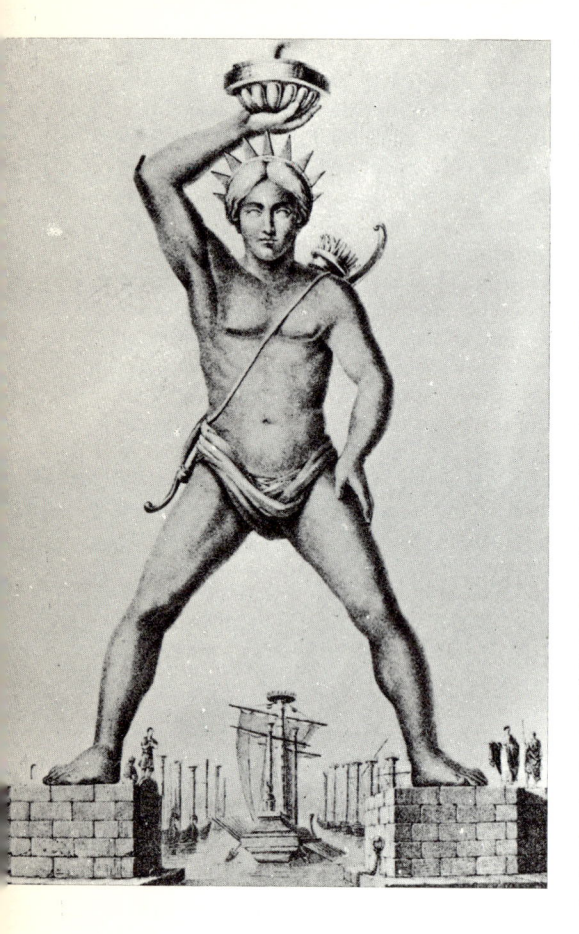

long voyages of the Phoenician adventurers, one of the first really large-scale voyages of discovery that we have reliable information about. On his return from this exciting voyage, Hanno inscribed the tale for future generations in one of the temples of his native town. The Greek translation of this Punic inscription, which is no longer intact, is called *Periplus* (The Circumnavigation) and has been preserved for posterity in the works of the Roman historian Pliny.

The expedition set off west from Carthage with all the strength it could muster. Sixty-seven fifty-oar galleys set sail, carrying "30,000 men and women, foodstuffs and other supplies." The fleet sailed past Gibraltar and south along the coast of Africa, probably beyond the river Senegal. Hanno's journal reads: "At night the land was full of flame and in the midst was a tremendous burning pyre taller than the rest which seemed to reach up to the stars. In daylight it proved to be a high mountain called Theon Okhema." This must have been the volcano Cameroon (13,350 feet), which last erupted in 1922.

The Phoenicians certainly did not encourage competitors on their long voyages. Competition could be squashed by clever lies and intimidation: in addition to the ordinary dangers which doubtless existed in plenty at the contemporary level of navigation and shipbuilding, they had invented ever greater and more terrifying supernatural perils to frighten off hopeful rivals. We can safely assume that such tales were the origin of the Sirens, Scylla and Charybdis, and many other imagined horrors and dangers. The people of antiquity were probably much less fearful than the classical world, and not afraid of setting off on long voyages; after all they had no idea how large their world actually was.

Mainly to back up their trade, the Phoenicians founded colonies in many places on the shores of the Mediterranean and its islands. The most well-known of these was Carthage, founded around 814 B.C. on the north shore of the African headland north of the present city of Tunis; it became a mighty power and the bustling center of contemporary navigation and managed to preserve its dominion of the western Mediterranean right up to the time that Rome began to be a serious rival. After the Third Punic War in 146 B.C. the Romans razed Carthage to the ground.

The importance of the Phoenicians to world history lies in the fact that they were the most advanced commercial nation of the ancient world and through their contacts with both East and West brought the goods and culture of the Orient to Europe. The Phoenicians invented purple dye; they

---

RADIOCARBON DATING, as the name suggests, is based on measurement of the radioactive beta-ray transmitted by a rare, radioactive isotope of carbon, C-14. This method, discovered in the 40s, has been used successfully in archaeology and produced some excellent results in the study of wooden remains. Carbon-14 dating is one of the methods by which natural science provides us with data on material as much as 30,000 years old. The findings have been reliable, though calculation of measurements must take into account the increase in carbon dioxide in the air caused by industry in the last hundred years, and postwar atom bomb tests, which also produce radiocarbon (about ten per cent of all the air's radiocarbon). The method calls for rather complex equipment.

---

taught Europe the glassmaking they had learned from the Egyptians, the Babylonian system of weights and measures, and the use of letters and numerals.

During the great flowering of antiquity—in the last two or three centuries B.C.—ships were larger and faster than ever before. We find mention of a ship of as much as 4,200 tons, which the Hellenes built for Hieron of Syracuse. The rigging and rudder system were also improved. In spite of these improvements, the voyage from Rhodes to Alexandria still took four days. One could get from Alexandria to Sicily in six or seven days, but it usually took twenty to twenty-seven days to Ostia, Rome's port. The average speed of cargo carriers was probably about four knots in fine weather.

Beyond the Mediterranean, connections were still slower. By sea and river from the Indus to Seleukeia on the banks of the Tigris could take forty days. Before sailors learned to make use of the monsoon wind, it could take as much as four to six months to sail the nearly 2,800 miles from Berenice, on the Egyptian side of the Red Sea, to the Indian peninsula.

The Greeks take to the water

On reaching the sea-encircled land of Hellas, the Greek tribes came into contact with seafarers and gradually learned the art of navigation and shipbuilding. They then started to compete with the Phoenicians, first in the Aegean and then in the central and western Mediterranean and the Black Sea. There are very few pictures of Greek merchant ships, so we have no real idea of the type. But we know that the Greeks, the second great seafaring nation of antiquity, won mastery of the eastern Mediterranean as early as the eight and seventh centuries B.C. The ancient Greeks became familiar with the winds of the Indian Ocean and its regular monsoon periods after Alexander the Great's expedition.

The great pillars of Hercules flanking the Straits of Gibraltar were believed to support the firmament at the edge of the land "pancake." Beyond them stretched an all-consuming abyss, a void. Penetration of the dangerous, unknown waters west of Gibraltar marked a revolutionary extension of empirical knowledge. The observations that mariners made there also resulted in decisive changes in the contemporary world picture. The wise Greek Pythagoras taught that the Earth, with all the other heavenly bodies, is shaped like a ball and that these planets circle the central fire, or Sun. Together with his fellow countrymen Herodotus, Aristotle, and Ptolemy, he also helped to create the basis for modern oceanic research. They took soundings, made charts, worked out distances with the

The Roman villa of St. Blase in Castroreale, Sicily. Mosaic with marine motif in the frigidarium. First century A.D.

aid of the stars, and made some progress in plotting the currents, tides, and winds.

Several Greek colonies developed on the shores of the Black Sea and the Sea of Marmara, and in Asia Minor, and good Greek harbors were built in southern Italy. (Long beforehand, of course—in the middle of the second millennium B.C.—the Etruscans had traded in these regions and held sway over the sea to the west of Italy, at the same time having contacts with many eastern countries.) There were so many Greek colonies in southern Italy that the people of the interior, too, started to speak Greek, and the entire area began to be called Greater Greece. The Greeks made long voyages west, even as far as Iceland and the Baltic, and east to the Indian Ocean and areas near the estuary of the Yangtze Kiang river.

It was while the Greeks and Phoenicians were competing fiercely for trade in the fourth century B.C. that the Greek Pytheas of Massalia (now Marseille) appeared on the scene. This geographer and astronomer fitted up what is believed to have been the world's first ship for marine exploration. Around 325 B.C. he sailed north past Britain, the Shetland Isles, and Iceland, as far as the coast of North

Norway, till pack ice blocked his path. Pytheas did not bring back gold or silver; instead, he produced the first description to survive of Scandinavia, or Thule, land of the midnight sun. His observations and experiences marked a great extension of the known world.

Even in those days shipbuilders were producing quite large craft. Thus King Ptolemy Philipator's armored ship (about 200 B.C.) is estimated to have been some 6,500 modern registered tons and 420 feet long. The ship Archimedes designed for Hiero II of Syracuse—the *Alexandria*—is thought to have been of a size corresponding to 4,200 modern registered tons.

The Romans appear on the scene

The spread of Roman rule in the Mediterranean was again a combination of trade and seafaring. The Romans were none too interested in maritime exploration, though, and this declined after the Greeks; and conquests were put before sea exploration. Old superstition and fear of the sea again dominated men's minds.

In Imperial Rome the Mediterranean was considered the inland sea of the Empire. It was the Roman's *mare nostrum* (our sea), on which, during the "Great Roman Peace" of the Empire, there were no political frontiers and hardly any dangers other than wind and weather to threaten peaceful seafaring. The Roman trading ships seem to have followed roughly one basic type, being round broad craft with tapered bows and a high stern that curved inward, rising up into a swan neck. From antiquity onward the boards were usually attached to the wooden frame in two different ways: the ships found in the Mediterranean are all carvel-built, the boards edge to edge; in the clinker-built method, particularly characteristic of northern shipbuilding, the edges of the upper boards overlap those of the lower.

Alexandria, rich and powerful all through the Empire, was the biggest maritime city, transporting corn, for instance, from the Nile valley to the Roman metropolis. Chapter 27 of the Acts of the Apostles describes Paul's eventful voyage in the late summer of 61 A.D. in a ship carrying wheat from Alexandria, which was shipwrecked near Malta before reaching Rome. The ship was so large that it took 276 passengers as well as its cargo. Paul went on from Malta by a ship carrying a picture of Castor and Pollux on its bows, which called at Syracuse, Rhegium, and Puteoli on its way to Rome.

Of the Romans' voyages to northern latitudes it should perhaps be mentioned that they discovered the Baltic around 65 A.D., during an expedition to Zamland, the coast of east Prussia, in the time of the Emperor Nero.

The Romans also held gladiatorial displays on water. They built amphitheatres round artificial lagoons *(naumachiae)*, on which galleys engaged in naval fights before an audience, which betted heavily on the result. Note the *corvus*, or boarding bridge, on the galley to the right.

About 150 years later the Frisians seem to have started trading between the Rhine delta and Scandinavia.

Greek, Syrian, Arab, Persian, and Parthian commerce at the beginning of our era was real world trade, as the "world" was understood then. It stretched on land far into the Asian interior and by sea from the Straits of Gibraltar through the Mediterranean and the Red Sea to the Indian Ocean and Malacca.

The disintegration of the Roman Empire after the Great Migration epoch led to the decline of navigation and shipbuilding. Piracy also put a stranglehold on Mediterranean seafaring at this period; it was practiced not only by Germanic vandals but also by Islamic Arabs from the north coast of Africa. After the Moors overran both sides of the Straits of Gibraltar in 711 A.D., following their conquest of Spain, they closed trade and navigation's natural gateway to wider waters, indifferent to the fate of established maritime traffic.

The Arabs and Chinese at sea

In those days the Arabs' trading territory extended from the Atlantic shores of the Pyrenean peninsula as far as southern China. Since time immemorial South Arabia had played a leading role in trade on the Indian Ocean and near by inland seas. This extensive Arabian seafaring was linked with the age-old Chinese navigation. From the seventh to the ninth century, Chinese ships made trading voyages as

Shipping in the time of Henry II (1216-1272). Picture: National Maritime Museum, Greenwich.

far as the Persian Gulf. With the rise of Arabian navigation, however, they gradually stopped sailing farther than the Indian mainland. The island of Ceylon (Taprobane of antiquity) seems to have played an important part in trade on the Indian Ocean as a halfway post, and even as a center. Arabian and Chinese seafaring was hardly up to contemporary European standards as far as the actual craft were concerned. In any case, the Chinese and especially the Arabs had a distinct start on the Europeans in navigation in the centuries before the Crusades, but they did not prove able to use it to full advantage.

Seafaring on the Mediterranean during the Crusades and after

For several centuries seafaring in the Mediterranean area languished. Then came the Crusades' era, when for nearly two centuries, from the end of the eleventh century onward, Christian expeditions of conquest were made to Palestine to win the Holy Land back from the infidel. Under the influence of the Crusades, Mediterranean trade was taken over completely by Europeans. The maritime cities of Italy, particularly Venice and Genoa, as well as Florence, now experienced a period of unprecedented richness and splendor. For several centuries the north of Italy was the most important center of world trade, mainly because of the country's very favorable position. These cities handled the transportation of and trade in Eastern goods, selling them to the increasingly prosperous countries of the West, and also shipped off innumerable crusaders to the Holy Land. One crusade ship alone involved anything from 1000 to 1500 passengers.

A great step forward was taken when the Straits of Gibraltar were won back from the Moors by Christian Spain. The first Venetian galleys—breaking the thousand-year boundaries of the Mediterranean's economy—reached the harbors of Flanders in 1318 and thus opened up a new era in the commercial and maritime life of the west coasts of Europe. In 1423 the Republic of Venice, a maritime trading city without par, had some 3,000 merchant craft and 300 warships, with total crews of 36,000 men. The Venetian ships were about 25 metres long, with two full decks and two short decks aft as cabins. The Genoan ships were smaller.

No one knows for sure when there began to be a distinction between merchant vessels and warships, but by the year 1000 it was a well established difference. It seems logical to link the origin of ships intended specifically for trading with the development of the first cities. There was obviously also a

The cog, fifteenth century Hanse ship.

time when shipbuilders tried to make the same vessel fulfill a dual role as merchant ship and warship.

The dominant role of the Mediterranean was of course of great significance for the history of the nations living around it. Cretan, Phoenician, and Hellenic seafaring, of such great importance to the history of culture, would not have been possible if these nations had not also had a military advantage over other coastal and island peoples.

For the whole of antiquity and most of the Middle Ages, the great oceans and regions beyond were unknown quantities to the civilized peoples of the

French color drawing, fourteenth century. Picture: Musée de la marine, Paris.

The nautical motif seal of the town of Staveren, 1246. Picture: Maritime Museum of the Netherlands, Amsterdam.

day. In the earlier Middle Ages ship types and navigational methods in south European waters did not develop to any great extent. It was not until the last centuries of the Middle Ages that Mediterranean seafaring started to come back into the limelight, and for some time, before the great voyages of discovery, experienced a kind of late flowering.

The most important changes in ships during that time were the transfer of the steering oar to the stern post to form a rudder, and the raising of the decks in larger ships. Larger sail area also meant more masts. As well as single-masted ships, a double-mast rig began to be used in large craft. Each mast still had only one sail, though. It was not until the fifteenth century, with the appearance of three- and four-masted ships, that several sails began to be used on the same mast, specifically an extra sail up on the main top. Ships also used a squaresail (spritsail) under the bowsprit in front of the bows.

Europe at this period was a complete world of its own. With time, however, what had been merely sporadic voyages developed established and regular occurrence, and certain regular channels of communication began to take shape even then.

Mainly in consequence of the Crusades, three large trading spheres gradually developed in Europe: a south European trading area in the Mediterranean countries, dominated by the Italians; a north European, or Hanseatic, trading area on the shores of the Baltic and North Sea; and, handling contacts between them, a central European area, consisting of the Danube and Rhine regions, northern France, and Flanders.

Seafaring in the north

In the meantime, seafaring had started developing rapidly far up in the north, in regions whose culture had long been influenced by the sea. This was natural enough, considering the economic and geographic position of Scandinavia: the English Channel, the North Sea, the Skagerrak and Kattegat, and the Baltic with its gulfs to north and east form an area in the north, comparable to the cultural sphere of the Mediterranean, on the shores of which we find the oldest monuments to the trade and seafaring of the Celtic, Germanic, Slavic, and Fenno-Ugric peoples.

The oldest settled regions in this area were the shores of the North Sea and Scandinavia. Compared with more southerly waters, the Baltic and the North Sea have less fortunate climatic conditions. The Mediterranean, for instance, has generally fine weather and hardly any tide. The vast areas of sea traversed by the Vikings, on the other hand, were the frequently storm-tossed

Amsterdam seal, 1418.

Purmerend (Netherlands) seal, fifteenth century.

Sea monster. Medieval drawing.

The Irish saint Brandanus (c. 484–587), the monks' Odysseus and guardian saint of seamen, whose saint's day is May 16. The picture shows St. Brandanus near Jasconius Rala.

high seas west of Norway. It is therefore natural that seafaring in this area developed later than in milder climes with clearer, brighter air. The fact of their climate makes the early seafaring achievements of the Norsemen all the more amazing; they were seamen of incomparable courage, endurance, and competence.

The geographical character of Scandinavia also played its part in the important, even revolutionary, historical events of the turbulent Viking period (c. 800–1050), which was of such significance to western Europe especially. As far as we know, the main reason for the Viking expeditions, as it was for the Great Migrations, was their fast increasing population, with its accompanying poverty, lack of space, and other problems. The Vikings did not voyage to other countries merely as soldier-adventurers, but also as settlers seeking a new homeland, and as traders.

From archaeological finds, we can conclude that seafaring was known as early as the end of the Stone Age—that is, about five thousand years ago—between all the shores of the North Sea (the British Isles, Norway, western Sweden, and Denmark). The Baltic islands of Gotland and Öland were also centers of trade between east and west in the Stone Age, as they have been in later times.

The natural conditions of the north made the Scandinavians not only farmers and sailors, but also shipbuilders. The Viking ships are world famous, but it is very difficult to get any exact information about the earlier craft from which these handsome ships developed.

Scandinavian petroglyphs have preserved for posterity a unique collection of pictures of craft from the Stone, Bronze, and Iron Ages, in other words from about 2-4000 years back. The oldest petroglyphs of boats, found in north Norway, are from the Stone Age. Wooden boats were possibly developed as thin wooden boards or sections gradually took the place of hides, fitted together in the same way as the latter. According to another theory, the Bronze Age boat developed out of the dugout by adding planks to its sides, when the original hull of the boat gradually narrowed and became the keel board. The distinctive construction of Iron Age boats, with the sides and ribs bound together, can be considered as supporting both theories.

Still, we know little of prehistoric northern ships. The horse's head figureheads of Phoenician ships were intended to repel the evil designs of demons. The high curving stem post decorated with an animal head, characteristic of Scandinavian ships as early as the Bronze Age, probably originated in the same kind of belief. Neither these nor Iron Age boats and ships used mast or sail.

Scandinavian shipbuilding

In the 7th and 8th centuries A.D. the craft of shipbuilding developed to a higher level in Scandinavia than anywhere else in Europe. The craft made there probably sailed better than all the other ship models of antiquity and the Middle Ages. By developing the keel the Scandinavians managed to make their ships both broad and deep. The keel made them seaworthy and stable, and also added to their ease of movement. Stability in turn made it possible to use a mast and sails on the open sea, and thus increased their range and speed.

Compared with other, generally clumsy, contemporary craft, the long, slender Viking ship was a real lightning ploughman of the seas. Its shape and

THE GOTLAND PETROGLYPHS. The island of Gotland has a number of monuments called petroglyphs, or rune stones, some of them possibly as old as the fifth century. They are large flat blocks of stone standing upright in the ground. Various symbols and scenes are carved on one side of each stone. The most usual themes are boats or ships full of armed men. The ships in the pictures ascribed to the sixth and seventh centuries show clearly a mast and rectangular sail. The petroglyphs, which are probably gravestones or memorials, are usually difficult to interpret.

5 The sea and man

the decorative dragon's head motif on its prow explain its nickname, "dragon ship." The Viking ships were open rowing or sailing craft, clinker-built from oak or pine, and well equipped for ocean travel. Their average length was 65 to 80 feet, with a crew of 70 to 100 men, and 20 to 30 pairs of oars. There were special warships (the *drake*, or *skeid*), traders (the *knarr*), and even pleasure ships. The warship, rowed with many pairs of oars, was narrower than the *knarr*, the merchant ship. The latter was primarily a sailing ship, and thus wider and higher. The celebrated warship *Ormen Lange* of the Norwegian Olav Tryggvessøn (d. 1000), who was elected king on his return from his Viking voyage, was probably 150 feet long, and rowed with 34 pairs of oars.

In late heathen times, the *snäkka* craft and smaller *skytte* sailing boats of the *ledung* fleets were developed from the Viking ships. *Ledung* meant a kind of naval service which the provinces on the Swedish shores of the Baltic and Gulf of Bothnia and around Lake Mälaren, with Gotland, were obliged to perform by supplying crew and food for naval ships, perhaps even by supplying the ships.

Old Viking ship finds

The three large ship burial grounds found around Oslo fjord have told us more about how the Vikings' sailing craft were built than any other ship discoveries. These open, clinker-built vessels, over a thousand years old, are amazingly well preserved and have been on display for several decades now in a specially built museum at Bygdøy, Oslo. The sites of the Oseberg and Gokstad ship burial grounds are in clay soil, which preserves wood well.

Valuable ancient ship finds have been made in other Scandinavian countries, too. Most recently, in 1962, five ships were found in Skuldelev, Denmark, in unique underwater excavations in the middle of the fairly shallow Roskilde fjord. These ships, three of which proved to be merchant craft, date from some time after the year 1000.

The profusely decorated and graceful Oseberg ship (found in 1904) is the finest product of Viking craftsmanship, and belonged to some powerful royal figure. The Gokstad ship (found in 1880), dated at around 850, is a structural masterpiece. Its length overall is 75 feet and maximum beam 16 feet. Devices corresponding to modern tackle were used to regulate the tautness of the sails, and the ship has a steering oar. The Gokstad ship seems to have no particular character. It could have been used as a warship, but could also carry enough cargo for sea transportation to pay.

In 1893 an exact copy of the Gokstad

ship was built in Norway. The Norwegian captain Magnus Andersen and his crew sailed this craft, called the *Viking*, across the Atlantic, and she was put on show at the Chicago world exhibition held the same year. The *Viking* proved to sail perfectly; in one day she covered 223 nautical miles.

If we measure the volume of the wood used on the ship and multiply it by the specific gravity of timber, we get a total weight of about 16,000 pounds for the Gokstad ship. To this we can add about 2750 pounds for rivets and standard fittings, which gives us a displacement of 8.5 tons. It has been estimated that the ship's mast, weighing about 800 pounds, was 30 feet long. From the length of the yard, the squaresail would have been maximum 40 feet wide. The old Scandinavian sail was of woolen broadcloth, which was not comparable to linen for durability. The cloth stretched with the pressure of the wind, and eventually the large sails swelled and tore.

The Oseberg Viking ship, ninth century, from the stern.

Stylized man's head. Woodcarving in the Oseberg ship.

The Vikings as seafarers

The Vikings were the best shipbuilders of their day and fearless seafarers in dangerous, icy waters. Navigation was as vital to them as all the other mariner's skills. Without compass[1], or charts, using only the stars, instinct, and their fine seamanship, they sailed to almost all the corners of the then known world. Their commercial voyages and raids took them first to England, Scotland, and Ireland, and then

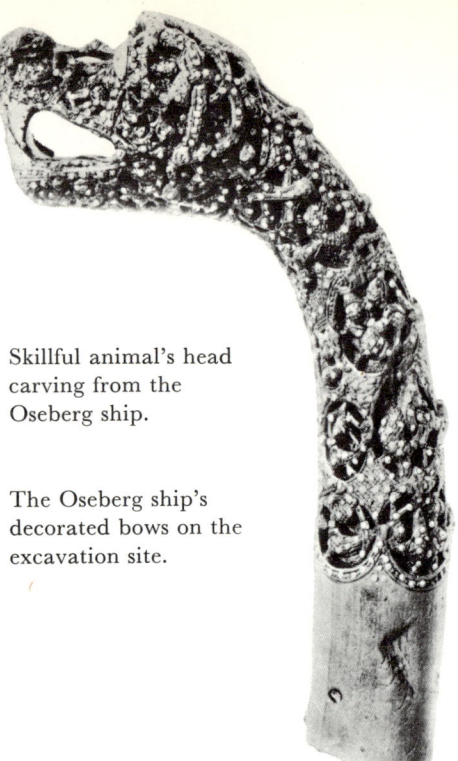

Skillful animal's head carving from the Oseberg ship.

The Oseberg ship's decorated bows on the excavation site.

to the coasts of the continent. Entering the Mediterranean, the Vikings also raided southern France, Italy, and North Africa.

From sagas and early Russian history it is clear that the Swedish and Norwegian Vikings knew, for instance, the Gulf of Finland as early as the ninth century. Thinking of the close contacts between the Norwegians and Arabs, it would not have been surprising if the Arabs had also known the Baltic, which they called Bahrvareng, "the *värings'* sea" (the värings were the Swedish

[1]Certain sagas do speak of a mysterious "sun stone."

Vikings). Relations between the Arabs and Vikings would seem to have been much closer than has long been believed possible. The main reason seems to have been a matter of fashion, as furs were very popular almost all through the Middle Ages.

Apparently the Vikings moved east into the Baltic before they went west. They plundered the land of the Wends, Prussia, Kurland, Estonia, and the Finnish coast. An important development was the infiltration of the Swedish Vikings up rivers into the heart of Europe. In Russia they first sailed to Novgorod, and then on along the waterways to the Black and Caspian Seas. Expeditions also ventured as far as Baghdad. In central Asia the Vikings came across caravans from China.

One of the biggest trading centers of the Viking world was the town of Birka on Björkö island in Lake Malaren, about 19 miles west of Stockholm. Our present, rather slight, knowledge of Birka and its trading connections comes from excavations in nearby burial grounds. The town went out of existence possibly before 980.

The Vikings made many discoveries in the course of their voyages on the Atlantic. According to Icelandic tradition many early discoveries—Iceland itself, Greenland, and the American continent included—were made by accident; the ships got swept off course by storms, were lost in fog, or went astray for some other reason. The Vikings settled in Iceland and Greenland, and in England, which they eventually overran. They founded the French province of Normandy, whose name also comes from the Norsemen, or "Normands."

In 1964 J.K. Tornöe published a book, *Early American History—Norsemen before Columbus*, in which he applies very detailed topographical analysis to the examination of old sources. According to this Norwegian scientist, the routes and landings of the Viking voyages of discovery must be completely reevaluated on the basis of the assumption that their ships could travel a good deal faster than had earlier been thought possible. The writer claims that the Vikings used the foresail, which would have considerably improved the sailing characteristics of their craft; they would thus have been able to reach a speed of as much as eleven knots, instead of the six knots formerly thought feasible.

Wherever the Vikings landed on their voyages, they struck terror and awe into the hearts of the inhabitants, as they were unscrupulous, violent ruffians as enemies, and as traders lacked the diplomatic patience of the Greeks, for instance. One extant source tells how, on June 8 in the year 793, a group of vessels was sighted off Scotland and the island of Lindisfarne. The Vikings had come: they plundered the

The Norwegian Viking Leif Ericson with his thirty-five men, setting off on his long ocean voyage around the year 1000.

period and without lasting significance for world history.

Yet just as theoretical physics teaches that neither matter nor energy can disappear but merely changes its form, so, too, the paths that man has taken cannot seem purposeless or wasted when seen in their proper, wider perspective. The old saying, He who knows not where he goes, goes furthest, holds good for the Vikings.

Trade in the Middle Ages

The goods in which international trade dealt in the early Middle Ages were already quite varied. The Scandinavian countries specialized in the export of furs, with Finland also selling salmon, dried fish, seal fat, dairy products, and, some opinion would venture, probably slaves. England sold metals like tin and lead, wool, and foodstuffs such as corn, butter, and cheese. Flanders and the Frisian Islands, which were northern Europe's leading commercial power in the eighth century, sold fine linen and woolen cloth in international markets, and the Baltic lands sold amber. The Franks were well known for their fine metal work, especially arms, which were a

island's monastery, killed cattle, slaughtered everyone who tried to resist, burned all the buildings, and left with all the island's gold and silver.

Before the Vikings' golden age ended they had settled areas from the Volga in the east to Newfoundland, across the Atlantic, in the west. The Viking story ended with the spread of Christianity into Scandinavia. With it, seafaring in the north began to decline. Great as this had been in the Viking days, it was merely a kind of transition valued commodity in other countries, the Saracens, for example, buying large quantities. The Franks also exported large amounts of foodstuffs, and slaves which they captured in the German interior. Various western European countries also sold precious metals. These products western Europe exchanged for the luxuries of the south and east: silk and cotton, purple dye, paper, sugar, perfumes, precious stones, decorative metal work, etc.

All commerce in the Middle Ages had to overcome many difficulties. These were troubled times, with little security or mutual trust. Sea trading, too, had its own obstacles to overcome. With no pilot stations, lighthouses, or sea charts, it was easy for a merchant ship to run aground. The feudal baron in whose coastal waters the shipwreck occurred had the right to seize the ship and its goods and to take its crew captive, usually releasing them only against large ransoms. As well as this unscrupulous plundering, many of the feudal aristocracy went in for piracy, which was one of the main plagues of seafaring right up to the nineteenth century, as indeed it still is in the waters of east Asia, for example.

Wrecking was a familiar phenomenon in northern latitudes, too. Even at the end of the Middle Ages the coastal population of Finland used to pray, "Lord, bless our shores with shipwreck." As "shipwreck" consisted in a ship's merely running aground, in many cases all the cargo was stolen and the ship burned. This barbaric custom was based on the primitive Germanic idea that the stranger has no legal redress and his property no owner.

The Hanseatic League and its might

Unstable conditions forced commerce to take such safety measures as its power and opportunities permitted. By the twelfth century at the latest, many German towns started to found *hanses*, or leagues, to protect and extend their trade. The Hanseatic League, which grew to be famous and mighty, was founded to protect and promote trade and navigation on the North Sea and the Baltic by the coastal towns of North Germany and a number of important inland trading cities. It had a large commercial and naval fleet, and waged independent wars.

The Hanse of course used all the usual types of contemporary merchant ship, but the most famous of them, linked firmly to the Hanse name, was the cog. This was a high, short, round-hulled and decked trader, with "castles" fore and aft. There were usually one or two masts, each with a single squaresail, or often with a rectangular sail on the aftermast. The cog was often armed as a warship, too.

According to the Swedish researcher

Sune Lindqvist, the cog type of vessel in the Baltic area goes back to pre-Merovingian times. It was probably an adaptation of the Roman merchant ship; the Scandinavian peoples have borrowed much more from the Romans than merely shipbuilding and maritime techniques. The actual vessel type was thus not uniquely Frisian, but a trading craft widely used for about a thousand years, from the days of the Great Migrations to the last centuries of the Middle Ages. However, the cog's dominant position in northern shipping is demonstrated, for instance, by the fact that towns founded far away from river estuaries (e.g. Turku, the old capital of Finland), which deep-riding craft could not reach, were moved nearer the sea. Toward the end of the fourteenth century the cog began increasingly to make way for the round-sterned galleon, or carrack, which took more cargo. The mizzen sail was an adaptation of the lateen sail used in the Mediterranean, and made for easier steering. Other innovations included the rudder and detachable lower sails ("ponette sails"). Castles were now a permanent feature of the ship's hull.

North European shipbuilding had used the clinker, or lap-jointed, method originating from the Baltic area; it had no serious competition until the end of the fifteenth century, in the flat-joint method (carvel). By the middle of the next century all large vessels were built by the latter method.

As the Hanseatic League grew more powerful, the age-old trade route from the Gulf of Finland along the Swedish coast and via Hedeby (earlier Sliesthorp) and Slesvik to eastern and western Europe was abandoned. Instead, goods began to be carried by way of the Lübeck, Hamburg, and Bruges harbors. Ever since the Iron Age the island of Gotland and its port Visby, in the middle of the Baltic, had been a center of trade between east and west. Later, Lübeck took over this Hanse town's status.

During the golden age of the Hanse in the fourteenth and fifteenth centuries, the League consisted of about forty towns—German and under German influence—from Cologne and Amsterdam to Visby and Tallinn, with mighty Lübeck at their head. The whole of north European trade at that period was controlled by the Hanseatic League, and it had large subdivisions in London, Bruges, Novgorod, Bergen etc. The maritime trade of north Europe was linked with the south in the early fourteenth century when Genoa, and soon Venice, Barcelona, and Palma, started to send convoys to Flanders and Britain.

Many factors accounted for the exhaustion of the Hanse's inner strength and the gradual disintegration of the organization. The great voyages of discovery and later the Thirty Years War played their part, as did the Hanse's poor organization, which no longer met the needs of the age. The loss of the League's privileged status and political significance abroad also speeded the breaking-up process. The gradual crumbling of the Hanse was only one part of the change taking place in the whole political and economic system of Europe.

The art and instruments of navigation

Maritime traffic presupposes navigational skill (Latin *navis* = ship, *agere* = set in motion) by which a ship's position and course can be fixed. The mariner of ancient times had no aids of any kind. Gradually man learned something of the movements and positions of the heavenly bodies and found them useful, because they permitted him to travel at night as well as by day. It was only after ships started using sand and water clocks, around 600 B.C., that it became possible to measure the speed and length of a voyage.

The oldest discovery showing a pilot is a model boat in Cairo Museum, found in a rock tomb about 4,400 years old. The crew includes a lookout standing in the bows (hands and sounding rod broken).

Over the ages seafarers provided themselves with specially built sea-

A hanging lamp made in the shape of the Pharos lighthouse, c. 100 A.D. Reddish-brown terra cotta, height 7 inches. Found in Faiyum, Upper Egypt. Collection of the Greek and Roman Museum, Alexandria.

VIKING. The exact origin of this word is unknown. Some scholars believe it may have meant "men of the bay." The sagas and Edda poems and the complex Skaldic poetry tell of the history and mythology of the Viking. The Norsemen themselves never used the word "Viking" as a general description for their peoples, nor did their neighbors—the objects of their raids.

marks to guide them on their way. It is thought that the first beacons burned on the Persian Gulf long before the Christian era. They were a kind of "eternal flame," using natural oil, tended by priests who gave sailors information about their routes. Homer tells us, around 950 B.C., about beacons lit to help sailors, but does not describe them further. A bare three hundred years later the Greek poet Leches mentions the lighthouse of Cape Sigeum at the Aegean Sea end of the Hellespont. As early as 400 B.C. there were lighthouses at the mouth of Piraeus harbor. About a hundred years later the famous Pharos of antiquity was built on the Nile delta, off Alexandria; this name has come down to posterity, and some languages have adopted it as the general word for lighthouse (French *phare*, Italian and Spanish *faro*). One of the Seven Wonders of the ancient world, the Pharos acted as "a column of fire at night, a column of smoke by day." Figures for its height vary greatly. The most reliable estimate is thought to be 475 feet, a very respectable achievement even by modern standards. The Pharos lighthouse was badly damaged in several earthquakes and finally destroyed altogether in 1375.

Seafaring did not start developing really rapidly until astronomical measurements, geography, and various equipment came to its aid. When distances and exact chronological measurements began to be used, scholars could start making maps of the then known world, relying, too, on the stories of seafarers. Thus came the first fumbling attempts to set down the outlines of known lands on paper. There were already several such maps in Herodotus' day (c. 450 B.C.).

Alexandria's Claudius Ptolemy holds a unique place in the history of cartography and sailing. He drew up the first map of the world around 160 A.D., the earliest attempt to put mapmaking on a scientific basis. Of course his map was very faulty and deficient by modern standards, but its great value is shown in the fact that it remained the official map of the world for an incredible period, some 1,400 years.

The oldest known sailing guide in Latin, a fragment of which has been preserved, is in a manuscript mentioned by Adam of Bremen in 1076. This itinerary describes a voyage from the Danish town of Ribe along the west coast of Europe via the Straits of Gibraltar to the Palestinian town of Akko (Acre).

The earth's magnetic field is used to fix a ship's course. The compass, whose importance to shipping can hardly be overestimated, made it possible to plan and execute longer voyages. The compass was already known in China in antiquity; it is explained in a Chinese dictionary dating from 121 B.C. The Arabs learned to use the compass in the eighth century, but it did not reach Europe, through the Mediterranean, until the thirteenth century and took still another century to get to Scandinavia. The West has the Arabs to thank for other devices, too: e.g., the hinged rudder (thirteenth century) and the astrolabe, invented by the Greek Hipparchos, which was used to fix the altitudes of the heavenly bodies. The first sea chart known was made by Petrus Vesconte in 1311, but it was not until ocean voyages became really common that more attention began to be given to the production of nautical charts.

The conquest of the seas

The advance from the Middle Ages into the modern period, the intellectual breakthrough of European man, was a period marked by a number of revolutionary inventions and above all by exploration and voyages of discovery, thanks to which the world opened up in all directions and began to look quite different. This was the dawn of the modern age. As the Crusaders had not succeeded in overcoming the barrier formed by the Islamic Arabs, individual adventurers set course for India and the other wondrous lands of the East, as harbingers of trade and Christianity—the two were easily combined.

From the end of the thirteenth century onward, Indian monks and merchants made journeys deep into Asia lasting many years. Explorers from this period deserving special mention were the Venetian merchants Nicolo and Maffeo Polo, and the former's son Marco, who made the famous expedition to Kublai Khan in China and returned by sea, learning much about the East Indies, India, and Ceylon.

The call of the Far East

It was, however, impossible even to think of making permanent contact with the mysterious East, whose fabulous riches were the dream of poor medieval Europe, by the tortuous overland route; the great Mohammedan barrier, which shut off the long land routes to the East, had to be circumvented in some way. And so arose the aspiration to find a sea route, either around Africa or across the Atlantic. Somewhere over there lay the island of St. Brendan, a paradise corresponding to the Islands of the Blessed and Gardens of Hesperides of classical antiquity, which the Irish monk had once chanced across.

By this time the compass was already in common use in Europe, and mariners were willing to venture into the open sea. Yet hardly a ship had crossed the Equator. It was thought that the regions beyond were mere sun-scorched wastes and that men and ships would be lost in the fierce heat. Terrible tales were told of sea monsters and currents of fire and water which dried into jelly and in which ships got caught and lost.

It was known, however, that south of India lay a great sea, the Indian Ocean. In old tales this ocean was said to circle Africa and link up with the western sea, the Atlantic. If this was true, then it was possible to get to India by sailing out to the Atlantic from the Mediterranean via the Straits of Gibraltar and then following the African coast, first south and then east. For a long time fear overcame any desire actually to make this voyage across the unknown deeps of "the green sea of darkness."

Then the Portuguese, whose interest in the sea had grown since the Italians started to sail to western Europe regularly in the fourteenth century, began to sail farther and farther south, especially along the west coast of Africa. When the expeditions sent out by the far-sighted, idiosyncratic scholar-prince Henry the Seafarer reached Cape Verde, the westernmost headland of Africa, in 1445, the news dealt a severe blow to earlier prejudices, and new hopes awakened. For the first time European man had reached the homeland of the black race, the Negroes, and had with amazement studied the luxuriant tropical vegetation that begins in these regions. The hot zone was not all waste land after all, but quite the opposite of a desert.

The sea route to India is discovered

The great goal—the discovery of a sea route to India—began to look increasingly attractive. In 1486 the Portuguese explorer Bartholomew Diaz reached the southernmost tip of Africa, which was later given the name Cabo da boa Esperaçna, the Cape of Good Hope. Spanish discoveries in the west soon after this urged the Portuguese to try their luck even further. In 1498, with three small ships, Vasco da Gama finally reached Malindi on the east coast of Africa and then, guided by an Arab pilot, sailed on to India and the harbor of Calicut on the coast of Malabar, then India's biggest port. The fact that the same amount of goods that could be bought for one ducat in Calicut cost five or six ducats in Alexandria and sixty to a hundred ducats in Venice gives us some idea of all that a direct sea route between Europe and India meant to European trade, and to Italy as its "middle man."

Throughout Indian waters the newcomers came across Arab sailors and merchants, who immediately sensed that the Portuguese were enemies to both their religion and their trade. They say that the first Portuguese to step ashore on Indian soil was greeted in Spanish by an Arab standing on the shore with the following words: "The devil take you who brought you here!" But there were other reactions. One Arab interpreter greeted the Portuguese in their own language: "Welcome to you all! Praised be God who brought you to this, the richest land in the world!"

The Portuguese were thus the first European seafarers to delve into the original sources of the treasures of the Orient. They had to dispatch considerable military might to India, but with the aid of their superior navigational and fighting power, succeeded in a couple of decades in superseding the Arabs and winning themselves a firm foothold for the pursuit of trade in several coastal regions of India. They also established bases farther east in the Indian Ocean.

Plenty of descriptions exist of the great enterprise of Indian shipowners, and of the vessels which sailed to Malacca and Indonesia across the Bay of Bengal, even carrying loads of horses. The travel memoirs of the enthusiastic globetrotter Ibn Batutan, from the 1330s, describe the huge junks which plied between China and India. He writes of their first class accommodations, bathroom, toilet, cabins, single and return reservations, etc., as if these were matters needing no explanation.

According to Marco Polo, the Chinese were more skillful shipbuilders than the westerners. Their sailing ships were usually four-masted, made of pine, secured with iron nails, and decked. Below decks were fifty or sixty cabins, where merchants could make themselves completely at home. The ships were divided into sections with waterproof walls. The joints were stopped with hemp and a mixture of lime and wood oil. Each ship had several different sizes of lifeboat, which were hung at the sides during the trip.

One intimation of the standard of earlier Chinese seafaring is that in 414 A.D. the Buddhist Fahien sailed by merchant ship in rare comfort from Java to Canton, across the South China Sea.

Seeking and finding America

One of the most well-known — if not the most well-known — dates in the history of exploration is 1492. Everyone connects this year with the discovery of America and Christopher Columbus. However, the story of the discovery of the New World is by no means so simple and straightforward. In the last few years there has again been widespread international debate on this question because of the discovery of a very interesting old map. The names of other early explorers of North America have been brought up and various theories put forward about the earlier settlement of the continent.

According to one ethnologist's hypothesis, America was first settled from Siberia via the narrow Bering Straits and the Aleutian island chain. It would have been possible to cross these straits — less than fifty miles wide — on a raft of tree trunks, particularly as the steep slopes of the opposite shore are visible from the mountain on Cape Dezhnev headland in clear weather. Russian historians claim that in 1451 Russian Cossacks under hetman Ivan Serafimov crossed the Bering Straits, horses and all, and founded the first European colony on the American

A leaflet published in 1493 depicts Columbus' arrival in America like this.

continent. On the other hand, we must not forget the possibility that the original home of the Eskimos of northern Canada could have been somewhere in the arctic regions of Europe. Very probably a land bridge joined the European continent to Greenland in the Tertiary Period.

Settlers could also have sailed to America in primitive craft from the islands of the Pacific. The latest conjecture points to the islands of Japan. In the January 1967 issue of *Scientific American*, the American anthropologists Dr. Clifford Evans and Dr. Betty Meggers argued that the peculiar symbols around the edge of pots found in Ecuador show that the Japanese—probably fishermen who had got lost—discovered America about 4,500 years before Columbus. The pieces of pottery would indicate Japan, since pottery of the same kind was typical of the prehistoric Jōmon period.

The Chinese, on the other hand, claim to have found America about 1,000 years before Columbus. A few years ago Peking Academy, in a letter to Jerusalem University, explained that according to Chinese travel stories, the Chinese discovered America around 500 A.D. The Chinese appeal to archaeological evidence in the discovery of the ruins of a Buddhist temple near what is now Mexico City, and also in Peru. The Hongkong journal *Wei Wei Pao* gave an account of an article published in 1961 in the Soviet journal *Knowledge is Power*, according to which the Chinese reached America via Alaska in the same century.

The famous seafaring and trading nation of antiquity, the Phoenicians, are also suggested as the discoverers of America. The outcome of recent research is that Dr. Cyrus Gordon, Professor of Archaeology at Brandeis University, who has specialized in the archaeology of the Mediterranean region, claims that the Phoenicians crossed the Atlantic and discovered both American continents as early

A Viking ship burial place in Gotland.
Next to it, "russes," semi-wild horses rather like ponies.

as 2,000 years before Columbus. Almost a hundred years ago a stone tablet, claimed to be Phoenician, was found in Paraiba, Brazil, but later vanished. A copy of its text was found some time ago in an old notebook. The text tells how twelve men and three women traveled from the Gulf of Akaba round the south tip of Africa to the Atlantic, intending to return home by the Mediterranean. However, the voyagers went off course in the Atlantic and ended up in Brazil. Dr. Gordon points out that there are many points of contact between the Indian cultures and the ancient cultures of the Mediterranean in the time before Columbus, which may have arisen from contacts between Phoenicians and Indians. These similarities include pyramids, a common architecture, and a 365-day calendar.

The Irish, too, have their own legends which tell how Irish monks, under their "Odysseus" Brendan—later the guardian saint of seamen—reached the coast of Mexico in small boats in the sixth century. According to some views, the legends of the Mexican and Central American Indians about long-haired and bearded gods are a direct reference to the Irish monks.

According to some data it looks as

The conquest of the seas 81

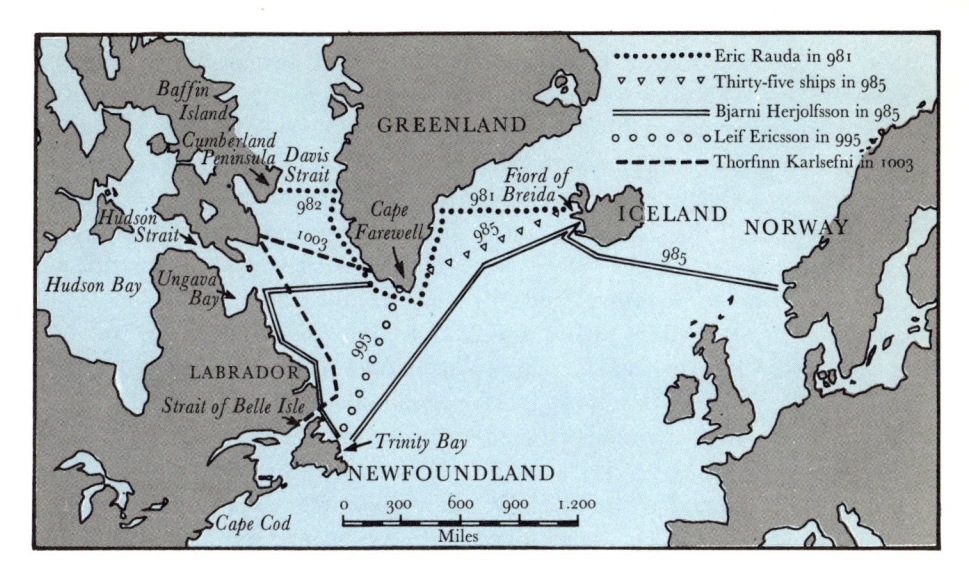

A map showing the routes of five Viking expeditions to North America from Norway and Iceland.

though the Irish could have visited Iceland around the year 795, long before the Vikings officially discovered it.

Probably the first European to see the continent of the New World was the Norwegian Viking Bjarni Herjulfson, whose ship got lost in a storm while trying to sail from Iceland to the colony founded on the south tip of Greenland. Bjarni, who was a trading skipper, not an explorer, did not go ashore anywhere. He probably found himself off the coast of what is now Nova Scotia, in 985. From there he turned north and sailed along the Newfoundland and Labrador coast to the tip of Baffin Island, crossed the wide Davis Straits and finally reached his father's colony in Herjulfsnes. Bjarni's ship's log has been preserved and gives us fairly exact information about this unique and eventful voyage.

It seems strange that the news that Bjarni brought to Greenland did not awaken greater interest among the Vikings. After all, forests grew in the unknown land, full of the valuable timber that Greenland lacked. The next Viking to set off was Eric the Red's eldest son Leif. Around 995 or 1000, he and his thirty-five men took only five days to sail to the fascinating new country, landing at Trinity Bay,

6 The sea and man

Newfoundland, Canada. The ship was loaded to the brink with birch and pine wood and with dried wild grapes, which grew in profusion on the island. For this reason Leif called it Vinland. Leif Ericson was given a hero's welcome back home and the honorary title Lucky Leif.

The old Icelandic sagas give detailed accounts of the adventures of Leif and his followers. The Norwegian archaeologist Helge Ingstad claims that he can finally prove the authenticity of the old story. During excavations in 1961–63 he discovered traces of Leif's expedition and the place where they lived on the north tip of Newfoundland. According to his research the Vikings not only reached Newfoundland but also spent several winters there.

Earlier researchers had come to the conclusion that Vinland was on the east coast of the American continent somewhere between Chesapeake Bay and Hudson Bay; they had usually decided on the Norwegian settlements on Cape Cod. Dr. Ingstad's research results and evidence are so convincing that Professor Julius Bird (curator of the American Museum of National History) and Professor Collins (a scientist at the world famous Smithsonian Institution) have accepted them entirely.

The knowledge Eric and his contemporaries gained about the western sea routes was never lost, and eventually spread throughout the seafaring countries of Europe. An old geographical map, the existence of which was announced by Yale University Library in October 1965, on the eve of Columbus Day, throws new light on this Viking voyage to America and adds confirmation to the old story. Yale University and the British Museum had studied the map for eight years following its discovery by an antiquarian bookshop in 1957. It is thought that the 8-by-16-inch map, in brown ink on parchment, which had been bound together with a medieval manuscript, was made by a monk in Basel around 1440. (It might be pertinent to mention here that there were participants from Scandinavia at the great church conference held in Basel in 1431–49.) This is the first discovery of a genuine pre-Columbus map showing the Vikings' Vinland. It is also the first known map to show the American mainland. The map is for this reason considered by many people to be one of the most important finds of the century.

"It is quite certain," writes Paul Herrmann, describing the adventurers who took part in the first explorations, "that technology has 'discovered' many things to us which were earlier self-evident. We therefore think it incredible that man was capable of crossing the open seas in

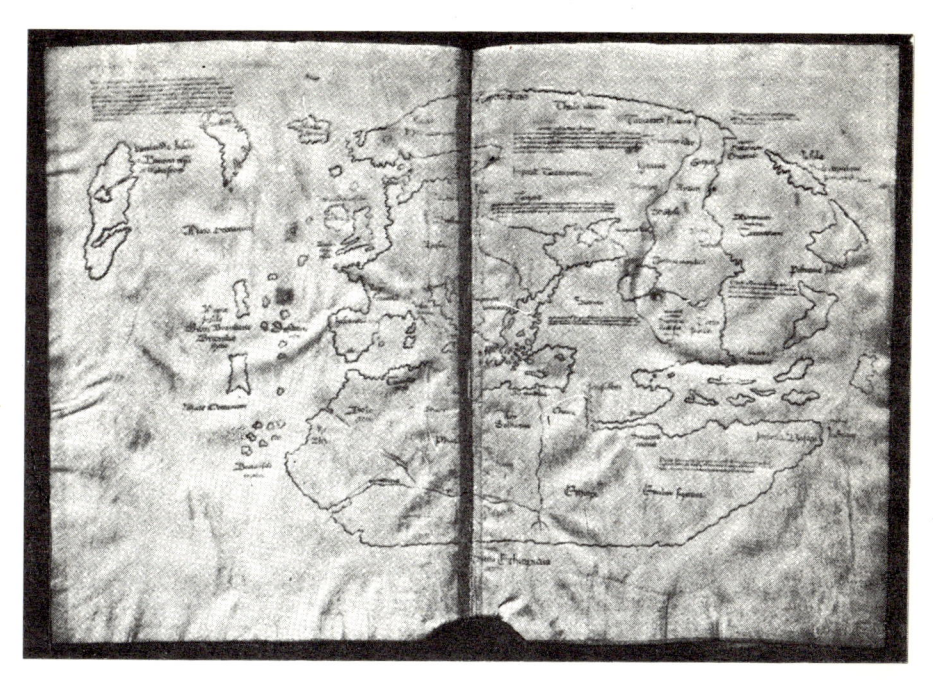

The oldest map showing America. It was probably made in Basel around 1440. It shows the large island of Vinland (Vinlandia Insula) to the west of Greenland. The two inlets are thought to refer to the estuary of the St. Lawrence river and Hudson Bay.

antiquity. But this is certainly the case, so we can also probably assume that white men sailed the Atlantic in the old days, too. The numerous finds made in the New World pointing to the existence of unknown, probably white-skinned people at a high cultural level could certainly be explained satisfactorily if this hypothesis were considered probable. In any case we should not forget that the many rumors in ancient Europe about the great land to the west on the other side of the ocean and of the voyages of discovery made there have been given added conviction by Thor Heyerdahl's expedition."

We can think of the "rediscovery" of North America in the fifteenth century as a new awareness of the existence of old routes, which had been long used and tested. It was certainly no mere coincidence, but linked more or less directly with old tradition.

Columbus and his role in the discovery of America

What, then, is the value and importance of Christopher Columbus, Genoan, famous mariner, writer, scientist, and soldier, in the light of the Viking voyages and recent map finds?

Backed and authorized by the Spanish king Ferdinand and his queen Isabella, the Columbus expedition, with three small ships and ninety men, left the little harbor of Palos (on the Rio Tinto river, near the point where it flows into the Bay of Cadiz) on August 3, 1492, on their first ocean voyage. On October 12 they sighted a small island, probably Watling Island in the Bahamas, to which Columbus gave the name San Salvador. Columbus thought he had reached India and called the natives Indians. The expedition pressed on, and by the 12th of the same month reached Cuba, which the explorer thought was a headland of the Asian coast. They sailed on to Haiti, which Columbus believed was Zipangu (Japan). From there, in mid-March of the following year, he set sail back to his home port. From this point onward, a whole new, almost defenseless, territory found itself at the mercy of the Spaniards.

On his second expedition (1493), Columbus reached the lesser Antilles, Puerto Rico, and Jamaica; on his third (1498), the island of Trinidad, and from there the Gulf of Paria on the coast of South America. On his fourth and last expedition (1502) Columbus discovered the east coast of Central America. To the end of his life he held firmly to the belief that he had sailed along the coast of east Asia. He thus never knew he had found America, and was wrong in many details, though right in the main.

During this century several attempts have been made to reconstruct the most famous ship in the history of the world's shipping—the *Santa Maria*, flagship of Columbus' first American voyage. Unfortunately we have no exact data on her dimensions and appearance, so the thousands of models made of the vessel are more or less incorrect. At best, they can only represent a vessel of roughly the same type and size as their famous original.

The *Santa Maria* was a small, round-sterned sailing vessel which could carry an estimated 80 to 100 tons. The director of the Museo Maritimo, José Maria Hidalgo, under whose direction as "genuine" as possible a copy was built in Barcelona for the 1964 New York World's Fair, gives the *Santa Maria*'s dimensions as: length overall about 77 feet (keel 51 feet), beam about 26 feet, and draft 6 feet. The ship had five sails, with a total area of some 3300 square feet. The *Santa Maria* was slower and rode lower in the water than both her smaller sister

The most famous ship in the history of sailing—the *Santa Maria*, flagship of Columbus' first Atlantic crossing.

ships the *Pinta* and the *Niña*. In his diary Columbus complains that it was too clumsy for voyages of exploration to distant seas.

Irrespective of who was the first European to set foot on any particular point of the American continent, Columbus was the first to make Europe aware of the great New World, and sparked off an invasion. Undeniably, Columbus must be given the credit for opening up the Atlantic route to European culture. He thus marks a very important turning point in the history of mankind. The fact that Columbus is known to have visited the port of London in early 1477, where he probably took part in an expedition to Iceland and there heard tales of the existence of countries across the ocean from seamen and fishermen, by no means detracts from the value of his discovery. Indeed, this just provides further proof of his dogged character, love of adventure, and innate sailing skill.

Facts remain facts. The Yale map, if its disputed authenticity can be vouched for, is mainly a valuable proof of what we already knew about the Norsemen's voyages, specifically the return trip of Leif Ericson.

As regards Columbus, we must always remember that he was not trying to find a new continent. He was obsessed by his ambitious dream of finding a fast western sea route to India and China. He was a man who dared to sail straight across the great ocean with firm faith in his own geographical theory, rather than cling to the coasts or sail from island to island.

The origin of the name "America"

Discussion of the disputes connected with the discovery of America could well also consider the question of whether it is proper to call it America, after the Italian Amerigo Vespucci, even though Columbus' role in the discovery of the New World was decisive. Vespucci, a mariner working for the Spaniards and Portuguese, took part in several voyages of discovery to South America. In 1507 his widely read travel letters were published in one Latin work called *Quatuor Navigationes*. Because of this work, the countries that Vespucci had seen became much more widely known than those discovered by Columbus. Vespucci was the first to write of the continent of the New World, that is, South America. The idea thus became accepted that it was Vespucci who had in fact discovered the new continent proper, while Columbus had found only a few new islands.

The German cosmographer Martin Waldseemüller (Latin, Hylacomylus) published a twelve-page atlas called *Cosmographia introductio* in 1507, in which he uses the name America, after Amerigo Vespucci, for the first time. We have this distant admirer, a school-

---

SEA CHARTS were the "keys to world power" and showed the "way to riches." They were therefore secret documents to be kept well hidden. The fact that the first sea chart now known was made by Petrus Vesconte in 1311 does not mean that there were none before that. The Dutchman Lucas Waghenaer edited the first bound collection of sea charts. The "Mariner's Mirror," published in 1584, covers navigation on the west coast of Europe from the Zuiderzee to Cadiz. For many years this collection guided Dutch, British, Scandinavian, and German seafarers in east Atlantic waters from the Canary Islands to Spitsbergen, as the new editions were expanded to cover the Shetland Isles and the Faroes, and even the Russian coast as far as Novaya Zemlya.

teacher in a small town of Lothringen, to thank for the name. America could—with every reason—have been called Columba, the name suggested by the Spanish bishop Bartolomé de Las Casas for the New World, in honor of the man who discovered it. This omission has since been corrected in that Columbus has been remembered in many names and other connections. The name America began to be used first in Germany and Austria, then in England. To begin with it meant only South America, but gradually extended its meaning to cover the whole New World. The name America did not become common usage until much later.

More explorations

The Spanish conqueror Vasco Nuñez de Balboa and his followers decided to work their way across to the sea that the "Indians" spoke of on the other side of their country. In September 1513, after crossing the Panama isthmus in central America, he became the first European to set eyes on the eastern fringes of the Pacific. The eager conquistador then waded into the water and ceremonially proclaimed this vast sea—the size of which he could not possibly guess—the property of the King of Spain, and gave it the name *Mar del Zur*—the South Sea.

The most audacious and important of the long-distance voyages was, however, that of the Portuguese Fernao de Magalhães, Ferdinand Magellan, who deserves a special place among the leading figures of geographical exploration. For instance, the oldest ocean depth measurements date from his day. With a Spanish fleet of five ships Magellan set off west in September 1519 and a year later sailed through the straits which now bear his name, between Tierra del Fuego and the South American continent. Finding himself in a region of "good winds," he gave the sea the name *el Mar Pacifico*—the Calm Sea. Sailing across this ocean he happened upon the Philippines, which thus fell into Spanish hands. In a fight with the natives there Magellan himself was killed, but his crew sailed on, south of Asia and Africa, and at last, in 1522, one ship and thirteen men straggled back to Spain.

The first circumnavigation of the world was completed, but at a heavy cost and with indescribable sacrifice. The plague of all seafarers, scurvy, caused by lack of fresh food, had of course been only one of many troubles.

The Finnish sailing expert and historian Dr. Eirik Hornborg, who died a few years ago, wrote: "This completed the world's three most important voyages. Columbus had shattered man's ocean horizons; as a pioneering deed his is the greatest of the three. Magellan had gone further, and with incomparable force of will sailed across the border line between East and West; of three heroic feats, his is the greatest. But thinking of immediate practical results, Vasco da Gama's expedition must come first."

Portugal becomes the leading sea power

For Portugal the discovery of a sea route to India and the East Indies meant a fast and immediate rise to prosperity and power. In a bare quarter century, making skillful use of his kingdom's good geographical position, King Emanuel succeeded in making Portugal Europe's most mighty sea power and Lisbon the most important commercial city of the continent. The main center of international trade and shipping had finally shifted from inland sea to ocean.

The heated conflict that broke out between the Portuguese and Spaniards around that time for possession of the trade routes and new lands incited the Spaniards, soon after Columbus' first expedition, to ask Pope Alexander VI to use his influence to bring about an agreement. In 1493 the Pope divided the globe into two spheres of influence. Under the agreement Portugal was to have all the new lands in the eastern hemisphere and Spain all those in the western hemisphere. The border line of longitude first ran just west of the Azores, but was later changed to the 48th meridian. This put Brazil in the eastern hemisphere and thus made her a possession of Portugal. This vital agreement—or to be more exact, papal decree—can be considered the birth certificate of European world politics.

The East Indies, mainly the coveted Molucca spice islands, became a bone of contention between Portugal and Spain and caused numerous voyages across the Pacific in the 1520s and later. By the end of the century the Portuguese especially, but also the Spaniards, had discovered not only the whole East Indies archipelago, and China and Japan, but also New Guinea, New Zealand, Hawaii, Tahiti, Samoa, the New Hebrides, and the Solomon Islands. Many of these places were quite soon forgotten, or "lost," and perhaps not refound until much later.

The growth of Spanish sea power

The Spanish and Portuguese voyages of discovery took them to lands whose valuable ore deposits and other natural products were a sore temptation to other European countries. But infinite riches from the newly discovered lands had permitted construction of massive fleets and thus of Spanish-Portuguese mastery of the seas; the others were left behind.

It was many decades before Europeans generally realized that this was a completely new continent. In our own time nothing less than easy connections to another planet would be comparable to the bright new vistas that gradually opened up to European eyes in the early sixteenth century.

The fact that Portugal gained her riches from trade too easily is one reason her might was toppled so quickly. In 1580 Portugal had the further misfortune of being annexed to Spain and thus involved in this kingdom's wars. Spain's Philip II, who was then at war with the Netherlands, hoped to deal the latter a death blow by forbidding them, in 1594, to dock at Lisbon to load up with Indian goods. But the Dutch merely started sailing straight to the Portuguese colonies themselves; before long they succeeded, one after another, in ousting the Portuguese from their bases.

The Spanish and Portuguese were the natural heirs of the discoveries in

THE TRADE AND MONSOON WINDS. The most settled winds are the trade winds, which blow from the northeast and southeast toward the equator. The trade winds set the equatorial currents moving round the globe. The direction of wind and water—like everything that moves, be it a ship, a bullet, or a bird—is affected by the rotation of the earth: this compels all movement in the northern hemisphere to the right and all movement in the southern hemisphere to the left. The combined effect of this and other forces sets currents into a slow rotating movement, clockwise in northern waters and counterclockwise in southern latitudes.

One important exception is the Indian Ocean. Here there are capricious monsoon winds, and the currents change direction at different seasons. The currents of the vast waters north of the equator move either east or west depending on which monsoon is in force. In the southern parts of this ocean, on the other hand, there is a distinct and characteristic circular, counterclockwise movement, south along the African coast and east with the west wind toward Australia, then north in directions that vary with the seasons, sometimes carrying water into the Pacific, sometimes bearing away Pacific waters.

the west, since they operated from an advantageous position—the edge of the Atlantic and the gateway to the Mediterranean. The Spanish conquerors followed in Columbus' wake and took possession of the fabled treasures of the New World's Eldorado. Expedition followed expedition, mainly driven by a craving for gold, the desire for adventure, and the missionary spirit. Some of these undertakings were peaceful scientific expeditions. Most, however, were military campaigns with the sole purpose of winning material benefits for the participants, mainly gold and fame, and new lands for their king.

These great gains and fast enrichment in the early decades of the sixteenth century made Portugal and Spain Europe's leading commercial, seafaring, and colonial powers. The transoceanic seafaring of these nations also involved a great deal of piracy, privateering, raids, and smuggling by the conquistadors. Goods so acquired could not be handled officially by the customs, or recorded in any other way, which means they do not appear in any statistics.

The products from across the ocean were almost all gold, silver, precious stones, and spices—in other words, goods of great price. For comparison, we could note that the main cargo of

THE ARCTIC NORTHEAST PASSAGE. The northeast passage between western Europe and the Far East, discovered by the Finnish explorer F. E. Nordenskiöld, was opened up, mainly experimentally, by the Soviet cargo ship Novovorones (3,700 G.R.T.). The ship left Hamburg on July 29, 1967 and reached Yokohama, 7,300 nautical miles away, on August 25. A Soviet icebreaker helped to open up a channel along the Siberian coast. The northeast passage shortens sea connections between western Europe and Asia appreciably, as the route from London to Suez to Yokohama is some 11,600 nautical miles long. The saving in time is about two weeks in one direction. To ensure safety at sea all ships must accept icebreaker and pilot accompaniment in the Vilkitski Straits at the northernmost point of the continent, Cape Chelyushkin on the Taimyr Peninsula.

The Russians were already sailing the Arctic Ocean in the fourth and fifth centuries and began their audacious voyages on the White Sea. From 1923 onward, Soviet vessels have sailed regularly from Vladivostok to the Kolyma and from 1927 onward to the gulf of Tiksi at the mouth of the Lena river. In 1932 the Soviet government proposed that the northern passage should be sailed in one stretch and the various separate Arctic links combined. In the next sailing season 43 ships used the passage, and in 1945 a good 150.

the Hanseatic League's ships was cheap bulk goods like salt and grain. The gold cargo that a single Spanish ship brought back from America could exceed many times over the total value of the Hanseatic League's grain cargo for a whole year.

European seafaring conditions revolutionized

The discovery of America and the opening up of sea routes to India had greater and more comprehensive effects on the cultural advance of the modern age than any other events. They completely revolutionized European seafaring and commercial conditions. A whole crowd of new goods appeared on the market to stimulate enterprise, and before long these products were in general, mass demand. The prices of Indian goods, which had been incredibly high, fell rapidly, and European prosperity grew.

This great turning point in world history soon produced a new type of man, too, typifiable as Columbus, Cortez, Copernicus, Pizarro, Erasmus of Rotterdam, or Dürer.

The Atlantic ocean now became an important factor in the economy of Europe, and the self-assertion of its countries grew rapidly. Their position had suddenly become much more central, whereas the Mediterranean regions, and in particular Venice and other Italian cities, lost their status as monarchs of the seas and became mainly centers of glorious memories. The main cities of Atlantic Europe—Lisbon, Madrid, Paris, London, and Amsterdam—became great metropolises, and growing ocean shipping began to increase the amount of traffic in other ports as well.

The great voyages of discovery to east and west were an incentive to voyages in other directions, too. In the late sixteenth century the British and Dutch started searching for a sea route to India through northern waters, one that would not tread on the toes of the Spanish and Portuguese. The explorers of the north east passage, hoping to make their way to east Asian waters via the north of Europe and Asia, discovered the Spitzbergen islands and Novaya Zemlya, but the ice barrier prevented them from getting farther east.

Almost four hundred years ago the British explorer Martin Frobisher tried to find a north west passage between the Atlantic and the Pacific—"the only thing still unachieved in the world that could make a highminded man famous and happy." He discovered the Hudson Straits leading into the bay of the same name and Frobisher Bay, which stretched into Baffin Island, but which he also thought was a sound. He and his crew explored the lands in the eastern part of the North American arctic archipelago, but the ice in the straits

The figurehead from the Finnish four-masted barque Hougomont in the Åland Maritime Museum, Mariehamn. The vessel was wrecked in Australian waters in 1932.

between the islands prevented them from sailing farther west.

As man had been sailing all round Africa and the other continents from the end of the fifteenth to the mid-seventeenth century, the idea inherited from ancient times that there was a large undiscovered Terra Australis, corresponding to the continents of the northern hemisphere, had to be abandoned. Most of the islands in the zone surrounding the Antarctic were, however, discovered during the search for this continent.

The Dutch fight their way into the lead

Before long it was the turn of the Dutch to become lords of the world's seas. As early as the first years of the seventeenth century they were making long voyages and reached the Australian coast; Willem Janszen sailed from Java to the Gulf of Carpentaria in 1606. The most important of their discoveries was made by Abel Tasman in 1642-43, when he found Tasmania and New Zealand and proved that the Australian continent was an island. By the mid-seventeenth century the West knew of the existence of all the continents except Antarctica.

Once the Dutch had decided to seek violent redress for the losses they had suffered on the American and East Indies routes, their navy conquered Java, the Molucca Islands, and Ceylon. They thus won sole rights to the world's richest spice trade, which the Dutch East India Trading Company, founded in 1602, developed energetically, along with other trade. Two years earlier the British had founded their own East India Company. Tough competition for the riches of the East Indies compelled the trading companies to engage professional oceanographers, who prepared the best possible sea charts of the day; information about shipping routes became closely guarded trade secrets.

The Dutch continued to wrest East Indian trade from the Spanish and Portuguese, and in the early seventeenth century Amsterdam took over Lisbon's status as the center of trade. After the defeat of the invincible Spanish armada in 1588, the Dutch also fought their way into the lead in ocean-going shipping. They not only took over trade and thus the oppressor's power from the hated Spanish and Portuguese; they also held sway over the most important European trade routes, and were the heirs of the Hanseatic League.

Holland's fast rise to greatness while fighting against Spain, then the world's

FIGUREHEADS go right back to the pre-Christian era. The ancient Phoenician galleys often had a carved representation of a dreadful sea monster or a horse's head at the prow. The ancient Egyptians, like the Chinese and other Oriental people, painted or carved "all-seeing" eyes on the bows of their craft. Greek mariners preferred gods and goddesses, whereas the Romans used the gods of mountains and rivers, e.g., a lion or crocodile. Since ancient seafarers considered their vessels living creatures, it was quite natural for them to try to give each ship the external shape of life. From this it was but a short step to the superstitious belief that the terrifying or fortunate force in a figurehead passed to those who had the job of designing and carving a new one. When rowed galleys appeared on the scene, the figureheads took on a somewhat more practical significance. Now their primary purpose was to act as a ram above water level. When sailing ships took the place of galleys, figureheads were no longer necessary in this sense, but their importance as a psychological weapon of warfare or attack was still great for centuries. The subjects of sailing ships' figureheads were many, but they were predominantly human figures. With steamships, figureheads disappeared, but in the last quarter century there has started to be a figurehead revival. We can thank one Norwegian shipping company for showing us that the streamlined form of modern ships can still be romantically heightened. An attractive custom that was in danger of oblivion has been revived by fixing cleverly designed cast steel figureheads to ships' prows.

mightiest maritime power, can be explained in many ways. By contemporary European standards she had a very high population density, which made for an easy division of labor. Another reason was that Holland and the Zeeland provinces were well located from the point of view of trade contacts, and the River Rhine formed a natural channel of goods transportation from Holland into the heart of Europe, and thence to the sea. Seafaring came completely naturally to this enterprising nation. Another very important factor was a new type of ship which could be sailed with a smaller crew and was more economical in many ways. Ships began to be built in series, which cut costs appreciably. Usually ships were owned jointly by many shareholders, which reduced the risk of heavy individual losses. In the wars between Sweden and Denmark, Holland was quick to help either side as necessary to prevent the vital straits from falling completely into the hands of either one. Her motive was obvious: three quarters of Amsterdam's wealth was invested in the Baltic trade; it was in fact the main source of Holland's riches.

Throughout the seventeenth century, when trade and navigation still went hand in hand, Holland held an unchallenged lead in these fields. Britain, who had the best chance of becoming a dangerous competitor, had seen her maritime trade crumble in the uncertain conditions of civil war and revolution.

Dutch control of trade in the North Sea and the Baltic made for busy shipping with the seafaring countries of the southwest. From there, the age-old Mediterranean technique of carvel shipbuilding became known to Scandinavia. This led to the development of a new type of craft—the caravel. Perhaps, indeed, there is a connection between the names.

Thanks to her extensive trading, Holland could afford to build up a great merchant fleet. In the 1630s this is thought to have consisted of nearly 35,000 vessels, or about two-thirds of the entire European merchant fleet at the time. According to one calculation, the Hanse merchant fleet at the end of the sixteenth century, before it went into a decline, totaled some 110,000 tons. In 1670, Holland could boast 600,000 tons; even in 1760 Britain had only 460,000.

Right up to the mid-eighteenth century the Dutch merchant fleet was probably the biggest in the world. From then onward this tiny country's merchant fleet began to decline, partly in consequence of the gradual silting-up of its harbors. Naturally enough, the small Dutch nation could not long cling to its dominion of the seas among its powerful neighbors. Yet although Dutch navigation did not in fact achieve anything shatteringly new, it was of great significance for the improvement and practical development of seafaring in general. It was a Dutch lawyer, too, who spoke out for men of all nations. The concept of "the freedom of the seas" of Hugo Grotius, founder of international law and modern philosophy of law, published his *Mare liberum* (Free Sea) in 1609 to rebut British, Spanish, and Portuguese claims to sole or prior rights to shipping and fishing on the high seas. In classical style he proclaimed: "According to international law, passage by ship shall be free to all men to all places."

In the 1730s there were two inventions of great importance to navigation: the reflecting sextant and the chronometer; science thus solved the problem of determining longitude at sea. Nautical charts also became more reliable. These important advances were made at a time when the British flag was moving into the forefront at sea.

The exciting sea novels of the British captain Frederick Marryat, who died in 1848, describe the "keelhauling" which was still used as a punishment on board ship in the last century. In orthodox keelhauling, the ship lay at a standstill — perhaps in the roads outside a harbor — and a rope was passed through the pulley tackle in the lowest yardarm and under the ship's keel into the similar pulley on the other side. The culprit was tied to the rope below the pulley with a lead weight attached to him. The rope was then suddenly released; the wretched seaman dropped into the sea and was "hauled" under the keel to the other side. When this vicious trick had been repeated as often as was thought necessary, the man was dragged onto the deck and often tied to the mast for his mates to deride. "Hauling" alone was a harsh invention, and often resulted in the loss of the victim's life. The immersion in a swimming pool that forms part of the modern "crossing the Line" ceremony is derived from keelhauling.

The famous British warship *Grâce à Dieu* (displacement c. 1,000 tons), popularly called the Great Harry, was completed in 1514 and then had 184 light cannon. In 1536–39 the vessel was completely remodeled.

Britain becomes the leading maritime power

The starting point for Britain's dominion of the seas was Cromwell's famous Navigation Act of 1651, which did a great deal of damage to Dutch seafaring. The Navigation Act laid down that goods from foreign countries being brought to Britain and her possessions had to be carried by British ships under British command, with a crew that was at least two-thirds British. By the late seventeenth century Britain had already proved her superiority in naval warfare.

There were, of course, many other factors working for Britain's development as the leading sea power in Europe and the world. One of the most important was the geographical position of the island realm as the continent's most westerly outpost. From the early seventeenth century onward Britain became the natural center for the evergrowing communications between the Old World and the New. Later — in the age of steam and industrialization — British seafaring was uniquely favored in that the entire kingdom was seated on top of what was possibly the world's finest coal field.

When we think of the natural advantages of any land that lies between two seas, and the country's good position otherwise from the shipping point of view, it seems strange that the sea has always been relatively unimportant to France's history and economy. The main reason is probably that, as a great agricultural country, France has always been self-supporting and felt no particular need to encourage imports. France's political aims and ambitions have thus been land oriented. Another factor was that Marseilles, Cherbourg, Le Havre, Bordeaux, and other French ports were not backed by great industrial areas, as were Antwerp, Rotterdam, Hamburg, London, and Liverpool.

At the end of the eighteenth century the world's merchant shipping consisted of tens of thousands of ships, but their average size was probably only around 100 tons. Even the biggest ocean-going vessels hardly exceeded 400 tons. Their slowness, divergencies from the route, long lay periods in port, etc., prevented the full use of this merchant fleet's capacity. A sailing ship used in transatlantic traffic, for instance, usually did only two return trips a year. Voyages to the distant waters of the Orient, to fetch spices, silk, precious stones, and other valuable goods, took far longer. Sailing ships which found themselves becalmed in the Tropic of Cancer, for example, often had to wait weeks for a wind.

Exploration in Pacific and Arctic waters

Because it was so remote and little known, the Pacific came in for relatively little attention in the first two centuries of the modern age. But after the mid-eighteenth century, interest in exploration of the Pacific and particularly Oceania, i.e. the vast archipelago in the southwest Pacific, grew tremendously, and expedition after expedition headed there.

One name in particular comes up in connection with Pacific exploration and oceanography — the British sea-captain James Cook, a leading figure in the history of exploration, whose expeditions taught the world about Australia and Oceania. Like so many other fearless explorers, Cook met a tragic end. On his third ocean expedition in 1779 he was stabbed in the back during a clash with the natives in Hawaii.

By the nineteenth century there were no longer any very important discoveries to make in the Oceania area. The

7 The sea and man

islands of the South Seas soon began to be visited by fast copra-carrying schooners, the best type of vessel for crossing the dangerous coral reefs. Around the middle of the century, the European powers also began to venture into the central Pacific. Besides Britain and France, the United States and Germany and finally Japan also started to appear on the scene to divide the spoils and watch over their interests.

The old dream of a northern passage leading straight to the riches of Asia tempted many expeditions to brave the icy wastes of the Arctic Ocean. The British, in particular, were trying to find a way to China through the north of Europe and Asia as early as the mid-sixteenth century. The ice barrier proved too great, however, and the men of ships that got stuck in the ice died of cold and hunger. Even so, these expeditions were not entirely profitless, as the waters of the Arctic Ocean proved rich in whale and seal. Finally the long-sought northeast channel was discovered by the Finnish-born explorer A.E. Nordenskiöld, who in 1879 sailed his ship the *Vega*, under the Swedish flag, through the Bering Straits to Japan and around Asia via Suez Canal to Europe. Even so, at that time the severe arctic conditions still prevented the northeast channel from becoming a significant link between Europe and the eastern parts of Asia.

Many nations—primarily the British—also searched for a northwest passage north of America. Expeditions followed one after another, but the natural obstacles north of America were incredibly great. The existence of a northwest passage was finally proved in 1835, but it was not until 1906 that a single ship, under the Norwegian Roald Amundsen, managed to sail all the way along and reach the Bering Straits. Thus voyages over many centuries, to both east and west, finally dispelled the mystery that had cloaked the Sea of Darkness for so long.

World history perspectives

The beginning of European ocean-going shipping was the preface to the continent's era of ascendancy in world history. Immediately after the first revolutionary voyages, in the age of the great explorations, the European colonial powers began to move into the limelight. Worldwide traffic and trade in a way originated from the colonialist enthusiasms of the sixteenth and seventeenth centuries. True commerce between Europe and the other continents, largely marked by common interests, has really only existed since the last century. The conquest of the seas was without exaggeration a much greater gamble than the conquest of the air, and cost incomparably more in human lives.

The British explorer James Clark Ross was the first (1841) to penetrate the Great Ice Barrier and to sail the coastal waters of the continent. The first team to reach the South Pole was led by the Norwegian Roald Amundsen, on December 14, 1911. Since then expedition after expedition has made research journeys to the Antarctic. To begin with, the goals were purely scientific, but eventually economic factors also came into the picture, as the Great Powers have their own particular interests to watch over. Apart from the coal and uranium hidden under the thick ice layer, the Antarctic proper has only a few material advantages to offer, as far as is known at present.

ANTARCTICA. Unlike the North Pole, which is in a frozen sea surrounded by vast oceans, the South Pole (about 9,000 feet above sea level) is on the globe's highest continent, washed by great stormy seas. Antarctica consists of the great continent itself, which is almost completely ice-covered, and the subantarctic islands in the sea surrounding it, totally some 5½ million square miles. Antarctic exploration has been complicated by the extremely severe climate, with its bitter cold and tempestuous storms. The Russian research station there reports measuring record temperature of minus 88.3 C in August 1960.

The governments which took part in the International Geophysical Year in 1959 signed a unique agreement, according to which the Antarctic is to be devoted to scientific and thus purely peaceful purposes. There are a total of sixty-odd research stations in the Antarctic belonging to twelve countries, with what might be called "occupation zones" held by Norway, Australia, France, New Zealand, the U.S.A., and Britain.

A quick, comprehensive survey of seafaring in antiquity and the Middle Ages and especially of the way people reacted to the sea as a link between people is bound to note some surprising differences for which physical features alone do not provide an adequate explanation; fundamental characteristics of human nature must also have played their part.

Babylonian, Egyptian, Indian, and Chinese navigation was relatively small-scale and limited, possibly because these old cultures did not devote much attention to it. On the other hand, the Phoenicians and Greeks were enthusiastic seafarers. Perhaps in the former case the complacency typical of older cultures which had reached a state of equilibrium was to blame. But why was it that the west coast of Scandinavia produced audacious and skillful mariners, whereas the west coast of Scotland, very similar geographically, has never been of any significance in this respect? And what power nourished in the hearts of the Malaysian-Polynesian race a love of seafaring and wandering, though they developed in similar conditions to the Melanesians and Negritos? Here again, writes the German ethnologist Heinrich Schurtz, we are confronted with cases in which secret forces of mind and character come to the fore and influence the advance of human history.

The different physical conditions under which various nations live have apparently influenced national character and qualities very much more than racial traditions. As the German researcher R. Hennig points out, "There have been just the same brave seafarers of the kind that the northern race has produced in such great numbers, among the Semites, Mongolians, and Malaysians. Yet it is completely indisputable that these and other nations have only proved themselves competent seafarers in places where their environment, their home background, has perforce developed strong-minded natures willing to brave the caprices of the sea, generation after generation. Does this not show that in similar conditions nations develop the same special characteristics, quite irrespective of the race that they happen to belong to? However, we have to admit that racial characteristics decide whether the advance is slow or fast."

The trials of life at sea

The beginnings and expansion of ocean-going shipping in the early centuries of the modern period required a completely different outlook from that in coastal and inland sea traffic, and the patriarchal conditions that had prevailed on board ship since the old days were undermined. Earlier, the skipper had been more of a leader than a commander, and in traditional style asked his crew for advice on the most important questions and followed the majority opinion. Later, the authority of officers grew and they became more remote from their men. The long distances sailed and the unwieldy crews called for a high level of discipline, and ships' command was strict.

There were new hardships on long voyages lasting several months or even years, which had been unknown on the old shorter coastal routes. Monotonous, rationed food which often went bad during the trip, the shortage of drinking water, and incredibly bad general sanitary conditions caused great difficulty and a high death rate on a slow voyage. In strange overseas ports the local diseases (cholera, yellow fever, malaria, etc.) could have disastrous consequences. Sometimes the entire crew of a sailing ship died of fever, some on land, others at sea.

Other great trials were the dangers of storms and of poorly charted or completely unfamiliar waters. We must also remember the low standard of navigation, which produced many miscalculations. The final straw was the danger of fire, a constant threat in wooden ships: after all, lighting and cooking facilities were very primitive.

In spite of all this, the heroic conquerors of the high seas, mainly the Portuguese and Spanish, set off boldly on their long voyages. In the middle of a tempest they had a childlike belief in their guardian saints, sang their Miserere, and died with the name of the Virgin on their lips. The bodies of those who died at sea were dropped over the side without further ceremony, into the bosom of the all-consuming deep. But for those who survived, life went on!

From sail to steam

The seafaring which influenced the cultural development of the human race over the centuries used sail and oar, particularly the former. Seafaring really began to be of significance for the history of the world when, at the end of the fifteenth century, it began to brave and conquer the oceans.

The late history of rowed vessels

Until the late Middle Ages, rowed craft, either as such or as combined rowing and sailing vessels, continued to be of great importance, particularly as warships. The low galley which originated in the seventh century rapidly became the most common type of warship, thanks to its fine fighting trim and seaworthiness, and was used right up to the beginning of the nineteenth century. The galley differed from the war craft of antiquity in that all its pairs of oars were at the same level. It was usually about 160 feet long, with one to three masts, lateen sails, and a poop construction in the stern. The rowers, or galley slaves (about 100 to 150 men), were either criminals carrying out their sentences or prisoners-of-war. A rowed galley could reach a speed of as much as five to seven knots. In the twelfth century galleys began to be powered mainly by sail, but rowers were always used in battle. There were also trading galleys and special galleys as well as war galleys.

The heyday of the rowed fleet lasted until the fourteenth century, when guns gradually began to take the place of the metal prow, or buffer, which had been the main weapon of sea warfare. Thereafter the rowed fleet fought an unequal struggle against the sailing fleet and gradually disappeared.

The sea and its dangers beckon

The seventeenth century was the time of Robinson Crusoe and the Flying Dutchman. The sea offered dangers and mysteries in plenty, but not enough to frighten off intrepid mariners. Holland's mighty fleet attracted seamen most, but other coastal nations also began to engage in navigation. The internationalization of the high seas was well under way.

The growing interest in ocean sailing could not, however, hide the fact that the main spheres of maritime competition, even in the 18th century, were coastal waters and the inland seas. Thus the north Europeans' "Spanish voyages" to the Mediterranean, primarily in search of salt, wine, colo-

MASK PAINTING. There was a great change in the decoration of ships during the Napoleonic Wars, the new style soon becoming international. Earlier, ships' hulls had been tarred and painted in various colors. Now they were painted black, the deck junctions marked out in white and the gun emplacements also painted around in black. Merchant ships which had no guns were painted in the same way. The idea was to make them look like warships and thus frighten off any pirates.

---

nial supplies, etc., in which Finnish frigates and other sailing ships also took part with growing enthusiasm from the 1730s onwards, were in fact coastal and inland sea traffic, though by Finnish standards they seemed like great voyages.

The most disgusting phenomena in seafaring at this period were the widespread piracy and the slave trade. The constant nightmare that haunted mariners in the sixteenth, seventeenth, and eighteenth centuries was the piracy that flourished on most seas and waterways. This sometime highly profitable pursuit was practiced mainly by the "barbaric peoples" of North Africa (Algeria, Tunisia, Tripoli, and Morocco), and by gangs of unscrupulous adventurers, the most famous being the West Indian buccaneers. With their well equipped and manned vessels, the pirates would make surprise attacks on peaceful merchant ships, kill or imprison their crews, and carry off the spoils to the nearest pirate harbor, where they were divided. Seamen taken prisoners were customarily sold as slaves.

The first Negro slaves were transported to North America in 1620. With the beginning of Negro slavery, the transatlantic slave trade really got going, mainly in the hands of the British from 1642 onward. It has been calculated that in the three hundred years of American history about four million Negroes were imported. The human loss sustained by Africa is much greater, however: due to the dreadful conditions on the voyage across the Atlantic, 15 or 20 per cent of the slaves are believed to have died.

The main sailing routes

In spite of the improvements made to sails and sailing ships over the ages, it was impossible for sailing ships to maintain regular services on any route because of the unreliable winds. On ocean voyages the route had to be planned to utilize the prevailing winds as effectively as possible: the trade winds blowing on both sides of the equator, the monsoon winds between Asia and Africa and Australia, which changed direction according to the time of year, and the west winds of higher latitudes.

Going from European waters to America, sailing ships still head south first so as not to have to progress against the southwest winds and the Gulf Stream. Southwest winds are so common and widespread in the north Atlantic, however, that it is usually quite difficult to sail to North America. If the ship's destination is Central America, South America, and Africa, she can take advantage of the steady northeast trade wind. Around the Tropic of Cancer the route divides, going west to the West Indies, south-southwest to the coast of Brazil and southeast to the southern part of Africa. The last mentioned is an easy trip: a ship is speeded on her way first by the north winds, farther south by the west winds, so sailing to Australia is no problem once she is past the south tip of Africa, the Cape of Good Hope.

The return trip from South Africa to Europe goes quite well to begin with, with the aid of the southwest trade wind, but sailing west around South America poses quite a problem because of the prevailing west winds. In early days many a ship had to spend months waiting for a favorable wind to get through the Magellan Straits or around Cape Horn to the west coast of South America. Once there, she was helped northward by the current along the coast of Chile and Peru and later by the southeast trade wind. Sailing to East Asia from

---

C R E W. The crew of a big sailing ship consisted of the commander, two mates, a carpenter, a sailmaker, and ten to sixteen men: able seamen, ordinary seamen, and cabin boys. There was also a mess crew: a steward and cook, and sometimes a cook-steward and mess boy, if the steward himself saw to the food. Smaller barques of about 500 G.R.T. had a crew of about twelve: captain, two mates, cook-steward, and eight seamen. A large four-masted barque (about 2,000 G.R.T.) needed a crew of about thirty.

---

the west is always difficult, as the route changes direction in the Malayan archipelago. Farther north the main dangers are the frequent violent storms, or typhoons. Sailing across the Pacific, ships must navigate so as to best utilize the trade wind and, sailing in the opposite direction so as to bypass these areas, aim either farther north or farther south, into the winds blowing from the west.

The journey from Australia to Cape Horn usually took about a month. As far as we know, the speed record for deep sea sailing vessels is held by the Finnish four-masted steel barque *Parma*, which in 1933 sailed from Victoria to Falmouth on the southwest coast of England with a cargo of corn in 83 days, and in 1936 from Europe to Australia in 73 days. She often reached a speed of 16 to 17 knots, and sometimes an average speed of close on 18 knots with good winds. The usual cruising speed of sailing ships was around 7 or 8 knots.

After a century or so of hard-won progress, sailing had reached a standard by the beginning of last century that could give a travel writer called Zimmermann cause to rhapsodize: "How great indeed is man at sea, how far above all other earthly beings! Even in the darkness of night he speeds across the vast world seas with the swiftness of an eagle. A glance or two at the stars, his compass, and his chronometer, a couple of calculations, and he is firmly fixed on his route. With scrupulous precision he fixes the exact point on those great, distant shores which shall be his destination. Thanks to the exactness with which the position of islands and harbors are marked these days, he reaches the places where he can get rest and provisions just as he would on land."

RIGGING. The following inventions can be considered important developments in the history of rigging: the raising of a new sail above the original single squaresail, detachable topmasts, the footrope and jackstay, which together produced a complete revolution in the rigging of sails, the adoption of wire, first in standing and later in running rigging, and finally the mechanization of sail handling in large ships through the patent block, brace, and halyard winches, and similar mechanical aids.

These words describe a level of seafaring to which no one today would entrust cargo or passengers. But even so, it was a long step from Magellan to Cook. The progress made in three hundred years was so great that the glowing praise of the passage just quoted is completely understandable.

With all their great improvements, though, ships were basically the same as in the early days of ocean sailing: a hull of wood, and rigging of wood, rope, and sailcloth. Such vessels main-

THE ROMANCE OF SAILING SHIPS. It is often claimed that our ports and harbors have lost most of their romance with the disappearance of high rigging and swelling sails. Though this is somewhat of an exaggeration, as romance is a subjective rather than objective concept, which lives on irrespective of human activities and procedures, the mechanization of navigation has given engine power an indisputable victory. At the same time certain features that have been cherished by the human mind, as well as being of historical significance, have disappeared.

Eirik Hornborg

---

tained contacts with America, the East Indies, China, and Australia; such vessels sailed round the globe on year-long whaling trips; such vessels made intrepid voyages into arctic and antarctic waters. The ocean-goers of this period were fully rigged ships with at least three masts: frigates and galleasses, barques and barquentines, schooners, brigs, and many more.

From the sixteenth century to the beginning of last century, shipbuilding advanced only slowly. Generally speaking, everything that could be achieved in the construction of wooden hulled ships had already been reached. Later improvements were details at best. The theoretical science of shipbuilding almost completely stagnated. When big new ships were being built, it was not possible to say with any certainty beforehand how well they would sail, etc. It was not until the eighteenth century that ship designers first enlisted the aid of mathematical calculations.

Engine-powered ships are planned

Though navigational skill and seafaring by sailing ship had made great progress, particularly after the great voyages of discovery, men dreamed of a vessel which would not have to rely on the wind. Food for thought had been provided long before by the first engines, fascinating new inventions capable of certain simple tasks. We have to go right back to the ancient cultures of Asia to find devices which could be called engines—mills, stampers, water-raising systems, etc. This is because only the simplest mechanical principles were known among primitive peoples.

Attempts were made even in the pre-Christian era to apply to shipping the principle that works a paddle wheel. The story goes that Claudius Caudex's Roman legions were carried to Sicily in ships whose paddle wheels were turned by oxen. A relief from around 527 A.D. shows a warship with three paddle wheels, each turned by two oxen. On the other side of the globe, Chinese sources mention paddle wheels turned by manpower in warships in the seventh, twelfth, and sixteenth centuries. One document in Munich (1430) describes a warship with four paddle wheels fitted on crankshafts turned by four men. Later in the same century the versatile Leonardo da Vinci drew up a number of plans for powering ships. The examples given would seem to be man's first random attempts to create a reliable mechanical way of driving vessels.

In June 1543 a sensational demonstration aroused amazement: the Spanish captain Blasco de Garay had built a ship which could move without sails. Emperor Charles V and his court were the audience when the 209-ton schooner *Trinidad* left Barcelona harbor into the wind, using rotating paddle wheels. The Emperor was delighted with the invention. Then he heard from experts that any ordinary sailing ship could travel at four knots, the top speed of the new dual paddle-wheel ship with its crew of fifty. Once the Emperor withdrew his patronage from the designer, the Inquisition began trying to find out whether he was in league with the devil. The infuriated Garay destroyed his ship's mechanism, gave up inventing, and retreated to a monastery.

Various plans for mechanical devices which would use human and animal labor to power vessels on the water are known to have been made in other countries—in England, for example, in the sixteenth and seventeenth centuries. All were doomed to failure. Greater power was needed before the principle was to have any practical application in ships.

Steam was the power source that solved the problem. In the early eighteenth century the French Academy announced a treatise competition on how a ship could be made to move without wind. In the treatise he submitted to the Academy, Abbot Gauthier explained that the steam engine was the only means then known which could hope to power a ship. Nothing could be proved, of course, until a feasible ship's steam engine had been successfully developed.

Antiquity's acceptance of the natural sciences and technology was minimal.

Paddle steamers on the Mississippi in the late nineteenth century.

For instance, the Alexandrian Heron, the versatile Greek mathematician and physicist, had perceived the applications of steam energy as early as 120 B.C. and built a device in which steam blown from two tubes set a ball rotating briskly, but he was still a long way from a steam engine proper. The devices Heron developed found their only useful application in the temples, when "miracles" produced by blown steam convinced the pious worshiper that his sacrifice had been received with favor by the gods.

The Frenchman Salomon de Caus, at the end of the sixteenth century, was one of the first to recognize how steam power could be used on land and water. His fellow countryman, doctor and physicist Denis Papin, gave a clear account of the principle of a steam-driven boat in 1685. He described a steam cylinder with a piston: this descended under the influence of air pressure when the steam below it condensed. The inventor assumed that the piston could be used to turn a boat's paddle wheel. In 1707 Papin is said to have made a trip in a small paddle-wheel boat on the Fulda river from Kassel to the Weser. In Minden, however, the shipowners who had sole rights to traffic on the Weser seized his boat and destroyed it. Contrary to common belief, the craft probably did not use a steam engine, but rather a hand-operated crank device.

The first steam engines

From the 1700s onward Britain has been one of the main centers of steam engine development. As early as 1698 Thomas Savery applied for a patent for one of the first steam engines. In 1705 another Englishman, Thomas Newcome, invented an "atmospheric steam engine" in which steam was used only to lift the piston; the atmospheric pressure above the piston then forced it down again. In 1736 Jonathan Hull gained a patent for an atmospheric steam engine of his own design which was supposed to rotate a paddle wheel fixed at the stern of a ship by means of a belt. The importance of Hull's steam ship was probably slight, but his experiments provided the stimuli for many other inventors.

The name of the Scottish mechanic and inventor James Watt will always be linked with the first really feasible steam engine, in which piston movement became a rotary action. He started his series of inventions and patents in 1769, when he made great improvements to Newcome's clumsy, heavy, and imperfect atmospheric steam engine. In 1782 Watt patented his dual-action vertical cylinder steam engine. In this engine, operated at low steam pressure, the parts both above and below the piston were connected to the steam-condensing apparatus. The steam then propelled the piston from both sides in turn.

It is a long step from the primitive working methods of those days to modern technology. For instance, Watt once wrote to a friend that he had drilled a really excellent steam cylinder: it was so exact that he could not get a florin between the piston and cylinder at any point.

Watt also created the unit of working effect still used today to measure engine performance, horsepower, in a practical way. He noted that a horse at a nearby brewery could raise a 75-kilogram weight (about 165 pounds) attached to the end of a rope passed round a block a distance of one meter (over three feet) a second.

It was Watt's fundamental and still valid achievement, which inventors soon started utilizing in various ways, that finally solved the problem of leashing steam as a general power source. When a much lighter and economical high pressure steam engine was developed which used the pressure of expanding steam instead of condensation and vacuum, it became possible to use the new power in various forms of transportation. Like many another invention, the steam engine, considered one of the greatest advances of mankind, was the outcome of brainwork, scientific research, and practical experiments over many generations. In its own day the steam engine formed a tremendous incentive to the development of industry, and its significance for shipping and railway traffic has been revolutionary. It finally permitted man to travel on the water irrespective of wind and weather.

Steamship experiments in Europe

In 1788 the Scot Patrick Miller constructed a hand-operated paddle wheel vessel floating on two hulls. When this proved far too cumbersome in practice, Miller went into cooperation with the steam engine constructor William Symington. The latter built him a two-cylinder steam engine with full accessories: the engine was installed in one hull and the steam boiler in the other. Two paddle wheels, fitted one behind the other between

The steamship Pyroscaphe, designed in Lyon in 1776 by Marquis Jouffroy d'Abbans, according to the original blueprints in the Paris Museum of Navigation. A. Ship, B. Steam engine, C. Shaft across hull, D. Double tooth wheel, E. Paddle wheels, F. Funnel.

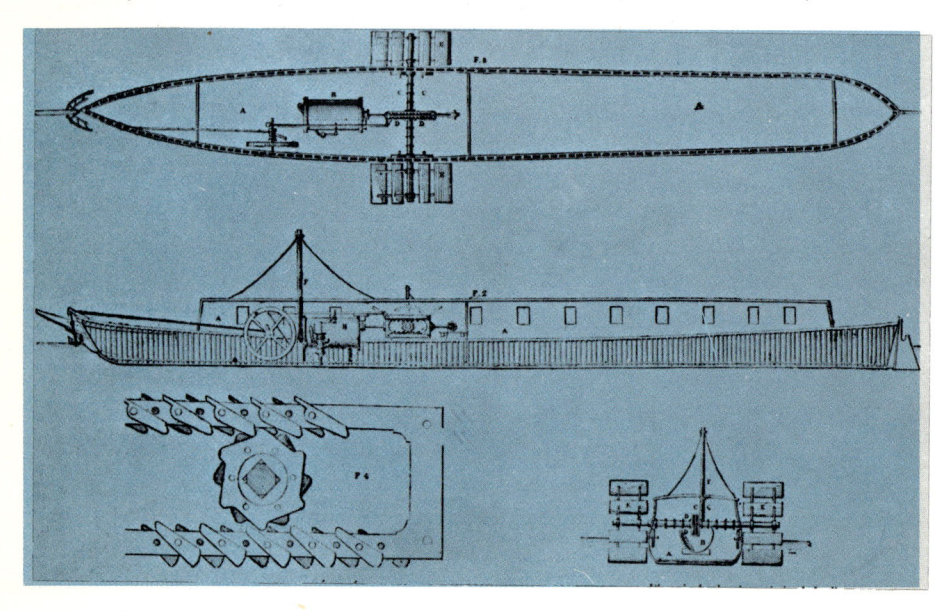

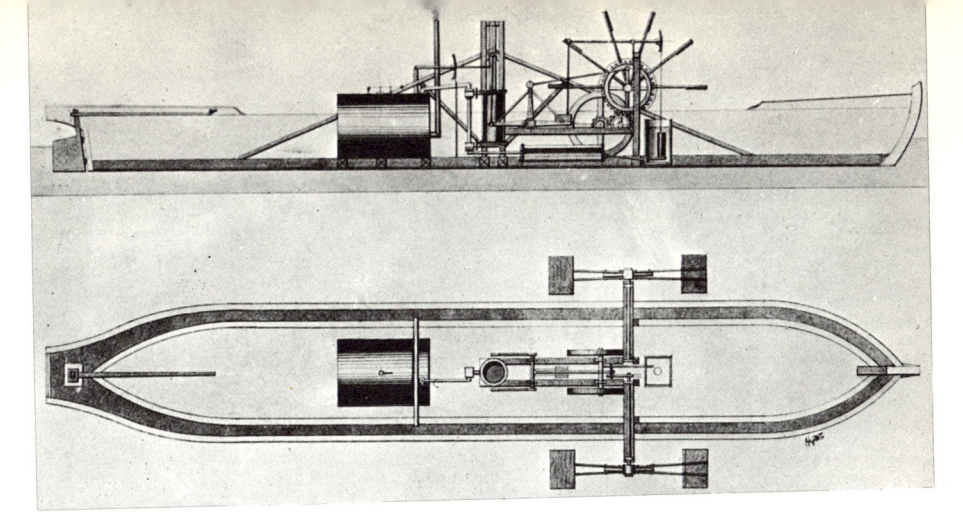

Robert Fulton's drawing of the paddle steamer he designed in Paris.

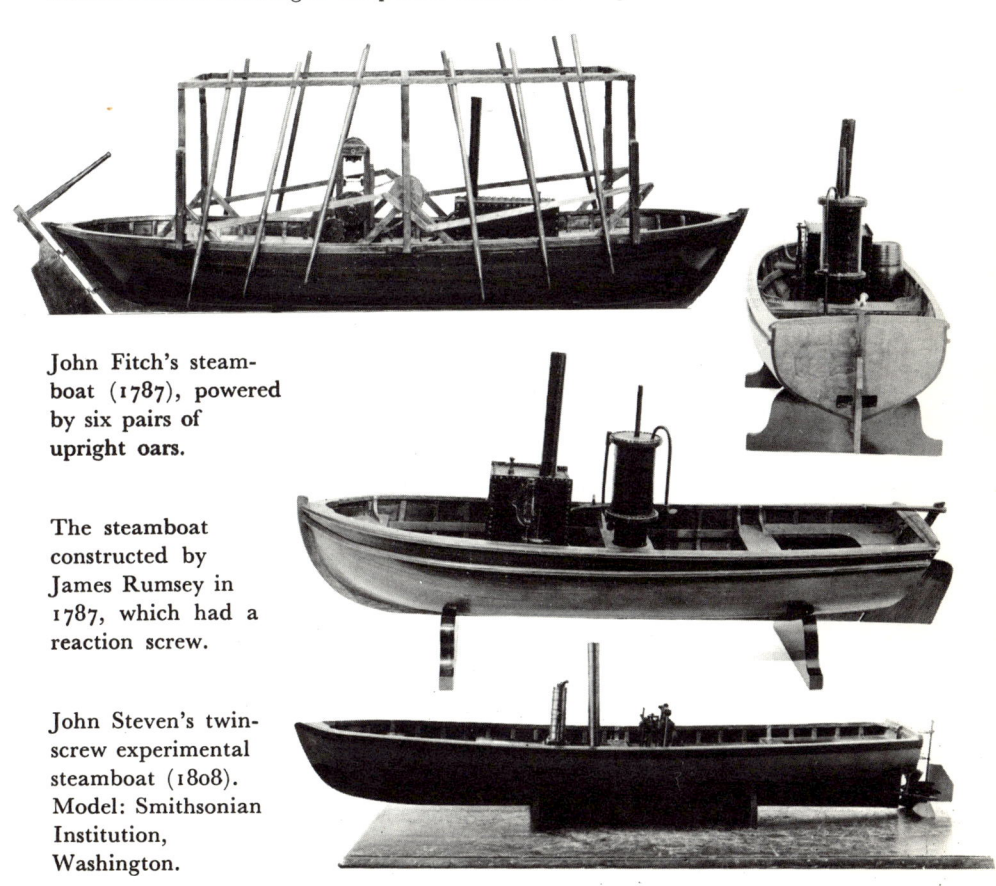

John Fitch's steamboat (1787), powered by six pairs of upright oars.

The steamboat constructed by James Rumsey in 1787, which had a reaction screw.

John Steven's twin-screw experimental steamboat (1808). Model: Smithsonian Institution, Washington.

the hulls, moved the steam boat forward at a speed of five knots.

In France, Count J. B. d'Auxiron fitted a two-cylinder atmospheric engine into a steamboat in 1774. Unfortunately the vessel sank before a trial voyage could be made. The industrialist Jacques Périer tried out a small steamship on the Seine in 1775, but the engine power was not enough to contend with the current.

Marquis Claude François de Jouffroy d'Abbans is usually considered a successful pioneer in fettering steam power for use in ships. In June 1776 he tried out his strange 42-foot-long, 7-foot-wide, nine-ton boat on the Doubs river. It had two engine-powered paddles in place of paddle wheels, one on each side, working in the same way as a duck's webbed feet. After this unsuccessful first experiment the Marquis did better when he built a bigger paddle-wheel ship, the *Pyroscaphe*, in which he installed Newcome's steam engine. The vessel was about 136 feet long and over 13 feet wide. To the immense wonder and admiration of his contemporaries, the *Pyroscaphe* actually traveled on the Saône near Lyon, even against the current, on June 15, 1783. The jubilation lasted only a quarter of an hour, for the hull gave way and water poured in. The boiler also proved unable to develop enough steam for a long journey.

Jouffroy failed in his attempts to

P. S. *Savannah* (1818), the first auxiliary steamer to cross the Atlantic or any ocean, built at New York with collapsible paddle wheels.

get the government to back his work, and the French Revolution interrupted his experiments for some time. In April 1816, Jouffroy gained a patent for steamboat construction, after which he began services on the Seine with his craft the *Charles-Philippe*.

Steamship experiments in America

On the other side of the Atlantic, the American John Fitch was granted a patent in Pennsylvania in 1785, under which he built a steam engine which powered a ship by means of a paddle wheel in the stern. The first trial was on July 27, 1786, on the Delaware River. Dissatisfied with this, the inventor designed a new type of steamboat, with an engine which powered twelve upright oars. The first voyage was on August 22, 1787, again on the Delaware River. The maximum speed was a modest three nautical miles an hour. The vessel was probably the first steam craft actually to travel on American waters, but technically and economically it was a failure.

Fitch went on enthusiastically with his experiments to develop a third and better steamboat. On June 16, 1790, he arranged an introductory trip on his 65-foot paddle steamer *Perseverance* for Governor Thomas Mifflin of Pennsylvania and other invited notables. Starting on June 14, the company ran the following advertisement in the Philadelphia *Federal Gazette* and other papers: "The steamboat is now ready to take passengers and is intended to set off from Arch Street Ferry, in Philadelphia, every Monday, Wednesday, and Friday for Burlington, Bristol, Bordentown, and Trenton, to return on Tuesdays, Thursdays, and Saturdays. Price for passengers, 2/6 to Burlington and Bristol, 3/9 to Bordentown, 5/3 to Trenton." This, then, was the beginning of the world's first regular steamboat line, some five miles long. The steamboat, which could reach six to seven knots, traveled several thousand miles on a regular schedule seven-

The British Channel steamer *Sirius*, which in 1837 sailed from Cork harbor to New York in eighteen days.

teen years before Robert Fulton launched his first boat.

Encouraged by this energetic entrepreneur, a company was even founded to build big cargo-ships. This premature enterprise soon collapsed, however. When Fitch did not even win support for his plans in France, he returned home a disappointed man and drowned himself in the Delaware, the scene of his eventful experiments.

Around the same time another American inventor was busy working on the steamship problem. James Rumsey gained a patent for a steamship of his own construction with a reaction screw. His first prototype had a steam engine and a pump which drew water in through the bottom of the hull and forced it out at the stern in a jet. The inventor demonstrated his steamboat in public for the first time on December 3, 1787, when it performed for a couple of hours on the Potomac River at around four knots. The vessel was never of any real practical significance, and constant bickering between Rumsey and Fitch about patent rights slowed down application of his idea.

Between 1790 and 1792 Samuel Morey built a small steamboat which successfully traveled against the current on the upper reaches of the Connecticut river. After several successful experi-

---

YACHTING has old traditions. Even the Roman Emperor Caligula had pleasure yachts on Lake Nemi. The Doge of Venice had a luxury galley on which he spent part of his time at sea each year. To begin with, yachting was only a sport for kings and the aristocracy. The City of Amsterdam in 1660 presented King Charles II of England with a simply rigged yacht. He had a whole fleet of similar yachts built and arranged races between them, thus creating the yachting concept. The first sailing club was founded in 1720 in Cork, Ireland; it later became the Royal Cork Yacht Club. In the nineteenth century, industrialists and businessmen, in particular, began to go yachting, and thus the sport of sailing gradually acquired its present popularity.

ments in New York, Morey built a steamboat equipped with a side paddle wheel on the Delaware in 1797.

Captain John Steves also played an important part in the development of steamboats. In 1803 he built the world's first twin-screw vessel, a steamboat not quite 30 feet long, but for one reason or another Stevens later gave up the screw. The fifteenth and final vessel to travel under its own steam before the appearance on the scene of Fulton was the paddle steamer *Phoenix*, built by Stevens with his father in 1807 (Hoboken, N.J.). The *Phoenix* traveled on the Hudson at some five knots.

The *Phoenix* started services on the Delaware, because for a number of years Fulton held sole rights to steamship traffic on the Hudson and on the waters of New York State in general. The *Phoenix* must have been the first boat to travel the 150 nautical miles from New York to Philadelphia, thus becoming the world's first steamship to have sailed the high seas.

A successful tugboat

In Britain, Lord Dundas wanted to substitute engine power for the horses that pulled craft along the Clyde canal and gave Symington the job of constructing a steamship. In 1801 the latter built the *Charlotte Dundas*, 55 feet long, 18 feet wide, and 8 feet in draft, which featured improvements of the steam mechanism developed by Watt and others and also improved the construction of the paddle wheels. In March 1802, this steamship, with a 10-horsepower engine, successfully towed two 70-ton vessels on the canal for six hours against a stiff wind. The achievement was greeted everywhere with great admiration, though the landowners along the canal claimed that the wash from the engine-powered ship damaged the banks. By order of the canal authorities, therefore, the tug had to stop operating after working successfully for about a year, and it remained in exile. Symington did not receive any other orders and died a poor man, like many another inventor-entrepreneur.

Robert Fulton and his steamships

Experiments aiming to develop feasible steamships continued with growing enthusiasm on both sides of the Atlantic. They were given a tremendous boost by the work of the American Robert Fulton, son of a poor Scottish-Irish immigrant of the same name, who was born in 1765 in Lancaster, Pennsylvania. Leaving America to try his luck in London, the mechanically inclined Fulton soon developed an interest in technical questions. His fellow countryman Rumsey gave the young man a job working with his steamship, and when Rumsey died shortly afterward, the youthful engineer, with growing enthusiasm for the steamship idea, worked on alone. In the spring of 1797 he went to France for the first time and spent four years there designing a submarine.

In November 1801, the wealthy United States ambassador to Paris, Robert R. Livingston, who had already carried out some unsuccessful steamship experiments back home, heard of Fulton. By this time, after hawking his inventions and suggestions for technical improvements around without success, Fulton was a disappointed and sickened man, but he agreed to remain in France with Livingstone's financial backing and to work on his designs for a steamship. Fulton experienced many more setbacks; rival inventors accused him of stealing their ideas, for instance. The persistent American was, indeed, more or less familiar with the achievements of his predecessors.

In spite of his problems, in August 1803 Fulton staged a trial on the Seine with a 58-foot steamboat. Invited guests included scientists and members of the French Academy. But the test met with only moderate success, for Napoleon, aware of Britain's overwhelming superiority on the seas, discounted talk of a successful submarine and steamship as idle boasts. If Napoleon had reacted to Fulton's invention with greater interest, comments the Danish physicist and inventor Poul la Cour, perhaps he

Robert Fulton (1765–1815), "father of steam shipping." Thought to be a copy of a painting by Benjamin West.

would not have ended up on St. Helena.

After all these disappointments Fulton thought it useless to stay any longer in France. Still financed by Livingston, he decided to continue his experiments in America, whose great rivers and lakes seemed made for shipping.

With maximum discretion and without mentioning his purpose, Fulton ordered a single-cylinder steam engine (18 horsepower), equipped with condensing apparatus, from the best-known

From sail to steam 117

In its original form the *Clermont* was something like this. The model in the Smithsonian Institution shows the remodeled hull (length 150′, beam 17′ 11″, and height at hold 7′).

manufacturer of the day, the British firm Boulton, Watt & Co., in Birmingham. The engine was the third that the manufacturer had exported.

Returning to his homeland in December 1806, after almost twenty years' absence, Fulton had a steamship built at Charles Brown's boatbuilding yard near the town of Albany, and then had it towed down the Hudson for engine-fitting on the outskirts of New York. Compared with its predecessors the ship was sizable: length 150 feet, width 13 feet, and draft 2 feet, with a displacement of 100 tons. The figures are those given by Fulton himself in a letter which was published in the *Nautical Gazette* as late as August 22, 1907.

Four years to the day after Fulton had shown his invention on the Seine, he launched his new vessel on the Hudson and made a short private trip in it. Then, and on the later historic maiden voyage from New York to Albany, the inventor called his ship by the simple name *Steamboat*. In later advertisements about services she was called the *North River Steamboat*. That winter the steamship was renovated so thoroughly that Fulton had to register it as a new vessel with the customs house. In the application papers the ship is called the *North River Steamboat of Clermont*. As early as 1810 we find *Clermont* alone, which later became the ship's established name. This brief history of the name is interesting because one sees conflicting information, both on the name and the ship itself, in print.

Strange as it may seem, Fulton's contemporaries did not take the revolutionary maiden voyage of his steamship seriously enough to write about it when it actually took place. Eyewitness accounts were not set down on paper until many years later, sometimes only at second hand. Only one newspaper, the *American Citizen*, published a three-sentence news item about the trip on the historic day, August 17th, 1807. This says the ship looked to observers more like a mere fraction of a ship, since everyone was accustomed to high-sterned sailing ships. Fulton's creation was long and narrow, and its aft deck rode only a few feet above the waterline.

The first attempt to set off was delayed by some slight fault. When this had been repaired, the trip along the Hudson proceeded to the full satisfaction of invited guests and the shipbuilder. With water spraying from its unshielded 15-foot paddle wheel, and smoke and sparks pouring out of its peculiar-looking funnel, the new river craft aroused wonder and some fear in observers gathered on the banks. Twenty-four hours later the "Fire Ship" anchored off Clermont, 110 nautical miles from New York for the night; at nine in the morning she continued to Albany, covering the 40-mile trip in eight hours. The *Clermont* had thus traveled at an average of 4.7 knots without using the sails with which she was equipped. The river sailing boats usually took four days to cover the distance that the Clermont had taken only 32 hours to complete.

Fulton's years of work as inventor and designer had at last produced results, and his dreams had come true. The *Steamboat* was not absolutely complete on the historic voyage, as the inventor apparently wanted her to be as light as possible. Soon, however, he fitted the deck with wooden sides, covered the steam engine, put beds in the cabins, strengthened the iron work, etc. On September 4, 1807, with fourteen passengers, the *North River Steamboat* set off on her first commercial trip. In mid-November the ship was brought up on land for the winter and the hull widened by four feet to improve stability. In her new form the ship's displacement is given as 182.5 tons. The ship was a good financial proposition and plied between New York and

The steamboat *Clermont* on the Hudson in 1810.

Albany until 1814.

Fulton, who died when he was only fifty, had plenty of detractors and rivals; the sailing ship skippers were jealous of the successful newcomer. Fulton knew how to make good use of the experiences and achievements of others; he never claimed that he had invented the steamship, but he was the first man to produce a financially feasible and successful steamship. The pioneering work of "the father of steamship traffic" marked the dawn of a new era in seafaring; steamship services began to run regularly and before long developed rapidly.

Fulton was the first inventor to have several ships in service simultaneously and whose ships sailed for more than one or two seasons. He designed and built a total of twenty-one steamships, including the world's first steam-powered warship, the *Demologos*, and the *Empress of Russia*, intended for passenger service between St. Petersburg and Kronstadt.

Fulton and Stevens' success signified the steamship's real breakthrough in America; five years after the first appearance of the *Clermont* there were already some sixty, and in 1817 about one hundred and thirty coastal and river steamers, with a speed of 6 to 7 knots. In 1826 there were some three hundred steamships and in 1839 a good seven hundred in inland and coastal service. The first American passenger steamer on the Great Lakes was the *Ontario*, built at Sacketts Harbor, New York, in 1817, which plied regularly between Lewiston and Ogdensburg for many years. The following year another famous inland water steamer, the *Walk in the Water* (the name given to it by the local Indians), was completed, and plied between Buffalo and Detroit.

In the early years of Fulton's first ship, it is estimated that the world's merchant tonnage in sailing ships was around three or four million registered tons. Some fifteen years later the figure was just about 5,300,000 N.R.T., with steamships accounting for only 10,500 N.R.T., or 0.2 %.

The beginnings of steamship traffic in Europe

The pioneering work of the father of steamships encouraged similar undertakings in Europe. On the east side of the Atlantic the place of honor goes to the Scottish spa owner Henry Bell, thanks to whose enterprise the first feasible European steamship was built on the Clyde in August 1812, by John Wood & Co. of Glasgow. This small paddle steamer, the *Comet*, equipped with a 3 to 4 horsepower steam engine, differed from previous paddle-operated vessels in that it had two paddle wheels on each side. The *Comet* carried passengers between Glasgow, Greenock, and Helensburg at about five knots. She was 40 feet long, 10 feet wide, and had a draft of about four feet with a 25-ton load. The hull plans reveal the lines characteristic of small packets at the time. Both passenger saloons of the *Comet* were very modest. The second-class saloon in the bows had only benches around the walls. In the first-class saloon on the aft deck, passengers at least had enough headroom to stand.

As far as we know, the second European steamer was the river boat *Elizabeth*, built in St. Petersburg, with British-made engines, in 1815. In 1816 the Johann Lange shipyard in Bremen built the paddle steamer *Die Weser*, also powered by a British engine. In the same year Sweden also produced her first steamship, when the British-born mechanic Samuel Owen, who had moved to Stockholm, fitted a screw engine in a small sailing ship.

The four-blade screw looked like the arms of a windmill, its hub was of cast iron, and the blades, about 3 feet long, were of birch. The four-knot *Stockholmshäxan* (Witch of Stockholm) was unsuccessful mainly because her boiler was too small, and things did not improve much when paddle wheels were substituted for the screw. Later, Owen built several steamers, among them the *Amphitrite* (1818), Sweden's first passenger steamer in regular service. She could take as many as 182 passengers.

Gradually, country after country acquired steamships and started steamer connections with other lands. As early as 1815 there was a regular passenger service on the Thames and Mersey rivers in Britain, and three years later Britain had a steamer connection to Germany and France. Owen's steam schooner *Stockholm*, which he had built and owned himself, started service between Stockholm and Turku in October 1821, offering the Finns their first sight of a steamship on their own shores.

The first steamers were built primarily for passenger traffic. Cargo proper, which took up so much space, was still carried by sailing ship.

The first Swedish steamship was the screw-propelled *Stockholmshäxan* (Witch of Stockholm), constructed by Samuel Owen (1816). Model made to a description by the builder's son.

The first British steam yacht *Comet* (1812) was in service in local Glasgow traffic. Her speed was five knots.

The first Russian steamboat *Elizabeth* on her maiden voyage on November 15, 1815 from St. Petersburg to Kronstadt.

The paddle steamer *Die Weser* (length 83 feet, engine power about 14 horsepower), the first German steamship, was built in Bremen in 1816.

The first Norwegian steamship *Constitutionen* (built in 1827 in Dover) was owned by the government and used in coastal service. Model in the Norwegian Museum of Navigation in Oslo.

The ship's screw, or propeller, was the outcome of long development. It was modeled mainly on the corkscrew and the arms of a windmill. As early as 1752 the Frenchman Daniel Bernoulli suggested that ships could be moved by a "screw wheel," which was a fair approximation of the propeller. In 1768, his fellow countryman Pauçton gained a patent for his "Archimedes screw," to be used for the same purpose.

Because of the many disadvantages of paddle-wheel mechanisms, a great deal of thought was given to the development of a suitable "screw" as a better and more reliable means of propelling a vessel. In 1785 the Englishman Joseph Bramah gained a patent for a device like a propeller. In his patent application he explained that a wheel with diagonal arms, like the slats of a smoke ventilator or the vertical sails of a windmill, could be used in place of a paddle wheel. This wheel could be attached to the shaft and submerged completely. When it was rotated in either direction, it propelled the vessel forward or backward, because the slant of the arms worked like oars, with equal force in each direction. The effect depended on the speed of rotation and the size of the wheel.

Engine-powered shipping developed particularly rapidly after the Swede John Ericson constructed a wheel propeller in 1836, probably on the basis

The tugboat *Ilmarinen*, the first Finnish steamship, built at the order of Nils Ludvig Arppe in Kitee, Finland, 1833. Length 85 feet, beam 13 feet, British 34-hp steam engine. From an aquarelle by J.G. Fabritius, 1830s.

of the Archimedes screw, and the Englishman Francis Petit Smith in the same year, but independently, produced the screw propeller; these were the first really practicable screws. In the mid-nineteenth century some thirty different types of screw had already been patented in various countries. Before long, paddle steamers found they had to make way for propeller-driven ships.

One factor illustrative of conditions in those days was that even in 1830 a special British Admiralty committee report claimed that only sailing ships were suitable as warships, though possibly steamships might succeed in the merchant marine. In April 1845, in hope of deciding the "paddle wheel v. screw" dispute, the British Admiralty arranged a tug-of-war between two steamers, each with a 200-horsepower engine. The result of the competition, held in calm water on the North Sea, was that the screw-propelled *Rattler* (888 tons) succeeded in towing the paddle wheeler *Alecto* (800 tons) stern-first at a speed of 2.8 knots.

Because the construction and maintenance of steamships was very much more expensive than that of sailing ships—the mechanism alone often cost more than the ship—shipping companies were formed to build them. Private individuals were not usually able to invest enough money in ship outfitting.

The revolutionary effect of the steam engine on shipping was not a sudden process, but rather a gradual acceleration. The first steamships were, after all, slow and expensive to run. With their uneconomical 1.5 to 2 atm. low pressure engines, steamships used a fantastic amount of fuel, which meant less profitable cargo space and the need to refuel at regular intervals. In the swell of the open sea, in particular, their paddle wheels were easily damaged. It was not until many new technical inventions and improvements had been made that steam became a really dangerous rival to sail.

In 1853 the British screw-propelled steamer *Argo* was the first engine-powered vessel to go around the world, taking 121 days. In the 1850s and 1860s the world's steam tonnage grew rapidly, partly as the result of the spread of the screw-propeller, but in 1860 still comprised only 6 per cent of the total world merchant tonnage. The larger ships preserved their sailing rig right up to the 1880s, though it did gradually simplify. Even as late as the

H.M. sloops *Rattler* and *Alector* in 1845, towing stern to stern to test the relative powers of the screw-propeller and the paddle wheel. The *Rattler* (screw-propeller) won.

The schooner *Royal William* (built in 1831 in Quebec) was the first steamship to cross the Atlantic by steam power alone. In 1833 it took nineteen days to sail from Pictou harbor (Nova Scotia) to Cowes, on the Isle of Wight in the English Channel.

1890s it was still possible to see sail being used as an adjunct to steam. It is thus impossible to state exactly when the engine stopped being an auxiliary and became the main source of power.

The history of the marine steam engine

A steam engine takes its energy from steam developed in a boiler. In a piston steam engine the steam travels from the engine input pipe into the slide valve chamber, in which a moving slide valve distributes the steam to each end of the cylinder in turn via steam passages. To begin with, the steam engine cylinders lay vertically or horizontally in the bottom of the ship, with the crankshaft high, but gradually engineers began to put the cylinders in a base and the crankshaft low down. This was important in screw-driven ships particularly, as the screw shaft could then be connected direct to the crankshaft. This engine location is nowadays the only one used, even in motor ships.

There has been a tremendous advance in steam engine power, fuel economy, etc. The consumption of coal in steamships has decreased relatively thanks to improvements in boiler and steam engine construction. The first change was to high-pressure engines (4 to 6 atm.). In 1854 the twin-cylinder steam engine was invented, that is, the dual expansion or compound engine, which improved the engine's efficiency appreciably. The steam first acted in the high-pressure cylinder, and then in the low-pressure cylinder. In 1877 the triple expansion or triple engine was invented, in which the steam expands in three stages. In this engine the steam goes in turn through high, medium, and low pressure cylinders.

The biggest marine steam engines ever built were quadruple expansion two engines. They were about 90 feet long and 43 high and produced 22,500 horsepower on the screw shaft. The passenger ship *Deutschland*, built in 1900 for the Hamburg-America Line, had four piston engines of this type.

Steam engine techniques reached their peak at the turn of the century, when other types of engine were still at an early stage of development. Since then more economical and more easily serviced engines (combustion engines and steam turbines) have gradually moved to the fore. Today, steam piston engines are used only in relatively small steamers.

Before the adoption of the twin-cylinder compound engine, steamers equipped even with the best types of engine were absolute gluttons. The Inman Line *City of Brussels* (3,747 G.R.T.), launched in 1869, consumed 95 tons of coal a day, whereas the compound engine of the *Spain*, a ship about the same size completed a couple of years later, managed on 53 tons.

A relatively slight increase in a steamer's speed raised fuel consumption enormously. If a ship could travel at twelve knots on 90 tons a day, doubling the fuel consumption produced only a third higher speed, that is, sixteen knots.

The steam engine's efficiency has

P.S.S. *Great Eastern* (1858), the Leviathan of the nineteenth century, with both paddle wheels and a screw-propeller. Though technically perfectly feasible, the ship was a complete failure financially. Lithograph by Picken according to Walters.

The first passenger steamer of the Cunard Line, the *Britannia*, in the ice of Boston harbor in winter 1840. Color lithograph by A. de Vaudricort, published 1844.

been improved greatly over the decades, for instance by adoption of the turbine, in which the exhaust steam from the engine expands to a very low pressure. The steam turbine mechanism's efficiency is about 30 per cent; that of a piston steam mechanism, between 12.5 and 21.5 per cent. Modern steamship boilers are heated almost entirely by oil. Oil heating is clean, simple, and needs little labor, as oil is easy to store and load. Less than 2 per cent of the world's tonnage now uses coal as a source of energy.

The changeover to metal hulls

The changeover from wood-hulled vessels first to iron and later to steel was in many ways a remarkable improvement. Designers recognized that timber, used for centuries, was not after all the most suitable construction material for ships, especially big ones. As early as 1787 the Englishman J. Wilkinson built an iron vessel about 70 feet long for the Birmingham canal in Staffordshire. In 1812–13 several small iron canal boats of the same type were built in England. In 1816 the Scot John Robinson designed the first iron sailing ship. Two years later, when the *Vulcan* was launched, the ceremony was watched by a huge crowd whose amazement knew no bounds when it became clear that the ship was not going to sink.

In those days, even many technically trained people still shook their heads at iron and for various reasons opposed

NAUTICAL MILE AND KNOT.

Rate, or speed, means the distance traveled in a certain time unit. In navigation the nautical mile is used as the unit of distance and the hour as the unit of speed. The international nautical mile (about 6,076 feet) is a more suitable measure than the land mile because it is in direct proportion to the latitude and longitude divisions of the earth. The nautical mile corresponds roughly to the average length of a minute of arc. The unit of speed, which gives the distance traveled in nautical miles by the ship in an hour, is called a knot. Its length in a log line is in the same ratio to the nautical mile as the running of an hour glass is to one hour.

Navigational theory distinguishes two speeds, viz. speed with relation to water and speed with relation to sea bottom. If the vessel is traveling in running water, its speed with relation to water is different from that with relation to the sea bottom. Speed with relation to water is determined by various instruments, which are called the log.

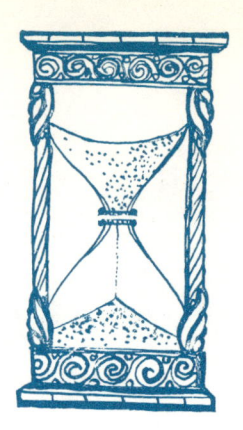

---

its use as the material for ships' hulls. They appealed, for instance, to the well-known fact that the specific gravity of iron is greater than that of water. They did not believe that a ship made of material heavier than water could float; in other words they did not understand the role played by the air inside the hull and other parts of the ship.

In 1821 the first iron steamship, the *Aron Manby*, was made in Horsley, Staffordshire, and transported in sections to London for assembly. From London the ship went on to Paris, and in 1822 started regular service on the Seine. The first iron ocean-going ship, the *Great Britain*, was completed in 1845.

By the mid-nineteenth century people realized that iron was an ideal material for building ships. Then the use of practical and cheap shipbuilding steel ("soft" steel produced by the Siemens-Martin process) began to spread: the first steel vessel was made in 1857 in England, and from the 1880s onwards it was practically the only material used for ship hulls. At the beginning of this century it was estimated that ships were made of 95 per cent steel and 5 per cent wood. An iron-hulled ship is only about half the weight of a wooden one of the same size, and a steel ship is a further 15 per cent lighter than an iron one. The special steel adopted some forty years ago has further reduced the weight of the hull by about 10 per cent.

Composite vessels, experiments with which began around 1870, aimed at reinforcing a wooden hull and deck with iron ribs, struts, etc. This form of building began to be used mainly in sailing ships and is still used for barges and small craft.

High-speed clippers appear on the seas

Though the revolutionary effect of steam power on shipping was already obvious in the first few decades of last century, the traditional sailing ship had by no means yet given up the struggle. In fact it was only then — on the threshold of the end of the sailing era — that the golden age of sail really began. Increasing competition from steamships, among other factors, meant that more attention than ever before began to be given to fast sailing, rapidly completed voyages, and efficient ship provisioning.

In those days a ship's most important qualities were its seaworthiness and its sailing characteristics. Docking and harbor work were not of the vital importance that they are today to a vessel's general economy. After all, a ship spent most of her time at sea fulfilling her role as a carrier. Stevedoring was handled by a cheap labor force, often the ship's own crew. No great attention was paid to cargo handling equipment, either. There was no development worth speaking of in this field throughout the sailing era, nor in the size of hatchways: these were kept as small as possible intentionally so that they would shut well and stay shut. The cargo holds were only opened and closed a couple of times a year. When they were closed, it was very firmly; the covered openings were sealed with oakum and pitch, numerous protective coverings spread over them and these held firmly in place with cross beams and sometimes even with a net.

A type of ship built specially for speed, the clipper, gave the Americans the lead around the middle of last century. More open-minded and unprejudiced than his European counterpart, the American shipbuilder, and specifically the true New England Yankee, began to develop a form of hull on principles quite different from established and orthodox practice. These fast, remodeled craft, sailing under the stars-and-stripes, soon aroused amazement, admiration, and envy among seafarers and shipbuilders all over the world. All the clippers were characterized by a much slimmer hull than had been known before, and an increase in rigging and sail area.

The clipper skippers were tough seadogs who extracted from ship, rig, and crew as much as they could give, and sometimes more. It was a risky game, but the risks had to be taken.

9 The sea and man

The Yankee skippers of Boston, New York, or Nova Scotia were the subject of debate, praise, and condemnation in ships' saloons and fo'c'sles, and in ports all over the globe. The American clipper commanders of the 1850s are said to have earned a bonus of 5 per cent of the trip's net revenue; a shipowner offered one skipper of the famous *Lightning*, built in Boston, an annual salary of £1,000: about $5,000, a lot of money in those days!

The name "clipper" seems to have been applied first to privateers fitted out in Baltimore during the War of 1812; these became known as "Baltimore clippers." The Americans, who had been building this kind of fast privateer while Britain was at war with Napoleon, made use of their knowledge of the sea to build ever faster merchant ships for their growing world trade and shipping. The California gold strikes in 1848 made it worthwhile building swifter and more numerous American sailing ships to cope with the great rush to the "Golden West," not only from Europe but also from the east coast of America. Though the clippers had to go around Cape Horn in the south, it was faster and safer to sail than to make the journey by wagon across the continent, where hostile Indians were among the very real dangers.

The shipowners of Boston and New York now enjoyed a real boom period: thousands of people were dreaming of a ticket to the Eldorado of the West, and their holds were full of general cargo and foodstuffs to feed the new inhabitants of the gold fields.

About the middle of last century, the American clipper had reached the peak of its development, its final flowering. Whereas in the early nineteenth century a 300-ton sailing ship was considered quite large, 600 tons was large, and 1,200 tons very large, the tonnage of the biggest clippers soon reached 2,000 tons or more.

The repeal of the Navigation Act forced British shipowners to make real efforts to preserve their lead, and competitive British clippers also started to appear on the seas. In the 1860s American clippers found they had real rivals in the British, mainly in ships built for the China tea trade. Designed mainly for the trade winds and East Asian waters, the British clippers were smaller, slighter, and generally slower than the American ships. It took them an average 135 to 145 days to sail from a Chinese tea port to the English Channel (14,500 to 15,000 nautical miles). On these and several other long-distance routes the freights were so good that the British and American clippers could often earn their own price on their first voyage.

The biggest clipper and the largest wood-hulled vessel ever built was the first four-mast barque, the *Great*

From sail to steam 131

An advertisement for the Panama–San Francisco route from the Gold Rush days, when the clipper *Martha Sanger* carried hopeful golddiggers to California. Either the ship in the picture is wrong or the text is, which calls the ship a brig.

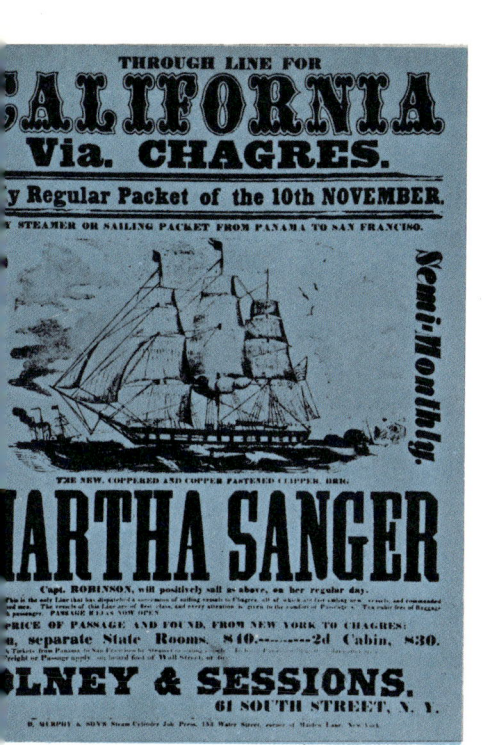

Republic, launched in Boston in autumn 1853 (4,555 N.R.T., length 325 feet, beam about 50 feet, sail area about 58,000 square feet). She had four decks, the top one spreading flat from stem to stern. The main yard was 117 feet long. It was once said of the ship that her masts were so high that young men who climbed up to the masthead were wrinkled old codgers when they came down. The *Great Republic* was the first sailing ship in which the engine power (a 15-horsepower steam engine) was used to help with work on deck. Even so she had a crew of 130. Because of a fire before her maiden voyage and various alterations, the ship never sailed in her original form.

Though the first iron-built ship dated from 1840, shipbuilding in iron did not really get under way until the 1860s. On the other hand wooden ships with iron ribs, or composite ships, were still popular in the 1880s; a copper lining could be used to protect the ship against the various forms of sea life which attached themselves to the bottom, causing great damage and detracting from the ship's sailing qualities.

Of all the clippers, the best known is the *Cutty Sark* (963 G.R.T., 921 N.R.T., length 210 feet), built in Dumbarton, Scotland, in 1896. After working some time in the China tea trade, she was transferred to the Australian route to carry wool. After an eventful history she was bought by Britain in 1938 and sailed under her original flag and name. In 1954 the *Cutty Sark* was towed to a concrete basin built for the purpose on dry land at Greenwich. There she lies, fully rigged as she was during her China tea trade days, as a museum ship and memorial to the ships and men of the great days of the clippers.

The *Cutty Sark* was a good sailor; at times she even exceeded 17 knots. However, the fastest sailing ship of all time is thought to have been the American clipper *Champion of the Seas*, of the Black Ball Line, which on her maiden voyage from Liverpool to Melbourne (about 13,400 nautical miles) in December 1854 sailed a record distance of 465 nautical miles in one day, for an average speed of over 19 knots.

Some of the biggest of all square-rigged ships (six barques and one frigate) had five masts. The latter was the steel-hulled *Preussen*, the world's biggest sailing ship without an auxiliary engine (c. 11,000 tons), which was built in Hamburg in 1902 and went down in a fatal collision near Dover in November 1910. This ship was 444 feet long and 52 ft wide, and her center mast was 222 feet high. The longest yards were 100 feet. She had 48 sails and a total sail area of 66,000 square feet.

Another great sailing ship was the steel-hulled gaff schooner *Thomas W. Lawson*, built in 1902 in America. This, the only seven-masted sailing ship ever built, could carry some 8,000 tons. She was 400 feet long and 54 feet wide. She had steam winches on deck to handle the huge sails, and she had a crew of only 18 men.

For the clippers, too, the relentless dictates of progress were unavoidable, though the changeover to engine-powered ships took place at different times and at different speeds, depending on region and route. The 1870s marked the beginning of the final and clearly perceptible decline of the sailing ship on the world seas. This was partly the result of the opening of the Suez Canal in 1869. Thanks to this new channel, distances from European harbors to the Far East shortened considerably, for instance from London to Bombay by about 44 per cent and from Marseilles to Bombay by 59 per cent. As well as the overwhelming competition from modern engine-powered ships, the general depression on the cargo market influenced developments. The first craft to disappear were the small and medium-sized wooden ships. The barques, whose tonnage ranged from a few hundred to about a thousand registered tons and which were still the nucleus of the Finnish merchant fleet, for example, in the 1870s and 1880s, were another type of vessel to disappear.

A few figures will give a better picture of the general trend. In 1870 Germany had 127 steamships and 4,320 sailing ships in ocean-going service, whereas in 1890 the corresponding figures were 815 steamships

The most famous clipper contest was the Tea Race among five loaded ships, from Foochow (China) to London in 1866. The winner of this 6,000-mile race was the *Taeping* (right), followed by the *Ariel* twelve minutes later. The trip took 101 days. The picture shows both ships fighting out the last stretch in the English Channel. Color lithograph by T.G. Dutton. National Maritime Museum, Greenwich.

and 2,779 sailing ships, and in 1899 there were 1,066 steamships and 538 sailing ships.

The late flowering of sail in Scandinavia

As they changed over to ships built of metal, the great seafaring countries also began to sell off their sailing craft. Since cheap ships were now available, sailing in Scandinavia experienced a period of fair prosperity for some time yet. The Finnish sailing fleet reached its greatest tonnage in 1876, when it was a good 303,270 N.R.T. When the supply of deep sea sailing craft dried up, the sailing ship era ended. The age-old alliance between timber, hemp, and sail finally broke up, after struggling with steam power for mastery of the seas for over half a century.

There were, it is true, still some steel sailing ships left in the twentieth century; the last deep-sea sailing ship to ply the seas under the Finnish flag, the Åland four-masted barque *Pommern*, was not removed from the shipping register until 1952. When World War I broke out, the American west coast and Australia were the only remaining shipping areas of any importance for long-distance sailing vessels. Everywhere else, sail was used relatively little in navigation. In the final years of their reign, deep-sea sailing ships were used mainly as carriers of bulk goods. They carried corn from Australia, rice from Southeast Asia, saltpeter from Chile. From Europe, their cargoes were usually coal, or from Scandinavia, timber.

Today it is rare indeed that one catches a glimpse of white sails on the oceans. One of the "last of the mohicans" is the three-mast barque *Gorch Fork* (built in Hamburg, 1958, and sailing under the West German flag), which is a naval cadet training ship.

The barque *Hercules* (c. 440 d.w.t.), which was the first Finnish vessel to sail around the world, under sea-captain P.G. Idman, in 1845–47.

The Finnish four-masted barque *Herzogin Cecilie* (built 1902, 4,350 d.w.t., length 334 feet) was one of the most famous names in Finnish deep-sea sailing.

The four-masted barque *Fennia* (built in Nantes, 3,135 G.R.T.) sailed for some four years with the Finnish Training Ship Co. Ltd. In June 1927, she suffered heavy damage in a storm in South American waters but succeeded in reaching Port Stanley harbor in the Falkland Islands and until recently acted as a floating wool store there. In 1968 the barque was towed to San Francisco, where she is spending her old age as a memorial to the sailing era.

During the twilight of deep-sea sailing, various attempts were made to fetter the power of the wind in other ways to propel ships. The German elementary school teacher and technician Anton Flettner, who invented the remote-control tank and a rudder type of special construction during World War I, was commissioned by the German Admiralty in 1924 to build a rotor ship. This experimental ship, the *Buckau*, had two cylinders, about 48 feet long and 11 feet in diameter revolving round a vertical shaft and rotated by two small engines. When the wind blew against the cylinder, a side pressure was produced by the Magnus effect, and this propelled the vessel forward. The *Buckau* crossed the Atlantic and aroused considerable attention in America. Another slightly bigger rotor ship, the 2,790 ton *Barbara*, was fitted with three cylinders and proved quite a success. But the efficiency of the rotor principle did not match that of screw-driven ships, and these experimental craft had disappeared from the seas by the 1930s.

The decline of sail

Basically the changeover from sail to steam was nothing more than the general process of mechanization which marked developments in the nineteenth century; it corresponded in navigation to the bitter but hopeless struggle being waged by other old and highly developed crafts and production methods against the relentless advance of industrialization.

Sailing ships held up bravely to the end, however, and even during the last century ocean shipping and world trade advanced primarily by means of sail. It was not until the early 1880s that steamships overtook sailing ships in the actual volume of world sea transport. Soon afterward, however, they won almost complete dominion of the seas.

Motor ships: beginnings and difficulties

The appearance of natural oil on consumer markets somewhat over a hundred years ago opened up great, new, and unimagined horizons for engines in various forms of transport. The steam engine gained a tough rival in the motor engine. In less than two hundred years, steam, the motor, and electricity have revolutionized industry and transport, gradually freed man from heavy physical labor, and at the same time created new employment potential and a different social structure.

The adoption of the combustion engine was preceded by scrupulous research, experiments, and adaptations. The French technician Jean Lenoir gave the "atmospheric combustion engine" he had invented a valuable start by manufacturing in 1860 a "motor which uses the air expanded by burning gas." This was a small, four-cylinder, four-horsepower gas engine using coal gas as fuel. The operating principle of the combustion engine is that the cylinder fills with air which is sucked into the cylinder when the piston moves upwards or is forced into it with a compressor; the gas mixture is then compressed when the piston moves down again.

NORTH ATLANTIC WEATHER SHIP NETWORK. This consists of 21 vessels, maintained by 22 member states of the ICAO (International Civil Aviation Organization). Each weather station covers a 10-square-mile area, which one ship patrols for a fixed period. Each ship remains in position for about three weeks, until it is relieved by another. In spite of Atlantic storms and other difficulties, the weather ships managed to remain in position for about 98 % of the time in 1967. Besides routine duties, the ships also provided medical and other assistance or advice, received some 950 sea and air SOS's and saved 17 people's lives.

A break for a smoke during sail work on the barque *Pommern* in Sydney harbor in 1928. Since 1953 the *Pommern* has been a museum ship in Mariehamn. Photograph by the author.

Cleaning the mast of the frigate *Suomen Joutsen* (Swan of Finland). Formerly the Finnish fleet's training ship, she has housed the State Seamen's Vocational School in Turku since 1961.

Manning a capstan in the time-honored way. Cadets replace the electric windlass to weigh anchor.

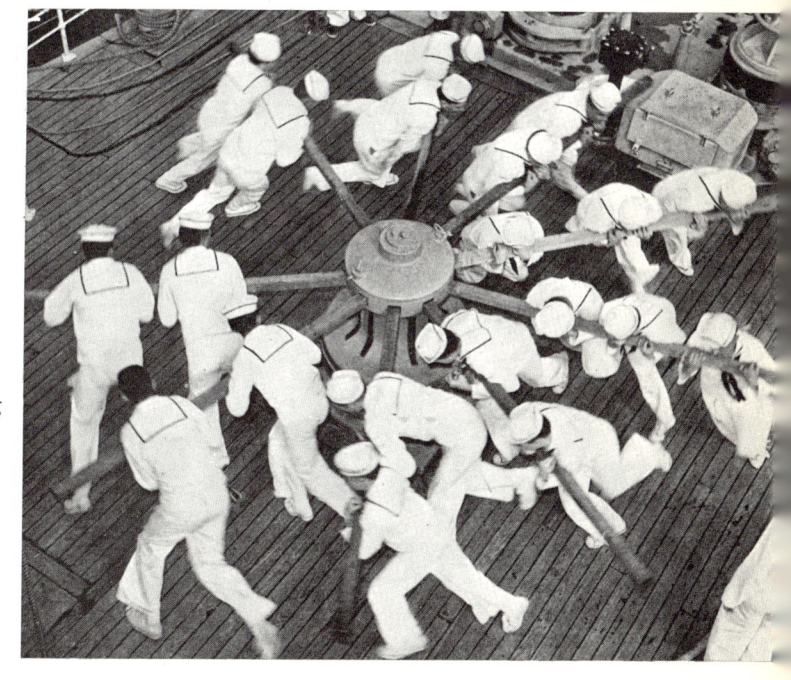

City Ice-Boat No. 1 was the world's first steam-powered ship built specially for icebreaking. The City of Philadelphia had this wooden-hulled paddle steamer built, and it started work on the Delaware river in December 1837.

The Danish icebreaker *Bryderen* (built 1884 in Sweden). The rigging and deck structure have been altered several times. The over 80-year-old ship now works under the Polish flag in Gdansk.

The four-screw diesel electric ice-breaker *Voima* (built 1954 in Helsinki, 3,480 G.R.T., length 271 feet, beam 63 feet, 10,500 shp) working in the Gulf of Finland. All seven of the Finnish government's present icebreakers have been built in Finland.

Lenoir's uneconomic and unreliable combustion engine lost its importance when the Benz, Langen, and Otto combustion engine became well-known. These German inventors worked with both gas and gasoline engines. The Frenchman F. Forest designed a special boat engine and tried it out on the Seine in 1870.

It was not until 1886 that the German G. Daimler built a small (2-horsepower) gasoline engine which corresponded to the modern idea of a combustion engine. To prove that his engine was reliable and economic, Daimler built a new 4-horsepower engine of the same kind in 1891 and installed it in a 26-foot long, 5-foot wide boat. Numerous tests were made with this boat, including a trip around Sicily which took 88 hours. Its gasoline consumption on this slightly over 56-nautical-mile journey was about 385 pounds, or about 0.5 kg per shp an hour. This event is generally considered the beginning of the combustion engine era. From Germany, engine building spread first to other parts of Europe, and soon to America and other parts of the world.

The engine industry first had to overcome many obstacles in most countries. There were difficulties, for instance, in the fact that the insurance companies considered the motor too dangerous, because its fuel—gasoline—is volatile, inflammable, and troublesome to handle in other ways.

The German Rudolf Diesel got the idea for a heavy-oil engine as long ago as 1878 while attending lectures as a young student. In his patent application of 1893 he explained the technical theory of building an ideal combustion engine based on the rotary process invented in 1824 by Officer-of-Engineers Garnot. Four years later his experiments with this new kind of revolutionary engine were complete, and in 1897 the first practicable diesel engine was constructed.

The diesel is a combustion engine in which the compression of the gases in the cylinder on the return stroke of the piston causes a temperature sufficiently high (about 800° C) to ignite a spray of fuel oil. This compression ignition engine differs from other engines in that it needs no spark to ignite the gases in the cylinder. A diesel engine can be two- or four-stroke. Its advantage over carburetor engines is primarily its higher efficiency. Another important advantage is that a diesel engine can use diesel oil, i.e. gas oil, as fuel. This is poorer quality but cheaper than gasoline or kerosene.

At the beginning of this century there were three kinds of marine engine in addition to the steam engine: the gasoline engine, the semi-diesel engine, and the diesel engine.

SAIL VERSUS ENGINE. Compared with the sailing ship, the engine-powered vessel is a newcomer without traditions. It fulfills its required task, is far more efficient than its predecessors, but it speeds through waters which the sailing ship had conquered. It is and will remain a "stranger" on the seas in some respects. The sailing ship, on the other hand, is a memorial to the struggles, trials and conquests, genius, courage and audacity, heroic exploits, sufferings and deaths of countless generations. The name of each part of the hull and rigging, each formality observed on board, each command given, is a piece of cultural history. With the disappearance of the sailing ship, an age-old branch of the tree of human culture withered and died. It was no longer needed. But the life span of the sailing ship was long and full of heroic deeds: from prehistoric times onward the sailing ship was the agent of cultural influences, the pioneer of ocean routes, a broadener of horizons, and a link between continents.

Eirik Hornborg

The first diesel ships

The German factories Maschinenfabrik Augsburg-Nürnberg and Friedr. Krupp were the first to experiment with diesel engines, in the time of Dr. Diesel. As far as is known, the world's first diesel ship and at the same time the first motor tanker was the *Vandal*, built at the suggestion of the Swede Marcus Wallenberg and financed by the Nobel brothers in 1903. The three diesel engines of this small vessel (total effect 360 horsepower) were built under licence by Nya A. B. Atlas, at Sickla, Sweden. The tanker worked in river and canal traffic in Russia, between the oil fields of Baku and St. Petersburg. She had a speed of seven knots with a 700-ton oil load. In 1907 the Swedish company A/B Diesels Motorer installed its first engine in the schooner *Orion*. The world's first diesel-powered ocean-going ship was the 1,000-ton tanker *Vulcanus*, built in Amsterdam in 1910. She had one six-cylinder, four-stroke, 450-horsepower Werkspoor diesel engine, which gave the loaded vessel a speed of eight knots.

Motor shipping gets under way

The ocean-going ship *Selandia* (7,385 tons, 5,057 G.R.T.), built by the famous Danish shipyard Burmeister & Wain for Det Østasiatiske Kompagni A/S is of greater importance, however. Each of her eight-cylinder, four-stroke diesel engines developed 1,250 horsepower, and the vessel could travel at almost eleven knots fully loaded. Her main dimensions were: length overall 383 feet, beam 52 feet, and height 30 feet. The *Selandia* set off on her maiden voyage on February 12, 1912. Her 20,000 mile journey to the Far East and back to her home port in Copenhagen marked the dawn of a new age in international shipping. The *Selandia* was in service almost thirty years, finally under the Finnish flag, when—under the name *Tornator*—she ran aground near Yokohama in January 1942 and was wrecked.

The next diesel-powered vessel was probably the Swedish *Suecia*, which was also completed in 1912. After this date the number of motor ships began to rise rapidly. After many stages of development, the diesel engine has become the most widely used marine engine. Big diesel engines are a source of power comparable to the steam turbine, even for larger tankers and fast cargo liners.

The latest diesel engines, the power of the largest exceeding 30,000 horsepower, can be used even in supertankers. The largest diesel-powered ship built so far is the tanker *Bergehus*, made in Japan in 1967, which is 202,557 d.w.t., 103,194 G.R.T., and 1055 feet long.

The diesel engine's lead in heat consumption has shrunk over the years because of the great advances made in steam technology. Even so, it has many advantages as a ship's power source. By far the most important for the triumphant progress of motor ships, which account for about two-thirds of the world's total tonnage, is the diesel engine's high efficiency. In the latest models this is as high as 41–44 per cent: this percentage of the energy in the fuel burned goes to the shaft and on to the screw to propel the ship forward.

Turbines as marine engines

The piston engine was a real power mechanism but at the same time an extremely complicated one, with its numerous heavy engine parts moving backward and forward. It is therefore understandable that there were many brains working on the problem of creating a mechanism which would turn power straight into a tortional movement, without a piston, crankshaft, etc. The invention of the turbine produced a mechanism in which the movement of some flowing substance (water, steam, or gas) works on a series of blades attached to a shaft.

In 1629 the Italian Johann Branca gave an account of a mechanism in which a jet of water rotated a paddle wheel. This action, or pressure, turbine was in principle the same kind as the device produced by Heron the Alexandrian 2,000 years ago. Both were mere curiosities, however.

The first feasible turbine was constructed in 1883 by the Swede Gustaf de Laval. This was, however, of less importance than the steam turbine developed in 1884 by the British engineer Sir Charles Algernon Parsons. A modern steam turbine—the reaction turbine—consists of a shaft or rotor lying in bearings, enclosed in a cylindrical casing. The shaft is made to rotate smoothly by jets of steam coming from nozzles located around the periphery of the cylinder; these strike blades, or buckets, attached to the shaft.

Parsons, who certainly had most influence on the development of the steam turbine into a marine engine, built the first turbine-powered ship in 1894, the steam yacht *Turbinia* (displacement 44 tons, length 99 feet, beam 9 feet), which was first fitted with one 2,000 shp turbine. But the revolution speed of the screw was excessively high; when this fault had been corrected and certain improvements carried out, the turbines proved competitive marine engines. The *Turbinia* was a tremendous success: she reached a speed of 34 knots, a really incredible achievement at the time.

Since the invention did not actively interest the Admiralty, Parsons arranged a historic demonstration at the great naval review off Spithead in 1897. The warships discovered to their amazement that the *Turbinia* could travel at a staggering speed, and even the destroyers which set off after her could not catch up with the gate-crasher. This occurrence provided the stimulus for the order of the first turbine destroyer, the *Viper*. The fast advance of the steam turbine as a marine power source was promoted around the same time by the invention of the "water pipe steam boiler." The first turbine merchant ship, the *King Edward* (551 tons), was built in Britain in 1901.

The steam turbine is in many ways better than a piston engine. It has very little vibration, especially compared with the diesel engine, and needs little space relative to its horsepower. Turbines do have the disadvantage that they can rotate only in one direction. As ships often have to reverse, particularly in harbors and docks, they have to have a separate reversing turbine which rotates the screw backwards. In large ships and at high engine powers the steam turbine has usually proved more economical than the diesel engine. The competition for the "Blue Ribbon of the North Atlantic" did much to promote the adoption of the steam turbine in ocean-going

The motor tanker *Bergehus* (built in Japan, 1967), the world's largest diesel craft. 202,500 d.w.t., 103,194 G.R.T., length 1056 feet.

The world's biggest ship at the moment is the 312,000 d.w.t. *Universe Ireland*, which is shown here arriving from her maiden voyage from Kuwait to the newly built Bantry Bay oil harbor in Ireland, in October 1968. Her record will be broken in late 1971, when a 370,000-ton mammoth tanker is due to be completed in Japan.

passenger ships. As long ago as the early decades of this century, large steam turbines had a relatively low fuel consumption. Ships whose engines had to develop at least 10,000 shp were therefore equipped with steam turbines, and smaller vessels with piston engines. Since then both types of engine have been greatly improved and developed.

The successful advance of the steam turbine actually began when the famous Atlantic passenger liners of the Cunard Line, the *Lusitania* and the *Mauretania* (1907), were fitted with them. The better of these sister ships was the four-screw *Mauretania* (30,696 G.R.T.), which held the Atlantic crossing record right up to 1929. In 1921 her system was changed over from coal to oil. Traveling at an average speed of 27 knots, the *Mauretania* developed about 108,000 shp. The last three knots consumed c. 600 tons of fuel (naphtha) a day, i.e. as much as the first 24 knots combined.

Recently the gas turbine has also been developed as a marine engine mainly in Britain and the United States. This produces high power relative to weight and space requirement, compared with other engines. The first gas turbine ship was the tanker *Auris* (12,250 tons) built in Newcastle in 1948 for Shell Tanker. In 1951 one of her four diesel engines was replaced with a 1,200-horsepower gas turbine, which can power the ship at 14.3 knots. On October 28, 1951, the *Auris* left Britain for Texas and Curaçao, then visited several European ports before returning to Britain, having sailed a total of 13,211 nautical miles.

Some gas turbine ships have been built since the *Auris*, but a lot of work and development is called for before the gas turbine can compete successfully at sea with the steam turbine and the diesel engine. No shipping company will be interested in a new type of engine unless it leads to considerable improvements in the vessel's overall efficiency. So far the importance of the gas turbine seems basically to be limited to its use in fast warships.

The *Turbinia* (1894), the first turbine-engined ship, did over 34 knots—an unheard-of speed—in 1898.

Nuclear energy in the service of navigation

In time, perhaps in the relatively near future, the gas turbine will already be a "classic" engine. The far-sighted might have had a presentiment of this as early as 1919, when the New Zealander Professor Ernest Rutherford successfully split the atom for the first time, thus creating the basis for modern nuclear physics. The first large-scale release of atomic energy was in a uranium reactor in Chicago in 1942. However, it was only when the first atom bomb was exploded peacefully in July 1945 in the Alamogordo desert in New Mexico, and the first military atom bomb was dropped with such destructive effect on the town of Hiroshima on August 6, 1945, that man's eyes suddenly opened to the tremendous fundamental forces he had set free.

The world's coal, natural gas, and oil reserves may well dry up within the next five hundred years. It is therefore essential to insure that coming generations can be independent of such sources of energy. This is all the more vital because with the fast rise in population and the rapid spread of industrialization, our energy consumption in the near future will be many times what it is now.

The application of steam power to the service of transport was a great event which had a revolutionary effect on both traffic and the development of military techniques around the middle of the last century. Now, on the threshold of the atomic age, we are facing a breakthrough of at least the same significance. The taming of atomic energy is a really tempting, though gigantic, task, with tremendous potential for both good and evil. When the uranium atom splits, it releases about

---

INTELLIGENCE CRAFT. A mobile vessel on the high seas is the best listening-in station for many intelligence tasks. It is relatively easy for it to carry heavy electronic equipment and a large technical staff, and to stay months at a time in position in important areas. The vessel is also usually safe in international waters, and even twelve nautical miles of territorial waters allow it to get near enough to carry out its intelligence work. Though destroyers are sometimes ordered into this "electronic warfare," the USA and the USSR usually use special craft for intelligence. It is claimed that the Soviet Union's trawler fleet, which is the biggest in the world, includes vessels with more electronic than fishing gear. Such special craft are very expensive. The United States intelligence ship *Pueblo*, seized by the North Koreans in February 1968, carried equipment said to have cost about 100 million dollars.

50 million times as much energy as when a carbon atom burns in a furnace. Another comparison is that when one uranium weight unit is split, two million times as many heat units are produced as when one weight unit of fuel oil is burned. No wonder, then, that engine designers are interested in the fascinating suggestions and propositions put forward by atomic physicists.

In practice, atomic power even today plays a very modest role compared with other sources of energy. Science and technology are, however, advancing at such a fantastically fast rate that today's vague gropings may well be tomorrow's accepted reality.

The release of nuclear energy has given a tremendous boost to the development of means of transport and communication. Faster progress has been made in the application of this energy than anyone could have guessed. At the moment atomic energy is used in steam engines and steam turbines, the only difference being that instead of the usual fuels, energy developed in nuclear reactions is used to heat the water.

The application of atomic energy in ships means a high and economic speed, practically unlimited operational range, and underwater, independence of the atmosphere's oxygen. The last-mentioned property in fact makes nuclear energy most useful as the power source in underwater vessels. Human capacities, with the need for foodstuffs, ammunition supplies, and spare parts, limit the operational range of nuclear submarines, however. The attainment of high underwater speeds depends on the general character of the vessel's water resistance properties. The harnessing of atomic energy to power ships has produced a real revolution in the concept of naval tactics and strategy.

The main attraction of nuclear energy is that fuel storage space can be greatly reduced and the ship need refuel as rarely as three times a year. Another important advantage of atomic ships on long voyages, particularly, is their great speed. Thirty years ago twelve knots was considered fast enough for cargo ships to travel. Today their speed must be at least 50 per cent higher. Each increase, however slight, is expensive and means more fuel storage space. Double the speed, and the oil needed is eight times as much. With this problem, the vast potential of uranium offers great advantages.

An atomic vessel has a nuclear reactor, or uranium pile, in place of a steam boiler, with sticks of heat-producing uranium fuel in a highly reinforced steel container. A cooling substance is used to lead the heat produced during nuclear fission to the heat exchanger, in which pipes full of water receive the heat and produce steam. The steam is utilized in turbines and

The nuclear-powered icebreaker *Lenin* in the Arctic Ocean at latitude 77°30′, and members of her crew enjoying the winter sun.

then passes through condensers back to the heat exchanger. The reactor thus acts as the "furnace" in an atomic ship.

The Americans were the first to gain experience of a nuclear-powered vessel. At the official launching of this craft on January 21, 1954, the Director of the United States Atomic Energy Commission said that this was the first time that the development of military weapons had produced instruments for the service of peace. The submarine was called the *Nautilus* after two predecessors of the same name. The first was the submarine designed by Fulton in France in 1801 and the second the imaginary vessel described by French novelist Jules Verne in his science fiction novels almost a hundred years ago, which traveled over 60,000 miles in the depths of the ocean. Some data on the *Nautilus*: displacement 3,764 tons on the surface and 4,040 tons submerged, length 317 feet, width 28 feet, speed on the surface 20 knots and

The world's biggest military craft is the American nuclear aircraft carrier *Enterprise* (built 1961), displacement 85,350 tons fully laden, length 1092 feet, and maximum speed 35 knots. The carrier's deck will take 70 to 100 aircraft.

The world's first nuclear-powered craft, the American submarine *Nautilus* (built 1955), on an exercise, at a speed of 20 knots.

Le Redoutable (France) was completed in 1967. Displacement 9,000 tons, length 416 feet, beam 34 feet, and speed twenty knots submerged. Crew of 135.

The world's first nuclear merchant ship the n/s *Savannah* (21,840 d.w.t.) looks just like a normal cargo and passenger ship.

The first German nuclear ship, the *Otto Hahn*, was completed in 1968 and is intended primarily for ore-carrying.

23 knots submerged, armaments 6 torpedoes, construction cost 65 million dollars. The hull is cylindrical and the bows blunt-nosed.

On January 17, 1955, the *Nautilus* made her maiden voyage from Connecticut to Long Island with a crew of 115. In summer 1957 she refueled for the first time, after traveling 72,500 miles, about half of this submerged. Her total fuel consumption was less than eight pounds of uranium (two pounds of uranium is a fist-sized lump). On July 22, 1958, the *Nautilus* set off from Pearl Harbor, Hawaii, intending to travel under the North Pole. On August 1, 1958, from the direction of the Bering Straits, the submarine dived under the ice and on August 5, 1958, surfaced in Greenland waters, having traveled almost 1900 miles in 96 hours.

In 1960 the American submarine *Triton* (5,900 tons) sailed around the world in 84 days, traveling the whole journey of over 40,000 miles underwater. During this time the vessel's only contact with the surface life of the oceans was what she could see through her periscope. It was nuclear energy, too, that made it possible, in 1962, for two American atomic submarines, the *Skate* and the *Sea Dragon*, to meet underwater at the North Pole, under the ice.

Over the last few years the United States has built a number of nuclear-powered submarines, many of them large and equipped with highly efficient weapons, among them Polaris missiles. There are at the moment about seventy-five atomic submarines complete and operational, plus a great

Aboard the British nuclear-powered submarine *Valiant* the Commander (center) studies the navigation chart.

The nuclear-powered submarine *Valiant* at Farlane, Gare Loch, at the end of a 12,000-mile underwater voyage from Singapore.

number under construction or ordered.

The Soviet Union has also built up nuclear submarine fleet of evidently well over fifty units, the three types of craft (speed c. 30 knots) probably being 5,600, 3,500, and 3,200 d.w.t. So far the British have built three atomic submarines, the first the *Dreadnought* (c. 3,500 d.w.t.) being launched on October 21, 1960, on the 155th anniversary of the Battle of Waterloo. France also has one atomic submarine, *Le Redoutable* (7,900 tons).

The first nuclear-powered surface vessel was built by the Soviet Union. On December 5, 1959, this tremendous ship, called the *Lenin*, was launched in the Neva at Leningrad. The displacement of this powerful polar icebreaker, completed in the autumn of the same year, is 16,000 tons, her length 435 feet and width 90 feet. Her energy source consists of three reactors, two of them in use simultaneously, the third in reserve. The atomic mechanism, with its protective coating against active radiation, weighs 3,000 tons. The steam turbines run by the heat from the reactors produce 44,000 shp. The *Lenin* travels at 18 knots in icefree water and can break eight-foot thick ice at an even speed of 2 knots. Her consumption of nuclear energy per day is about 45 grams of uranium, and the vessel can go three days at a stretch without refueling. The *Lenin*'s main duties are to assist merchant shipping in the difficult ice-packed route between Murmansk and the Bering Straits on the Arctic Ocean.

The keel of the first atomic-powered merchant ship was laid in Camden,

N.J., on May 22, 1958. At the launching on the Delaware on July 21, 1959, the vessel was named the *Savannah*, after the first engine-powered ship to cross the Atlantic. The *Savannah*, built primarily for experimental purposes, was completed in 1962. The ship is 21,840 d.w.t., 13,890 G.R.T. and 7,513 N.R.T., her length about 590 feet and beam 80 feet. As well as her crew of 66, the ship can take 60 passengers in twenty cabins and about 9,000 tons of cargo. The atomic reactor, located in the middle of the ship and carefully shielded, can produce steam power for the turbines for three-and-a-half years of uninterrupted sailing, or a distance of over 360,000 miles. The ship refueled for the first time in Galveston in August–September 1968. The 20,000 horsepower developed by the two steam turbines propel the n/s (= nuclear ship) *Savannah* at about 21 knots by means of a five-blade screw. By mid-1967 the *Savannah*, whose construction costs proper came to about 48 million dollars, had cost the American government a total 100 million dollars.

The *Savannah* made her first visit to Europe in summer 1964, when she called at certain West German and British ports. She has since made goodwill visits to over forty ports. The ship was not originally intended as a paying venture, but as an experiment in the use of this new source of energy in peacetime service. In the three years in which the *Savannah* has been in regular scheduled service, she has carried a total of only some 110 tons of cargo.

The keel of the world's third nuclear-powered merchant ship was laid in Kiel in September 1963, and at the launching in mid-June 1964 she was given the name *Otto Hahn* after the famous German chemist and nuclear researcher who had recently died. Because of delays caused by financing and some subcontracting, the ship was not finally finished until autumn 1968. She is 15,000 d.w.t., about 560 feet long, 76 feet wide, and has a draft of 30 feet. The reactor has a 50,000-horsepower turbine, which gives the ship a speed of sixteen knots. The *Otto Hahn* is also fitted with a diesel engine. She cost about 13 million dollars including development costs, and was financed by the West German government, certain of the north German Federal states, and Euratom. The *Otto Hahn* is being used for two purposes. On the one hand she operates as an ore carrier; on the other she provides constant research material. She has a crew of 78, but also has space for about 30 scientists and researchers.

In 1968 Italy started to build a combined supply and ammunition ship; this will be the fourth nuclear-powered surface vessel in the world. Japan's first nuclear-powered ship will be primarily an experimental vessel; she should be finished in March, 1972.

BY ROWBOAT ACROSS THE ATLANTIC. It sounds unbelievable, but two men rowed across the Atlantic in the summer of 1896. They were George Harbo and Frank Samuelson, two tough Norwegians who had moved to New York. They made the more than 3000-mile trip from New York across the ocean to Le Havre in two months in a 18-foot open boat with no sail.

This ship will be 8,350 G.R.T., but her capacity will be only 2,400 d.w.t. and her overall length about 420 feet.

Apart from nuclear surface merchant ships, so far very few surface vessels have been built for military purposes. There are only four, all in the United States Navy. The world's biggest warship, the aircraft carrier *Enterprise* (displacement with full load 85,350 tons) was completed in 1961. With her eight reactors she is capable of speeds exceeding 30 knots and can go five years without refueling, if her turbines and four screw shafts are working properly. The other atomic surface ships are the missile cruiser *Long Beach* (1961, 16,250 tons) and the frigates *Bainbridge* (1962, 8,700 tons) and *Truxtun* (1966, 9,050 tons).

The application of nuclear energy to ships has obviously fully lived up to the hopes entertained for it for a decade and a half, though we are still only at the beginning. The many valuable advantages gained in military craft have already been demonstrated. The adaptation of the new power source to merchant ships looks promising, though there are still many unsolved problems, primarily financial feasibility.

The advance being made in this sector is fast; the *Savannah*'s reactor, for instance, is already out-of-date. With modern technology it is possible to create nuclear energy systems which need even less space and develop a high speed. The pressure water reactor will probably make way for lighter types of reactor, and in some fifty years surface vessels may well find a rival in fast underwater merchant ships. Some estimates say that by 1980 over 10 per cent of the world's merchant shipping will be using atomic power.

According to research done in the United States, the use of nuclear energy as a ship's power source is already economic, particularly in tankers and ore-carriers, if long distances and high speeds are required. Nuclear-powered tankers and container ships may on certain conditions be competing with corresponding ships using traditional energy sources as early as the 1970s; this appears from a research study on the use of nuclear energy in ships and navigation which the German company GKSS published in 1967.

Shipping companies in various countries seem, however, to be mainly of the opinion that at the moment we are still quite far away from economically feasible use of nuclear energy. Big shipbuilding countries with plenty of capital are, however, keeping the demands of the new age in sight so that they can attain and maintain a leading position in the construction of nuclear-powered ships.

Busy shipping canals

The main shipping routes run from west to east. Yet the continents spread roughly lengthwise, from north to south, forming natural barriers which force ships to make long detours. Man has tried to overcome these obstacles right from the early days of shipping. When planning routes from one sea to another, he has understandably devoted great attention to any narrow isthmuses offering a possible shortcut between seas or continents. There are now several man-made maritime canals across such land barriers, of varying importance to shipping depending on how busily trafficked the seas are which they link and on the amount of time saved by using the canal.

Though there were a few in antiquity, canals are mainly a product of the modern era. The idea of linking the Red Sea and the Mediterranean with an artificial canal is four thousand years old. The plan was implemented for the first time, we believe, during the reign of Pharaoh Sesostris III around 1880 B.C. The present Suez Canal, oldest of the maritime canals and by far the most important, was completed in 1869 by the French engineer Ferdinand de Lesseps. The Regent of Egypt granted a 99-year concession to the international canal company, but in 1958 the President of the United Arab Republic, Gamal Abdul Nasser, nationalized (by compulsory surrender) the Suez Canal Company for ever.

The Suez Canal is a single-level canal, and its present length is 107 miles, about 24 miles of this along the Bitter Lake. The canal's width at waterlevel ranges from 500 to 700 feet, and its maximum depth is about 40 feet. The average passage takes about 15 hours, and three parallel channels have been built for passing, at Port Said, Ballah, and Kabret (on the Bitter Lake). Canal traffic has grown steadily, except during wartime. The total tonnage of ships that have been through the canal was over 50 million N.R.T. in 1947 and 100 million N.R.T.

in 1954. The traffic figures for 1966 were: 21,250 ships with a total tonnage of 274.3 million N.R.T., 241.9 million tons of goods traffic, mostly oil. The ten most important countries—Italy, Britain, France, Holland, the USA, Belgium, West Germany, the Soviet Union, Spain, and Denmark—account for about 4/5 of the canal's total goods traffic.

The importance of the Suez Canal to world economy is very great, so the events of June 1967 and its continued closing have caused many disturbances in world trade and traffic. The European countries have benefited most from this canal. The saving in distance ranges between 17 and 59 per cent and in fuel from 50 to 70 per cent, depending on the ship's capacity, speed,

TONNAGE. The measure of a ship's capacity is the registered ton (= 100 cubic feet). The Moorsom system makes a distinction between the ship's total, or gross, registered tonnage (G.R.T.) and its net registered tonnage (N.R.T.). Calculation of gross tonnage takes in roughly all the areas below the deck or decks and the permanent deck structures: practically speaking the vessel's entire volume or cubic content. Net tonnage is gained by deducting from the gross tonnage all the areas necessary for making the ship move, such as the engine and boiler rooms, fuel, foodstuffs and water stores, tool and equipment stores, officers' and crew's cabins and messes, with alley-ways. This gives the "money-making" part of the ship's volume which in most countries forms the basis for pilotage, lighthouse, harbor, canal, and other maritime dues.

Displacement is the volume of water displaced by the ship, and gives the total weight of the fully laden vessel up to the loadline. Displacement is given in metric or British (i.e., long) tons, according to the system of measurement used in the country where the ship was built. Displacement can be divided into two main groups: the vessel's light weight and its dead weight (d.w.t.). Dead weight expresses the vessel's capacity in tons. This figure includes the weight of all the possible cargo (= ship's loading capacity) plus all the fuel, foodstuffs, water supplies, etc., and the weight of crew and passengers, that the ship can take without sinking below the freeboard mark put on the ship's side by the authorities.

As a general rule it can be said that when referring to cargo ships we mainly mean dead weight capacity (carrying capacity), or weight in tons. Passenger ships are usually referred to in G.R.T., which Lloyd's, the UN, and many corporations also use in ship statistics. The size of military vessels is given without exception as displacement. The standard displacement tells the total weight of a fully fitted warship with crew, supplies, armaments, and boiler feed water, though excluding fuel. When these are all taken into account, we get the permitted, or full, displacement.

cargo, and of course destination.

A plan has been drawn up in Israel for the construction of a rival to the Suez Canal. According to preliminary data this single-level canal, 160 miles long, would link Ashdod on the Mediterranean with the port of Eilat at the northern corner of the Gulf of Akaba. It has been estimated that this ambitious project, which will call for considerable investment, would take about twelve years to build.

A dream of four centuries became true in the summer of 1914, after many reversals, just after the outbreak of World War I, when the American cargo ship *Ancon* sailed across the Central American isthmus via the new Panama Canal. This canal, which links the Atlantic (Caribbean Sea) with the Pacific, was built in ten years, like the Suez Canal. The canal is about 50 miles long, from Colon to Balboa, 300 feet wide at its base, and at least 40 feet deep. Ships take 7 to 8 hours to go through the canal, which has many locks. The Canal operates like a company, the sole shareholder being the United States government, which has leased the 16-mile Canal Zone from the Republic of Panama. About 12,000 ships and 70 million tons of goods pass through the canal every year.

Compared with Suez, the Panama Canal is of relatively little importance to European trade. On the other hand, the journey from the economic centers of the American east coast to the countries of East Asia, Australia and the west coast of America has been cut considerably. From New York the voyage to San Francisco has been cut by about 61 per cent, to Valparaiso by 44.5 per cent, to Yokohama by over 38 per cent, to Hongkong by 33 per cent, and to Sydney by about 24 per cent.

The tremendous growth in traffic, with the cumbersome lock systems, has made the Panama Canal impractical in many respects. Military and political considerations have also given the United States government serious cause for building a new canal. No unanimity has yet been reached on the location of such a canal, however. The Nicaragua region is the main candidate.

Of the European maritime canals, the Kiel (or Kaiser Wilhelm) Canal is worth special mention, mainly because it is important to all the countries round the Baltic. The canal was excavated in 1887–95 across the lower part of the Jutland peninsula, from Brunsbüttelkoog near the mouth of the Elbe, to Holtenaus on Kiel Bay. The canal was extended considerably in 1909–15. The 61-mile passage will take vessels up to 1000 feet long, 130 feet wide, and 31 feet in draft. The locks at the ends of the canal are about 1200 feet long, 145 feet wide, and 45 feet deep. As the canal cuts the distance from the English Channel to the Baltic by about 240 nautical miles, it is busily traveled. Nearly 80,000 ships a year use the Kiel Canal and make this shortcut between the North Sea and the Baltic the world's busiest maritime canal. Its goods traffic is considerably less than Suez's or Panama's, however.

When the world's most expensive waterway, the St. Lawrence Seaway, was opened in June 1959, after five years of construction, the realization of this long dreamed-of project was of particular advantage to the economy of the countries who built it, Canada and the USA. At the same time the rest of the world was given the chance of delivering goods right to the heart of a marketing area comprising 40 million people. The total length of the 16-lock seaway, leading to the Great Lakes, calculated from the Atlantic via Lakes St. Louis, St. Francis, St. Lawrence, and Ontario, the Welland Canal, and Lakes Erie, Huron, Michigan, and Superior, right to the town of Duluth in the state of Minnesota, is about 2,342 nautical miles, 300 miles longer than the length of the Mediterranean. The magnificent work of extension and new building done on this waterway, formerly only of slight significance, has made it possible for big ocean-going ships to penetrate right to the industrial centers of the interior. The maximum ship size permitted at the moment is: length 708 feet (before, 249 feet), beam 74 feet (12 feet) and draft 25 feet (14 feet). In 1965 a total of 10,558 vessels passed through the St. Lawrence. Its goods traffic comprised 60 million tons, over two-thirds of this carried by American or Canadian ships. Because of ice, the traffic season is only from mid-April to the beginning of December. It has been estimated that the costs of the renovation of the St. Lawrence Seaway will be covered in fifty years by the canal dues.

Passenger ships in ocean service

It was only when world trade began to develop in the early nineteenth century that regular passenger and cargo services became necessary. The growing need for punctual, regular, and systematic traffic was the main factor working toward the foundation of shipping lines, and it was the steam, coal, and iron era that made such services possible. In the last few decades, in particular, scheduled services have become such an important feature of merchant shipping that economic life would not run smoothly without them.

The beginnings of transoceanic services

The world's first regular ocean shipping service was opened by the American Black Ball Line in January 1818, when the sailing ship *James Monroe* set off on the 3,000 mile trip from New York to Liverpool. Regardless of weather or insufficient cargo, the ships of the Black Ball Line set off promptly twice a month on the days given in the timetable. It was of course impossible to give a fixed date of arrival because of the unpredictability of the winds. The regularity of the Line's departures was really quite remarkable 150 years ago, though British packets had sailed the Atlantic before the American War of Independence.

The American packets, with the ships of the Black Ball Line in the lead, remained the "Aristocrats of the Western Ocean" right up to the mid-nineteenth century, when British steamships started to take over their routes. Before long, fast-expanding and superior steamship traffic forced the legendary packets off the world seas.

Earlier steamship traffic was mainly for passengers, but soon the steamships also began to carry mail and general cargo on a fixed timetable. To begin with, scheduled traffic was of significance only in a relatively narrow sphere — on the great rivers, the coasts of the major seas, and finally on small enclosed seas like the North Sea and the Baltic.

The first engine-powered ships cross the Atlantic

There was an interval of a quarter of a century after the maiden voyage of the *Clermont* before the first engine-powered ship made an actual ocean crossing: the famous American frigate *Savannah* (320 G.R.T., length 110 feet), which in 1819 made the crossing from Savannah, Georgia, to Liverpool in 27 days, 11 hours. In fact her 90-horsepower engine was auxiliary to her sails and was used only for a total of some 85 hours. Early engine-powered ships often found it necessary to resort

A fine sight in New York harbor, 1829: a packet of the Black Ball Line returning from England. On the foretop sail is the Line's symbol: a black ball.

to sail, as the unreliable mechanism and weak paddle wheels were inclined to break down in heavy swell and stormy weather.

The pioneer transatlantic paddle steamer *Rising Star*, built in Rotherhithe in 1821, was intended for use as a warship in the Chilean revolution. She was the first steam warship, and the first vessel to use steam on the Atlantic in a westerly direction. By the time she arrived in Valparaiso, the first steamer to enter the Pacific, the revolution had succeeded and the Spanish Navy had departed: therefore *Rising Star* was never used as a warship.

The first French steamer to cross the Atlantic was built of wood at Rouen in 1824 and launched under the name of *Galibi* for the merchant service. She was, however, renamed *Caroline* on her transfer to the French Navy. The ship sailed from Brest to Cayenne in French Guiana.

The first steamship to sail the Atlantic under Dutch command was the schooner-rigged *Curaçao*, built in Dover. She sailed from Hellevoetsluis, near Rotterdam, in April 1827, bound for Paramaribo in Dutch Guiana.

Across the Atlantic by engine power alone

There are conflicting data on the first ship to cross the Atlantic by steam alone. However, the honor would appear to go to the schooner *Royal William* (1370 G.R.T.) built in Quebec in 1831, which had an 18-foot–diameter paddle wheel driven by a 200–horsepower auxiliary engine. Originally the ship was intended to ply between Quebec and Halifax, but she was later sent to London to be sold. The *Royal William* left Pictou harbor (Nova Scotia) on August 18, 1833, with a crew of 36, seven passengers, and a cargo that included 324 tons of coal. Nineteen days later, traveling at a mean speed of six knots, she reached Cowes on the Isle of Wight in the English Channel, after a difficult trip.

In spite of this pioneering voyage by the Canadian ship, it was believed to be almost impossible for a steamship to manage the trip from Liverpool to New York (just over 3,000 nautical miles) without refueling en route. The famous British ship designer Isambard Brunel thought differently, however. He had built the Great Western Railway and suggested at a company meeting that the railway be "extended" by steamship as far as New York. He was a convincing and strong-willed character and carried his idea through; in 1837, in Bristol, the first steamship to be planned specially for Atlantic traffic was built—the *Great Western* (1320 G.R.T.).

The British Queen Steam Navigation Company, so named in honor of the newly crowned Queen Victoria, was also founded in 1837, but engine construction difficulties delayed completion of its first steamship, the *British Queen*. However, the company, determined to beat the *Great Western*, hired the canal steamship *Sirius* (703 G.R.T., length 206 feet, engine power 320 horsepower), which was originally intended to ply between London and her home port, Cork harbor. The *Sirius* left London on March 28, 1838, and overtook her rival on the Thames. She then steamed to New York, with 40 passengers and a crew of 35, in 18 days, 10 hours, during which time she used 24 tons of coal a day to keep up her mean speed of 8.5 knots. Just a few hours later the *Great Western*, which had crossed the Atlantic from the mouth of the Avon in 15 days, 5 hours at a mean speed of 8.8 knots, also steamed into port. It was a very close fight, however, as during the final stretch the little canal steamer ran out of fuel and had to feed her boilers with bulkheads and furniture from the cabins.

The arrival of the two ships in New York harbor threw the town into a state of unprecedented excitement and enthusiasm. This first race for what is called the Blue Ribbon of the Atlantic

FLAGS were originally used for military purposes. They originate from battle signs used in antiquity. Compared with these old signs used by kings and military commanders, national flags are very much more recent. The oldest national flag in use is the Danish flag (1219), followed possibly by the Swedish and Dutch flags. Of the flags of the world powers, America's is the oldest, dating from 1777. The French tricolor dates from 1794 and the present British flag from 1801.

---

constituted a vital incentive to the development of regular transatlantic service.

Transoceanic connections develop

The real originator and energetic developer of ocean-going steam traffic was the Canadian Samuel Cunard, who founded the still-operating shipping line in 1839. The first ship of the British and North American Royal Mail Steam Packet Co. (later known by the name Cunard Steamship Co. Ltd.) was the three-masted barque *Britannia* (1,156 G.R.T., 740 horsepower), which left Liverpool on July 4, 1840. At a mean speed of ten knots, she reached first Halifax and then Boston, taking a total of 14 days, 8 hours for the trip. The ship could accommodate 115 passengers and 225 tons of cargo. The return trip to Liverpool from Halifax, at a mean speed of 10.7 knots, took ten days. The *Britannia* was soon joined by her sister ships *Acadia*, *Caledonia*, and *Columbia*. As one steamship after another crossed the Atlantic, a network between various ports gradually began to build up. Before long, additional shipping companies were founded to handle overseas connections, and former companies extended their activities to wider horizons. There was fierce competition between them over ships' size, speed, comforts, and ticket prices. Ever since, the world's biggest and fastest ships have plied between Europe and America.

While Atlantic traffic was being built up, traffic connections were also beginning with the East–India, the Far East, Australia, and Oceania. A review of some of the well-known ship-

11 The sea and man

SHIPS' LIGHTING originally consisted of oil lamps. They were not much, but even so passengers grumbled when they were extinguished at ten each night. In 1872 the White Star Line tried out gaslight in their new ship *Adriatic*. The smell made the passengers seasick, so this improvement had to be abandoned. The first electric light was used in the *City of Berlin*, of the Inman Line, in 1879. The advance was a sensation in Atlantic traffic, though in fact the *City of Berlin* had only six electric lamps altogether.

---

ping lines founded last century is enlightening: P. & O. Company, originally the Peninsular Steam Navigation Company (1837), the Royal Mail Steam Packet Co. (1839), the Pacific Steam Navigation Company (1847), Hamburg-Amerikanische Paketfahrt-Aktien-Gesellschaft, usually abbreviated to Hapag (1847), B. I. (1855), Anchor Line (1856), Norddeutscher Lloyd (1857), Compagnie Générale Transatlantique (1861), the White Star Line (1869), the American Australian Line (1870), Holland-Amerika Line (1871), Red Star (1872), the Orient line to Australia (1877), the first direct line to New Zealand (1883), etc.

The magnetic attraction of the great Californian gold strikes has been mentioned elsewhere. Shortly afterward (1851), the first important gold strikes were made in Australia. The news spread rapidly overseas and adventure beckoned. Large numbers of fortune hunters from various parts of Europe set off on the long and difficult journey to the other side of the world. There was a tremendous rise in the emigrant traffic of British shipping companies, but this relied largely on sailing ships (packets) for many years to come.

The first steamship, the *Sophie Jane*, had already reached Australia from Britain in May 1831 and was shortly put into coastal service in New South Wales. In the same year the first steamship was built in Sydney—the *Surprise*. She went into service between her home port and the Parramatta river.

As passenger traffic on the North Atlantic developed, the speed record on this stretch became a tempting object of competition. Thus the first actual race for the Blue Ribbon of the North Atlantic dates back just over a hundred years, though rivalry between sailing ships crossing the "duck pond" goes back much further.

In fact there is no actual Blue Ribbon, though today there is an elegant trophy. The Knights of the Garter, Britain's highest order, wear a blue silk ribbon, which explains why English idiom uses "blue ribbon" as a term of admiration.

The Cunard Line's *Acadia* crossed the Atlantic in 1840 in 11 days, 4 hours at an average speed of close on 9.5 knots. Fifteen years later the *Adriatic* of the American Collins Line (1856, 3,670 G.R.T.) did the same journey at a mean speed of about thirteen knots. She was the last wooden-hulled paddle steamer built for Atlantic traffic. The last iron-hulled paddle steamer built for the Cunard Line, the *Scotia* (1862, 3,870 G.R.T.), crossed the Atlantic from New York to Queenstown in 8 days, 3 hours at a mean speed of fourteen knots. The *City of Brussels* did the same trip in under 8 days in 1869. An average speed of fifteen knots was exceeded for the first time by the steamship *Baltic* of the White Star Line (3,707 G.R.T.) on a trip from America to England in 1873. It was 1882 before the sixteen-knot record was broken by the steamship *Alaska* of the Guion line (6,400 G.R.T.). Two years later the steamship *Oregon* of the same line (7,375 G.R.T.) exceeded a mean speed of 18.2 knots and sailed from Queenstown to the Sandy Hook headland (off New York) in 6 days, 9 hours, 42 minutes. Inman & International's steamship *City of Paris* (10,506 G.R.T.) was the first to reach a mean speed of twenty knots, in 1889, and four years later the Cunard Line's s/s Campania (12,950 G.R.T.) traveled from Sandy Hook to Queenstown in 5 days, 12 hours, 15 minutes at the magnificent mean speed of 21.8 nautical miles an hour.

Shortly after Queen Victoria's Jubilee, in 1887, competition among the Atlantic shipping lines really got fast and furious. One after another, they proclaimed their ships finest and fastest. Until then the British and American shipping companies had dominated the field, but now a dangerous rival appeared on the scene: Germany, which had developed into a powerful, highly centralized nation after winning the Franco-Prussian War.

The first important achievement of their energetic new shipyards was the world's first twin-screw ocean steamship, the *August Victoria* (7,661 G.R.T., length 455 feet) built in Stettin for Hapag in the late 1880s. This ship proved faster than its compeers, and soon afterward (1890) the same shipyard's *Fürst Bismarck* was threatening the supremacy of the Cunard Line's *Umbria* and *Etruria*. She was the first ship to cover the distance between Southampton and New York in under 6 days and for a short time held the coveted Blue Ribbon. In 1885 the *Etruria* had sailed from Queenstown to Sandy Hook in the record time of 6 days, 5 hours, 31 minutes.

In the early days the Blue Ribbon route was rather imprecise and changed from year to year. The route still varies from season to season; a more southerly route is sailed in early summer because of icebergs.

In 1935 an international committee representing Britain, France, and Italy was formed to draw up the rules for the challenge trophy and to act as its custodian and awarding body. What had been a mere figure of speech became a concrete reality, thanks to the generosity of a British M. P., H. K. Hales. The actual trophy depicts the sea god Neptune seated on a marble base surrounded by mermaids who are holding up a globe, around which is a blue silk ribbon.

To prevent ships of the line from sailing too fast in crowded waters in an attempt to win the trophy, the committee made the Bishop Rock lighthouse in Cornwall the departure point for ships leaving from the English Channel, the Fastnet lighthouse for ships from Liverpool, and the Cape Tarifa lighthouse for ships leaving from the Mediterranean area. The common destination point in American waters was the Ambrose lightship (a permanent lighthouse since 1967) off New York. The distance between Bishop Rock and Ambrose is 2,942 nautical miles.

The actual Blue Ribbon race is run from east to west, but horsepower is also pitted against horsepower in the opposite direction. The winning ship must be able to hold the record continuously for three months before she gains possession of the trophy, whose splendid full title is the North Atlantic Blue Challenge Trophy. The prevailing currents and winds in the North Atlantic make the Europe-America trip slower than the opposite direction.

In 1892 the French appeared on the Atlantic scene with their fast passenger ship the *Touraine*. In 1893, recognizing its own capacities, the Cunard Line had two new passenger ships built, the *Campania* and the *Lucania*, both of them fast, beautiful craft. The sailing era had now been left behind for good. Two simple masts and two graceful high funnels gave these ships their distinctive and engaging appearance. The 12,950 G.R.T. sister Cunarders, one of which did nearly 22 knots, were now the fastest ships on the Atlantic.

Then once again the Germans took the lead. Norddeutscher Lloyd's steamship *Kaiser Wilhelm der Grosse* (14,349 G.R.T.) won the Blue Ribbon in 1897 with a speed of over 22 knots, and the trophy remained in German hands for another ten years. The Cunard Line's turn came again in 1907 when their four-screw turbine steamers, the sister ships *Lusitania* and *Mauretania* (31,938 G.R.T., 70,000 shp), became the first ships to speed across the Atlantic in less than five days, at a mean speed of 24 knots.

It is on the North Atlantic that passenger traffic has always developed most dynamically. Even before the World War I began, the ever-growing amount of passenger traffic on this great main channel of communication was the main object of shipping companies' ambitions. In spite of international regulations and agreements on ticket prices, North Atlantic routes became the scene of fierce competition, forcing the shipping companies to produce ever larger, speedier, and more comfortable ships and more regular, punctual, and efficient service. In 1912 the first ship of over 50,000 G.R.T. was seen on the Atlantic, the German *Imperator*, which fell into the hands of the British after the war and was renamed the *Berengaria*.

Increasing emigration engaged a great deal of tonnage quite early and played its part in the development of navigation by creating the conditions for regular line traffic. The stream

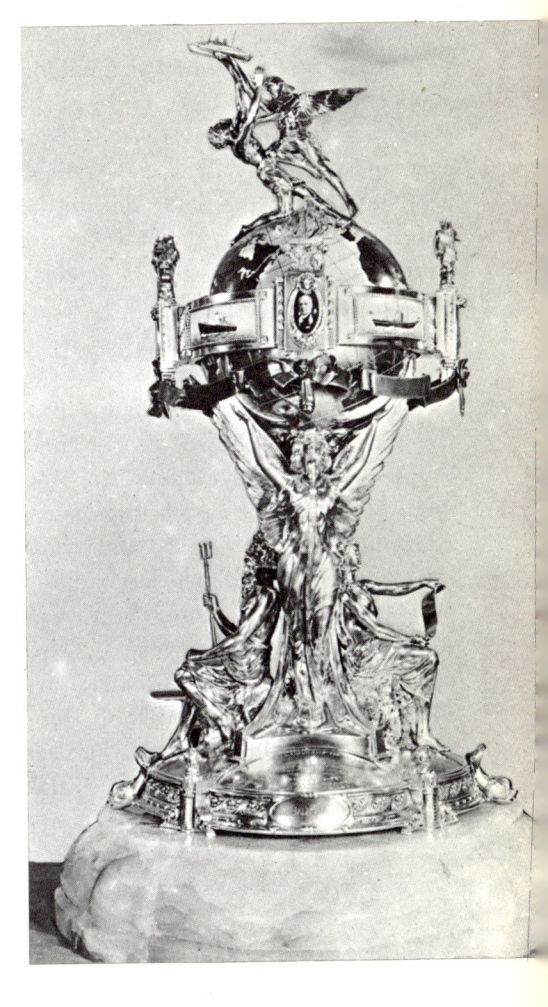

The magnificent and valuable challenge trophy presented to the winner of the "Blue Ribbon," donated by the British M.P., H.K. Hales, in 1935. The silver trophy shows the sea god Neptune sitting on a marble base surrounded by mermaids. The latter are supporting a globe in their uplifted arms, around which is a blue silk ribbon.

of European emigration continued to swell; in the 1830s around half a million people moved to the USA, in the 1840s about 1.4 million, and in the 1850s over 2.7 million. In 1892 608,500 people moved to the States and in the peak years 1906, 1907, and 1913, the figure was over a million. The amount of mail and general cargo, as well as ordinary passengers, also began to grow.

The fast expansion of Atlantic passenger traffic is shown clearly in a couple of comparative figures: in 1900 there were 671,126 such passengers altogether (between-decks and third class, and second and first class cabins); by 1913 the corresponding figure was 1,858,605. Most passengers in this tremendous flood were emigrants traveling west. German and British shipping lines were still accounting for over half of all Atlantic passenger transportation in 1913.

The World War brings great changes

During World War I building of merchant ships was almost at a standstill. Most of the big passenger ships had been turned into military craft: some into armed cruisers, some into troop carriers, some into hospital ships. A large number of ships were also sunk.

After the war Germany was left practically without her own merchant fleet. German ships which had sought safety in neutral ports were interned, and ships in American ports were seized when the USA joined the war. Under the Treaty of Versailles these ships were later divided up among the Allies. When the war broke out, the uncompleted *Bismarck* passed into the hands of the White Star Line and was renamed the *Majestic* (56,621 G.R.T.). The giants *Imperator* and *Vaterland* became Cunard's *Berengaria* and the U.S. Line's *Leviathan*. The *Columbus* turned into the White Star's *Homeric*, etc. Many other, smaller vessels changed nationality, and with it their shipping lines.

The war put an almost complete halt to international passenger traffic, but with peacetime and the return of more stable conditions, bans and restrictions on traveling began to be lifted, passports and visas became easier to get, and finally tourist travel was actually encouraged. With the steep drop in the number of emigrants, North Atlantic passenger traffic changed in character after the war and became more evenly distributed in both directions. The tremendous transferences of property and changes in the distribution of wealth that took place during the war and the postwar period, the fast development of means of transportation, and the fact that it physically became much easier to get from place to place put travel within

NAVIGARE NECESSE EST;
VIVERE NON EST NECESSE.
Plutarch says that Pompey (106-48 B.C.) had been sailing far afield buying corn for Rome from Sicily and Africa. On the return trip such a violent storm blew up that the sailors refused to go aboard. Pompey was then the first to leap aboard, and shouted the famous "winged words" above, which in translation mean: "To sail is vital; to live is not." The saying expresses a sense of duty that scorns self-preservation.

---

the reach of millions of people who earlier had had no chance of enjoying it.

Fiercer competition between shipping lines

Soon after the end of World War I international passenger traffic began to revive, and the big shipping companies again engaged in fierce competition, particularly on the main Atlantic routes. In July 1929 Norddeutscher Lloyd's four-screw turbine steamship *Bremen* won the Blue Ribbon on her maiden voyage from Bremerhaven to New York at a mean speed of 27.8 knots, wresting it from the *Mauretania*, which had held the Ribbon for 22 years, longer than any other vessel. The *Bremen* was record size and top class in other respects; she was 51,731 G.R.T., 930 feet long, 100 feet wide, and produced over 125,000 horsepower. The ship could take some 2,200 passengers, as well as a crew of 950. The *Bremen* was destroyed during the bombing of Bremerhaven in 1941.

By the end of the 1920s international passenger traffic had attained a new level of prosperity that lasted right through to the end of the next decade — even taking into account the setbacks that were the consequence of the international economic crisis. Before long, there was some degree of crowding and even overloading at times during the tourist season proper, particularly to the most popular tourist countries of Central Europe. One consequence was the growing interest of the traveling public in new and more remote countries, such as Finland.

In 1938 there were a total 309,591 passengers from Europe and North America; 258,352 traveled in the other direction. These figures reflect the decrease in emigration and the increase in tourist travel.

Before September 3, 1939 — the outbreak of World War II — the Blue Ribbon changed hands another three times among four-screw turbine steamships. The first was the Italian line Società di Navigazione Italia's *Rex* (51,075 G.R.T.), which broke the Atlantic record in 1933, covering the distance from Gibraltar to New York in 4 days, 13 hours, 58 minutes at a mean speed of 28.9 knots. She was the first vessel to receive the actual challenge trophy for the Blue Ribbon record.

The world's biggest passenger liners

The French now made a name for themselves in the Atlantic contest, though they had earlier been satisfied with providing the best possible service at sea without seeking to break any records. In 1935 France built the biggest passenger ship ever, the four-screw turbine steamship *Normandie* (86,496 G.R.T.), which fulfilled the long-time builders' dream of a ship over 300 meters (935 feet) long. The *Normandie*'s unusual appearance and many new features as well as her vast size made the ship a fine achievement in the history of shipbuilding; designers had succeeded in harmoniously combining a modern shape with French elegance and polish. She was the first great ocean liner with a turbo-electric engine, and her four motors, producing 160,000 hp, gave the ship a speed of 32 knots. In 1937 the *Normandie*, pride of the Compagnie Générale Transatlantique, established an eastward Atlantic record by covering the distance between the Ambrose lightship and Bishop Rock in 3 days, 22 hours, and 7 minutes at a mean speed of 31.2 knots, thus winning the coveted Blue Ribbon.

A year earlier, the Ribbon had been won by Cunard White Star Ltd.'s *Queen Mary* (81,235 G.R.T.), which had set up a record of 3 days, 23 hours, 57 minutes at a mean speed of 30.6 knots, for the east–west crossing. After the *Normandie* broke the *Queen Mary*'s

One of the most magnificent of modern passenger liners is the 45,733 G.R.T. P. & O. Orient Line *Canberra* (1961), here seen berthing at Circular Quay, Sydney. Her maiden voyage between Belfast and Sydney, including calls at other ports, took 27 days. The ship can take 2,290 passengers, more than any other passenger ship. She has a crew of about 960.

The French line Transatlantique's passenger liner *Antilles* (19,228 G.R.T., speed 26 knots, 1952) plies the route Le Havre—New York.

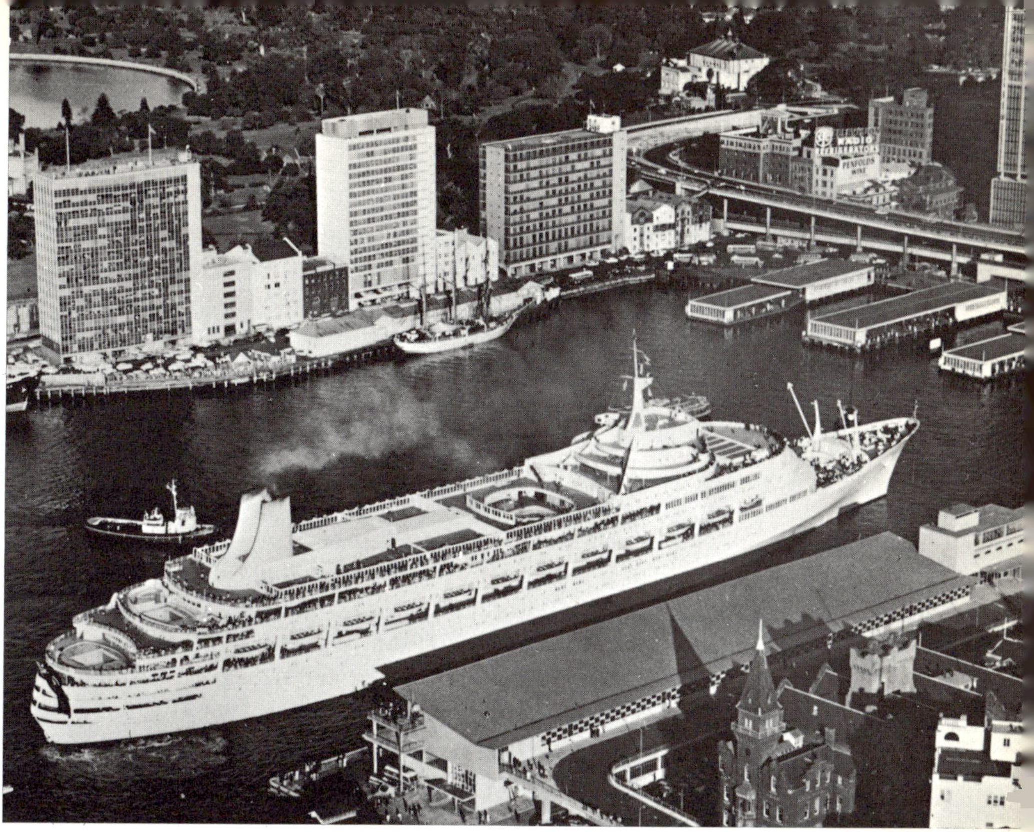

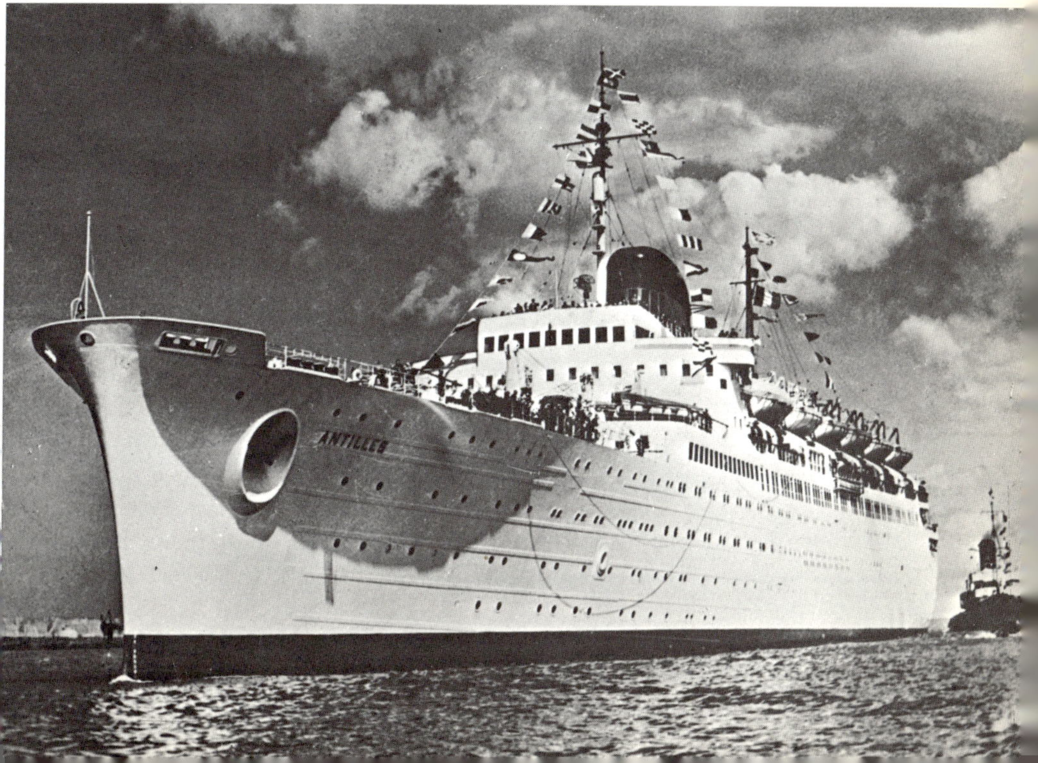
ANTILLES

record, the two ships successively snipped a few minutes off each other's time. The *Queen Mary*'s fastest Atlantic crossing from west to east was 3 days, 20 hours, 42 minutes in August 1938. She used some 1,100 tons of fuel oil a day to produce her cruising speed of 28.5 knots with her 160,000-horsepower engines.

Many experienced old travelers claim that with the disappearance of the *Normandie* and similar prewar luxury liners a distinctive, elegant world was lost that has not been rediscovered in the latest superliners. The year 1939 was the "fin du siècle" for a certain level of ocean passenger traffic.

Passenger traffic branches out

World War II had still greater and more far-reaching consequences for international passenger traffic than the first Great War, enormously thinning the ranks of the giant ocean ships. The *Normandie*, for instance, caught fire in New York in February 1942, while she was being turned into a troop carrier. The famous Atlantic liners of the inter-war years—*Bremen, Rex, Conte di Savoia, Empress of Britain, Majestic, Berengaria, Leviathan*, the first *Mauretania, City of Paris*, and many others—have also disappeared from the seas, as well as ships on more distant seas, e.g., the *Orford, Orama, Oronsay*, and *Orcades*.

The shipping lines in western European countries have, however, rapidly renovated and modernized the ships that survived the war and also built new and better passenger liners to meet ever-growing passenger demands. In addition to both Atlantic and Pacific scheduled services, cruises have recently attracted large numbers of passengers to these luxury liners. Many lines run cruises to the Caribbean, the Mediterranean, and the North Sea and Baltic area in the off-peak seasons, and in summer sail as far east as Helsinki and Leningrad.

Technical improvements have done much to improve liners on long-distance routes. The general design principle of the passenger areas in large ships is basically the same as it has always been, but there have been great changes in décor and atmos-

---

LIGHTHOUSES. The first unmanned nuclear-powered lighthouse was built near Baltimore, Maryland, in Chesapeake Bay, where it has been working since May 20, 1964. The high-power generator was designed to work nonstop for ten years without maintenance.

One of the most remarkable lighthouses was built at Kishbank, Ireland, in 1967. It is 180 feet high. The lighthouse structure includes a helicopter field, quarters for ten men, radar equipment, observation rooms, etc., and, most important of all, a 2.000.000 candelas "light."

ALONE ROUND THE WORLD. The first man to sail alone round the world was 51-year-old Joshua Slocum, an old salt who had advanced from cabin boy to captain. In an old model sailing ship which he had renovated himself, the *Spray* (c. 12 G.R.T., length about 33 feet), he set off from Boston on July 1, 1895, and after an eventful voyage returned to Newport harbor on July 3, 1898. He did not stay at home very long, but set off for Australia, where he got married and with his wife sailed 6,000 nautical miles across the Pacific. Fourteen years later he again felt in need of solitude and prepared his old ship *Spray*. He set off from Bristol, Rhode Island, aiming primarily for the Orinoco river in South America, but no one has heard of him since.

In summer 1969, an Englishman succeeded in rowing across the Atlantic single-handed in the east–west direction.

---

phere. Atlantic ships usually offer three classes, but the largest long-distance vessels generally have only two (first and tourist class). The names second and third class are no longer used; instead, the terms cabin class and tourist class are employed. These not only sound better, but also have in fact substantially improved comforts and amenities. Democratization of conditions and attitudes has also meant that lower prices are not the only appeal of the tourist class. Many wealthy people also prefer its more casual atmosphere, its freedom from social cliques, obligatory forms of dress, and other formalities.

Floating luxury hotels

The noble company of mammoth liners was headed by Cunard White Star's *Queen Mary* and their *Queen Elizabeth*, the world's largest passenger ship today (83,673 G.R.T.), often erroneously called the former's sister ship. The *Queen Elizabeth* was at the completion stage when war broke out and was not put into civilian service, after war duties and necessary alterations, until October 1946. Next in order of size comes the C.G.T. flagship *France*, completed in 1961 (66,348 G.R.T., length 315.5 m), the finest achievement of French shipbuilding.

The Italian turbine steamship *Michelangelo* (built in Trieste in 1965, 45,900 G.R.T.), represents modern passenger shipbuilding at its best. Construction costs were about 4.3 million dollars. The ship can take 1,775 passengers and has a crew of 720.

The great Atlantic passenger liners are so splendid and comfortable that they are often called floating hotels. Yet this is perhaps a simplification. It would, after all, be difficult to find hotels on dry land which could compete with these ships in quality of service or in size. No other community of 1500 to 3000 people exists which could offer such a vast and willing machinery of service as a luxury class ocean liner.

It is only the fastest Atlantic passenger ships that do not carry cargo. "Second class" liners on Atlantic routes, and even luxury liners on long-distance voyages, are greatly dependent on cargo. It is not economically feasible to build such fast passenger ships for the South American, South African, Indian, Australian, New Zealand, and Far East routes as for the short run to New York.

Since the days when the first vessels crossed the Atlantic by steam power alone, there has been a good 60-fold increase in tonnage and 4-fold increase in speed in passenger ships. After World War II many predicted the end of the great liners. The same prediction was made about 3,500 G.R.T. vessels after the Crimean War over a hundred years ago. After World War I the idea was current that people no longer had the money or the desire to travel by luxury ship. The French

The first class lounge in the passenger liner *Michelangelo*.

Line (C.G.T.) received a great deal of sympathy because under the agreement it had made with the French government it had to complete the *Ile de France* (43,152 G.R.T.), work on which had been interrupted by the outbreak of war. Yet when the ship was completed in 1927 she became a great favorite on the New York route.

Improved new liners are still appearing, particularly in traffic between Europe and the east coast of North America (specifically New York). New vessels completed in recent years include the Israeli *Shalom* (23,338 G.R.T., 1964), the Norwegian *Sagafjord* (24,000 G.R.T., 1965), the Greek *Oceania* (34,000 G.R.T., 1965), the Italian sister ships *Michelangelo* and *Raffaello* (45,900 G.R.T., 1965), the Russian *Aleksandr Pushkin* (18,821 G.R.T., 1966), the Greek *Queen Anna Maria* (26,300 G.R.T., 1966) and the British *Queen Elizabeth 2* (65,863 G.R.T., 1969).

Gigantic ocean passenger ships, of recent years mainly built by Britain, Italy, and France, are very expensive undertakings. The first two ships mentioned above, built in France, each cost about twenty million dollars. The motorship *Kungsholm*, the new flagship of the Swedish-American Line and the biggest passenger ship in Scandinavia (750 passengers), cost the line about seven million pounds and is

Looking as fresh as when she arrived 31 years ago, the *Queen Mary* passes the New York skyline on September 22, 1967, on her farewell voyage to California.

said to have caused the John Brown shipyard in Clydebank a three-million-pound loss. In general only big, wealthy countries can permit themselves this kind of luxury and self-advertisement, and then usually only with government subsidy. The race to build bigger and bigger passenger ships has been abandoned; ships built recently are under 50,000 G.R.T., averaging about 30,000 G.R.T.

It is estimated that the profitability of big passenger ships has deteriorated. Cunard ships like those already mentioned have sustained growing losses in the 1960s. As a result, both "Queens" have had to make way for newer, more practical vessels.

Details of the "Queens" roll of honor

In September 1967 the *Queen Mary* made her 1001st and final Atlantic crossing. Sold to America for 3.5 million dollars, she steamed to Long Beach, California, where she has since been turned into a floating hotel, maritime museum, and conference center, at a cost of thirteen million dollars. In the thirty-three years between launching and retirement, the *Queen Mary* performed a multitude of other duties as well as passenger traffic; during the war she was a troop carrier, a G.I. bride ship, a hospital, and a British command ship. The distance she traveled corresponds to eight return trips to the moon—3,807,277 nautical miles. The *Queen Mary* carried a total of 2,114,000 paying passengers and almost a million soldiers.

The *Queen Elizabeth* stopped sailing in November 1968. In July 1969 Cunard sold her to an American combine for 8.6 million dollars. There are plans to turn her into a hotel and congress center in Florida.

The *Queen Elizabeth* could carry a total 2,288 passengers—822 first class, 668 second class, and 798 tourist class—and a crew of 1,266. The passenger liner *France*, on the other hand, can take 2,048 passengers and has a crew of nearly 1,000.

The first class of such a ship does not have cabins in the usual sense. The tastefully decorated, comfortable rooms have wide beds on softly carpeted floors. The pampered modern passenger has so much comfort, variety and amusement available to him in cabins, saloons, decks, swimming pools, gymnasiums, dance halls, and cinemas all over the ship that he is literally swamped in entertainment for the four or five days of his Atlantic crossing. The ship's "Main Street" can offer various shops, outfitters, salons, repair shops, etc. There is a daily ship's newspaper. The meals deserve special mention, as the shipping lines make them a leading

THE GYROCOMPASS AND RADAR. The magnetic compass is not a completely satisfactory direction indicator. It was not until the gyrocompass was invented in 1908 that navigation gained an instrument that showed the right direction in all conditions. An essential aid for safe long-distance voyages, the gyrocompass began to be used widely after World War I.

World War II gave impetus to the development of radar into a feasible device by which a ship at sea could be located. Almost all new ships are now fitted with radar, as are most old ones, and particularly all passenger ships. In peacetime shipping, radar increases safety considerably.

The bedroom of a first class suite in the s/s *United States*.

The turbine steamship *United States* arriving in New York harbor from her maiden voyage in 1952 after breaking the Blue Ribbon record, crossing the Atlantic in 3 days, 12 hours, 12 minutes.

means of competition. Their dozens of dishes and delicacies constitute real luxury, even extravagance.

An 80,000-ton vessel is really huge; even seen from afar, the two-funnel *Queen Elizabeth* or the three-funnel *Queen Mary* are most impressive. A ship like this has ten decks above water level and two decks below. The distance from the keel to the top of the funnel is some 180 feet. The focus of the ship's daytime life, the promenade deck, is 715 feet long. The *Queen Mary*'s hull is held together by ten million rivets. She has four screws and sixteen steam turbines, which develop 200,000 horsepower, giving her a normal speed of about 28 knots. She has twenty-two lifts. The hollow rudder weighs about the same as two railway locomotives, and each screw is 20 feet in diameter. On an ordinary crossing the ship would carry about thirty-five tons of flour, ten tons of bacon and pork, seventy tons of game and other meat, four tons of cheese, eight tons of marmelade, and fifty-six tons of coffee, tea, and sugar. These figures alone provide a revealing picture of the scale and needs of a modern ocean giant.

Speed and the latest developments

In many respects the American turbine steamship *United States* (53,329 G.R.T.), some of whose technical detail still seems to be veiled in secrecy, represents the latest advance in high-speed Atlantic giants. When completed the ship represented something quite new in marine design, primarily because she is a tremendously large passenger ship which can easily and rapidly be turned into a troop carrier. The *United States*, which is said to have cost eighty million dollars to build, is as fire-proof as modern technical aids can make her. She can also be said to be a floating advertisement for American interior decoration, ornamentation, and fittings.

On her maiden voyage in July 1952 the *United States* made the fastest west-east Atlantic crossing on a Blue Ribbon route: 3 days, 10 hours, 40 minutes at a mean speed of 35.6 knots. In the opposite direction she also broke the record with a time of 3 days, 12 hours, 12 minutes. The Blue Ribbon has since been held by the *United States*.

May 1969 witnessed the maiden voyage from Southampton to New York —after some difficulties during the trials—of Cunard's newest ocean liner, the versatile twin-screw *Queen Elizabeth 2* (65,863 G.R.T., speed 28.5 knots), built both for transatlantic service and cruising. Costing some 30 million pounds, she is probably the last giant liner of her type and marks the end of an era. She was dimensioned to take the locks of the Panama and Suez canals. Cunard claims proudly that its *Queen Elizabeth 2* guarantees Britain's lead in the passenger shipbuilding industry: every possible technical ad-

12 The sea and man

178 The sea and man

The passenger steamer *Monterey* (14,800 G.R.T., speed 20 knots, 365 passengers) of the American Matson Line makes six-week round trips to the South Pacific from San Francisco and Los Angeles, stopping at Bora Bora, Tahiti (picture of Papeete harbor), Rarotonga, Auckland, Sydney, Noumea, Fiji, Niuafo'ou, Pago Pago, and Hawaii.

A T S E A. "I love the sea, the great, open, ever-ready sea. I love the powerful and secret sea. Great sea, I drink you into my soul: now though you cast yourself in flamelike mountains of black hate, with the stony gray sky above; now though you shimmer like a gentle lap of brightness, beneath the vast blue heavens. Now you bring joy to the human breast, now engulf man in an infinite, tearless longing. Sea, sea I love, of you I drink my soul full."

Volter Kilpi

vance was utilized in her construction. The *Queen Elizabeth 2* takes 2,025 passengers and a crew of about 900.

Although passenger traffic across the Atlantic is increasing all the time, in the last twenty years shipping has had a tough new rival in the aircraft. With the growing popularity of fast jets, in particular, air traffic has become of prime importance: in 1958 air traffic overtook shipping for the first time in the number of passengers carried across the North Atlantic (see statistical data on p. 180). Aircraft have also gained in significance as freight carriers in recent years. This is particularly true of mail and valuable goods, or those calling for fast transportation.

The fiercer competition between air and sea has forced the shipping companies to make every effort to improve their service and preserve their competitiveness. The adoption of the reduced-rate economy class in air travel is a particularly serious threat to passenger ships, which have started to offer similar arrangements with many added comforts. Even before the last war it sometimes happened that a passenger ship on an Atlantic or Australian route was made one class throughout.

While ordering new and more attractive passenger ships for the main routes of passenger traffic, many shipping companies have considered it in their interest to collaborate with the airlines, for instance by becoming minor or major shareholders in them.

The airlines as rivals of sea traffic

The statistics below throw light on recent developments. The shipping figures are those given by the Trans-Atlantic Passenger Steamship Conference, and the air traffic figures (scheduled services and charters) those compiled by the International Air Transport Association (IATA).

	By ship				By air			
	West-east	East-west			West-east	East-west		
Year	1,000 passengers		Total	Change %	1,000 passengers		Total	Change %
1936			598					
1937			659					
1938			568					
1946	(estimated)		300				105	
1947	»		415	+38			209	+99
1948	211	290	501	+21	99	154	253	+21
1949	285	367	652	+30	122	151	273	+ 8
1950	316	375	691	+ 6	146	171	317	+16
1951	288	422	710	+ 3	153	189	342	+ 8
1952	350	494	844	+19	208	240	448	+31
1953	379	513	892	+ 6	243	280	523	+17
1954	400	538	938	+ 5	272	309	581	+11
1955	425	537	962	+ 3	330	362	692	+19
1956	424	587	1,011	+ 5	382	453	835	+21
1957	437	590	1,027	+ 2	447	572	1,019	+22
1958	447	517	964	− 6	598	694	1,292	+27
1959	419	462	881	− 9	724	816	1,540	+19
1960	433	466	879	—	920	1,009	1,929	+25
1961	392	393	785	−11	1,049	1,127	2,176	+13
1962	415	405	820	+ 5	1,252	1,335	2,587	+19
1963	393	417	810	− 1	1,362	1,474	2,836	+10
1964	353	362	715	−12	1,705	1,846	3,551	+25
1965	315	334	649	− 9	1,971	2,121	4,092	+15
1966	277	326	603	− 6	2,236	2,464	4,700	+15
1967	245	259	504	−16	2,640	2,865	5,505	+17

Cargo ships in world shipping

The world economy would not have been able to develop to its present level without international shipping. There are two main reasons why shipping is important. First, the seas divide the world's continents and thus make shipping an essential, and for goods transportation usually the only, form of transport. Secondly, shipping is the best means of mass transportation. A ship is still the cheapest form of transport, whether the criterion is use of motive power or the weight ratio between means of transportation and cargo. Over long distances shipping costs are only a fraction of rail transportation costs. In spite of the tremendous development that has recently taken place in overland and air traffic, the seas, once the only highways of world traffic, have still preserved their significance as our most vital traffic channel.

Modern society in the civilized countries is dependent on an uninterrupted and regular import and export of consumer goods, machines, and a wide range of finished and semi-finished products. Raw materials such as corn and fuels are still largely supplied by sea in huge seasonal waves of transportation. They are purchased in large quantities, stored, and used gradually during the wait for the next consignment. Whole shiploads are brought now and then throughout the year, sometimes at frequent intervals, but on the whole irregularly. All the other goods which raise our standard of living and increase our comfort level, however, must reach their destination without interruption or disturbance. Because of the vast diversity of trade and the character of scheduled goods traffic, such products cannot be imported or exported from one place to another in whole shiploads. These goods are carried in innumerable consignments from innumerable ports to innumerable destinations. The great complexity of this work of transportation has to be handled by scheduled traffic.

The scope of shipping

With the development of international trade and its rapid advance in the last few decades in particular, merchant shipping has grown considerably. There are no exact comparative data available on the extent of world traffic. As early as 1929 it was estimated that world shipping, which is quick to reflect fluctuations in international economies, carried a round total of 470 million tons of goods a year. Because of the universal depression in 1932, the total fell to 350 million tons. Thereafter shipping gradually revived and

THE CREW OF A MERCHANT SHIP. The above-decks command consists of the Master and the first mate, the latter closely followed by the second and third mates. The Master must have his captain's papers, and he holds the highest authority on board. The first mate's most important duties include supervision of stevedoring (loading and unloading) in port. The rest of the above-decks crew consists of a bosun, a carpenter, able and ordinary seamen, apprentices, deck hands, cabin boys, saloon boys, and kitchen assistants. The engineering command consists of the chief engineer, who must be a qualified man in big ships, and a first, second, and third engineer. The ship's radio officer is considered on a level with the rest of the ship's officers. Other crew on the engineering side are the engineer assistants, greasers, donkeymen, and apprentice mechanics. A larger vessel will also have an electrician, motorships a turner, tankers a pump operator, etc. The galley crew includes a chief steward with one or more cooks, cook-stewards, second cooks, saloon stewards, mess boys, kitchen assistants, and cabin cleaners. The purser handles money matters on a passenger ship. The female domestic staff includes a manageress, cook, assistant cook, mess girls, waitresses, cleaners, and pantry girls, and in passenger ships a cold cook.

in 1938 reached the same figure as in 1929. Ten years later 490 million tons were transported, and in 1950 the figure was a good 550 million tons. Later developments in international seaborne shipping and the division of goods carried into dry goods and oils in the period 1951—68 was as shown in the attached table, according to the UN Office of Statistics.

The figures given show that between 1938 and 1966 goods transportation by sea rose 3.7 fold. In the same period the world's merchant fleet tonnage rose 2.5 fold, its transportation capacity also rising considerably with improved technical equipment, higher speeds, etc.

Most of the 47,500 and more merchant ships of at least 100 G.R.T. now in use are of course cargo ships. These vessels carry goods day and night between the world's innumerable ports, either in tramp traffic or in scheduled services.

The biggest shipping countries in 1968 (in million G.R.T.) were Liberia (25.7), Britain (21.9), the USA (19.7), Norway (19.7), Japan (19.6), the USSR (12.1), Greece (7.4), Italy (6.6), West German (6.5), France (5.8), Holland (5.3), and Panama (5.1).

Cargo ships and their work

Although the main work of cargo ships is the transportation of goods, many of them also carry a certain number of passengers; regulations specify a maximum of twlve. Since the war this form of travel has enjoyed growing popularity, for a cargo ship offers a fine opportunity for making an enjoyable, peaceful voyage, visiting many ports in various countries. Many newer cargo ships, however, have given up passenger facilities proper (apart from the "company cabins"), as they have not proved economically feasible.

Cargo ships can be divided into three main groups: general cargo ships, bulk cargo ships, and tankers. General cargo ships usually carry a large variety of goods for numerous different customers. Their capacity is not usually very great; 6,000–8,000 tons is considered an economic unit. If the ships were larger there would not be enough cargo for them at their ports-of-call—there is not always enough now. The shipping companies are showing an increasing tendency toward frequent services—a little at a time, but often. Bulk carriers, on the other hand, are getting bigger, as they carry large quantities of such raw materials

International sea-borne shipping 1951-68

Goods loaded by type of cargo

Year	Dry cargo mill. tons	% rise	Oil mill. tons	% rise	Total mill. tons	% rise
1951	385	—	255	—	640	—
1952	375	−3	285	12	660	3
1953	385	3	295	4	680	3
1954	410	6	320	8	730	7
1955	480	17	350	13	830	14
1956	520	8	390	11	910	10
1957	510	4	420	8	930	6
1958	480	−6	440	5	920	−1
1959	490	2	480	9	970	5
1960	540	10	540	13	1,080	11
1961	570	6	580	7	1,150	11
1962	600	5	650	12	1,250	9
1963	640	7	710	9	1,350	8
1964	720	13	790	11	1,510	12
1965	770	7	880	10	1,650	9
1966	800	4	950	9	1,750	7
1967	888	11	1,000	5	1,888	8
1968	980	10	1,120	12	2,000	6

Figures for 1967 and 1968 are estimates

The steam turbine ship *American Charger* (1967) is a super-efficient container cargo ship. 11,244 G.R.T., 6,673 N.R.T., 13,583 d.w.t., length 556 feet, beam 75 feet, draft 31 feet.

as ore, coal and coke, corn, and fertilizers, and speed is not usually the important factor.

There has been a great advance in the technology of cargo ships in the last fifteen years. When clouds began to gather on the shipowner's and shipbuilder's horizon in the Korean War and the first Suez crisis, the shipping industry began to branch out into daring new ventures. The adoption of new ideas and technical innovations in the shipbuilding industry has accelerated competition. One stimulus has been the long-term and low-interest credit granted to customers ordering new vessels. This phenomenon, in itself to be considered unhealthy, has probably tempted many shipping companies into much more audacious gambles with regard to ships' size and technical level than would have been the case had they had to pay cash. In 1966 Japan produced a 91,000-ton dry cargo ship (length 850 feet, beam 123 feet, draft 45 feet), and even larger craft have at least been ordered.

Some ten years ago nineteen knots was considered a high speed for a cargo ship of the line. Today speeds are as high as twenty-five knots. The increase in speed has called for new kinds of hull construction. Laboratory tests have given designers valuable tips. For example, a blunt-nosed bulb below water level in the bows reduces the ship's resistance to water and promotes an even higher speed, or alternatively saves engine power and fuel.

Ships have been specially built for the transportation of various dry bulk goods such as corn, sugar, and ore. They do not usually use derricks. If the cargo is corn, it is unloaded by means of suction devices, whereas coal, ore, or sugar is moved by means of grabs or similar equipment. General cargo ships are designed so as to be suitable for the transportation of as wide a range of goods as possible. Live cattle, whale, motor vehicles, coal, bananas, paper, and, most recently, containers (unit loads), are some examples of cargoes for which special ships are built. One of the newest ships for carrying live animals is the 9,000-ton *Centaur* (1963), which can take 700 head of cattle and 4,500 sheep. The ship is equipped with hygienic and worksaving feeding devices and pen-cleaning gear. Progress has also been made in the transportation of timber. Loose boards are troublesome to handle and take up too much space. Fastening timber into bundles weighing up to two or three tons has proved a practical and economical solution.

The rise in the sea transportation of motor vehicles has done much to promote the advance of transportation techniques. For water transportation within Europe, for instance, ships have been built with several decks and a direct drive-on, drive-off system. The most efficient method of transporting European cars to the United States is by specially constructed bulk vessels with removable car decks which permit the transportation of bulk goods on the return trip. Ships built for paper transportation are fitted with a new type of crane for better and faster loading and unloading.

The breakthrough of container traffic

In today's increasingly industrial society, distribution and transportation costs are so great that in Finland, for instance, they can account for a higher percentage of the final market price than actual production costs. The rationalization of transportation and efforts to reduce the reliance of transportation on capital have therefore become highly topical issues. Over the last ten years this has led to the adoption of unit loads in industry and commerce, that is, the amalgamation of small consignments into larger entities. Developments began with the flat and gradually led to the emergence of unit loads and the container.

The use of containers does not influence actual transfer costs, but it does make for considerable, even vital, reduction in docking and stevedoring costs. It is obvious that the automation and rationalization of cargo handling, for instance by using unit loads, provide the best way of reducing costs at the moment; automation actually on board ship comes second. The basic factors involved in the favorable solution of the container question are standardization, coordination, and cargo calculation regulations.

The development of the world's merchant marine

According to data compiled by Lloyd's Register, the world's merchant marine (vessels of at least 100 G.R.T.) has developed this century according to the table below. The statistics apply to the middle of each year. There are no figures for the war years 1915–18 and 1940–47. For the various countries' order of size, see p. 182.

Year	Steam- and motorships No.	G.R.T.	Sailing ships and barges No.	G.R.T.	Total No.	G.R.T.
1900	15,898	22,369,358	11,712	6,521,043	27,610	28,890,401
1901	16,528	24,008,883	11,471	6,410,569	27,999	30,419,452
1902	17,156	25,859,987	11,274	6,387,254	28,430	32,247,241
1903	17,761	27,183,365	10,948	6,266,186	28,709	33,449,551
1904	18,467	28,632,684	10,692	6,102,727	29,096	34,735,411
1905	19,153	29,963,392	10,421	5,985,168	29,574	35,948,560
1906	19,877	31,744,904	10,017	5,752,026	29,894	37,496,930
1907	20,746	33,969,811	9,295	5,421,188	30,041	39,390,999
1908	21,550	35,723,095	8,833	5,159,622	30,383	40,882,717
1909	21,909	36,473,102	8,505	4,942,295	30,414	41,415,397
1910	22,008	37,290,695	7,935	4,593,428	29,943	41,884,123
1911	22,473	38,781,572	7,511	4,337,942	29,984	43,119,514
1912	23,217	40,518,177	7,012	4,062,937	30,229	44,581,114
1913	23,897	43,079,177	6,617	3,874,051	30,514	46,953,228
1914	24,444	45,403,877	6,314	3,669,668	30,758	49,073,545
1919	24,386	47,897,407	4,762	2,988,863	29,148	50,886,270
1920	26,513	53,904,688	4,971	3,376,112	31,484	57,280,800
1921	28,433	58,846,325	4,753	3,115,649	33,186	61,961,974
1922	29,255	61,342,952	4,662	3,017,311	33,917	64,360,263
1923	29,246	62,335,373	4,247	2,822,898	33,493	65,158,271
1924	29,024	61,514,140	3,919	2,505,129	32,943	64,019,269
1925	29,205	62,380,376	3,700	2,257,706	32,905	64,638,082

1926	29,092	62,671,937	3,513	2,109,350	32,605	64,781,287	
1927	28,967	63,267,302	3,198	1.922,525	32,165	65,189,827	
1928	29,387	65,159,413	3,021	1,795,246	32,408	66,954,659	
1929	29,612	66,407,393	2,870	1,666,919	32,482	68,074,312	
1930	29,996	68,023,804	2,717	1,583,840	32,713	69,607,644	
1931	29,952	68,722,801	2,392	1,408,239	32,344	70,131,040	
1932	29,932	68,368,141	2,315	1,366,169	32,247	69,734,310	
1933	29,515	66,627,524	2,185	1,292,661	31,700	67,920,185	
1934	28,964	64,357,792	2,033	1,218,820	30,997	65,576,612	
1935	29,071	63,727,317	1,908	1,158,655	30,979	64,885,972	
1936	29,197	64,004,885	1,726	1,058,758	30,923	65,063,643	
1937	29,524	65,271,440	1,659	1,014,584	31,183	66,286,024	
1938	29,409	66,870,151	1,581	976,360	30,990	67,846,511	
1939	29,763	68,509,432	1,423	930,227	31,186	69,439,659	
1948	29,340	80,291,593			29,340	80,291,593	
1949	30,248	82,570,915			30,248	82,570,915	
1950	30,852	84,583,155			30,852	84,583,155	
1951	31,266	87,245,044			31,226	87,245,044	
1952	31,461	90,180,359			31,461	90,180,356	
1953	31,797	93,351,800			31,797	93,351,809	
1954	32,358	97,421,526	no figures available		32,358	97,421,526	
1955	32,492	100,568,779			32,492	100,568,779	
1956	33,052	105,200,361			33,052	105,200,361	
1957	33,804	110,246,081			33,804	110,246,081	
1958	35,202	118,033,731			35,202	118,033,731	
1959	36,221	124,935,479			36,221	124,935,479	
1960	36,311	129,769,500			36,311	129,769,500	
1961	37,792	135,915,958			37,792	135,915,958	
1962	38,661	139,979,813			38,661	139,979,813	
1963	39,571	145,863,463			39,571	145,863,463	
1964	40,859	152,999,621			40,859	152,999,621	
1965	41,865	160,391,504			41,865	160,391,504	
1966	43,014	171,129,833			43,014	171,129,833	
1967	44,375	182,099,644			44,375	182,099,644	
1968	47,444	194,152,378			47,444	194,152,378	
1969	50,276	211,660,893			50,276	211,660,893	

The Ford Motor Company's giant ore carrier, the *Henry Ford II*, steams through a drawbridge as she departs from the Rouge plant for upper Michigan and Minnesota iron ore fields.

In the few years since it emerged from the experimental stage, container traffic has expanded with amazing speed. This is particularly true of Atlantic traffic, where there are already a large number of cargo ships specially fitted out for this purpose. According to many shipping people, container ships will be carrying the bulk of all trade between the USA and Europe in the next ten years. Within twenty years they will probably dominate ocean shipping routes throughout the world.

Several big ports and even smaller harbors are building quays with the necessary equipment so as to be ready for the changeover from ordinary cargo ships to container ships which carry their cargo in great "boxes" and can be stevedored automatically. Special container harbors are being built or planned in many countries. A container harbor was, for instance, completed in 1969 in Southampton, the center of English transoceanic passenger traffic, for large ocean-going ships.

There has been considerable standardization in the size, customs clear-

An ocean vessel moves toward the Atlantic through the St. Lambert Lock. The site of Expo '67 can be seen in the background.

ance, insurance, and interchangeability of containers in just a few years. Sea transportation proper accounts for only the smallest proportion of the costs involved in this door-to-door traffic chain. According to research carried out by Norddeutscher Lloyd, the transportation costs for a particular general cargo on the route New York—Bremerhaven were distributed as follows: land transport in the USA 37 %, land transport in West Germany 14.5 %, warehousing at both ports 12 %, loading and unloading at both ports 25 %. The sea transportation accounted for a mere 11.5 %, though the freight charge per ton/nautical mile for general cargo from the USA to Europe is among the world's highest.

The greatest advances in container transportation have been made in the United States, the pioneer of this form of transportation. Huge terminals have been built, particularly in New York harbor, and several American shipping companies have established container ship lines between American and European ports. Container quays built

The beauty of modern technology on the Finnish tanker *Tervi*.

primarily for coastal traffic are being extended and others constructed with an eye to transports from European ports.

The fast rise in the number of container ships, especially in United States tonnage, brings with it some economic and other problems, according to the British Chamber of Shipping 1967 report. We can expect the near future to face us with a number of difficulties, some legal, some technical. There are also a number of unsolved questions brought up by the effect of container services on traditional liner conferences and pricing policy, freight, the general principles of negotiation between firms offering container services and the shipping companies, and the relations between container firms which do not own ships and those which do.

Oil transportation and tankers

Oil transportation and distribution have brought up many problems which were still largely unknown a hundred years ago. In 1860 a historic cargo crossed the Atlantic: the brig *Elizabeth* carried 224 tons of kerosene in wooden barrels from Philadelphia to London.

The space taken up by barrels and their tendency to leak set inventive minds working on designs for a ship which could carry bulk oil in specially built sections or tanks in its hold. The first ocean-going tankers were the iron-hulled sailing ships *Atlantic* and *Ramsay*, built in Britain in 1863, which could each carry slightly over 1,000 tons of oil. A special feature of these ships was that their hollow masts allowed for cargo expansion.

The first engine-powered tanker was the Belgian *Vaderland* (1872), a kind of mixed cargo ship. The inventive owners had designed her so that she could carry emigrants to the USA and bring back oil to Europe. The authorities considered this arrangement too dangerous, however, and in fact the records do not indicate that the *Vaderland* was ever used for oil carrying.

The Swedish shipbuilding industry can probably claim the honor of constructing the world's first actual steam tanker, in Motala, 1878, on the initiative of Ludvig Nobel. This tanker, called the *Zoroaster*, loaded 250 tons of oil in individual tanks. In four years the Nobel brothers' fleet consisted of a dozen or so tankers (the biggest about 800 tons), which operated on the Caspian Sea and the Volga. The steamship *Ferguson*, built in 1885, is thought to have been the first engine-powered ship to carry kerosene in fitted tanks.

The new era in ocean-going tankers was begun by the *Glückauf*, built in England in 1886 for Deutsche Amerikanische Petroleum Gesellschaft by the German Wilhelm Anton Tiedemann. This vessel was revolutionary in construction and very up-to-date in many respects: for instance the engines and the crew's quarters were in the rear of the ship; she had a bulkhead which followed the center line, and lateral bulkheads. By contemporary standards her proportions were impressive: loading capacity 3,020 tons, 2,307 G.R.T., length 315 feet, beam 37 feet, and speed fully laden 10.2 knots. The ship was certainly epoch-making, and she soon began to be copied widely. The *Glückauf* sailed successfully up to 1893, when she was wrecked near New York.

M/s Finlandia (Helsinki, 1967), the new flagship of the Finland Steamship Company, is a combined car and passenger ferry. She has room for some 800 passengers, about 320 cars, and over 800 tons of container cargo. Main data: 8,168 G.R.T., 4,035 N.R.T., length 497 feet, beam 65 feet, and speed 22 knots.

The basic design of the *Glückauf* was so successful that it was retained practically unchanged right up to the early 1920s. One of the basic structural weaknesses of tankers—their lateral strength limited their length—was then eliminated by increasing the number of oil tanks and thus also augmenting the number of bulkheads, and it was not long before tanker size gradually grew.

In the early decades of this century the world's tanker tonnage grew rather slowly. At the turn of the century, tankers accounted for a total capacity of 0.5 million tons, with an average vessel size of about 5,000 tons. At the outbreak of World War I, total tonnage had quadrupled and average size had risen by about 1,000 tons. Before World War II the world's tanker tonnage included some 1,500 ships with a total capacity of some 16.5 million tons. The biggest individual tankers were the 22,600 ton *William Rockefeller* (1921) and *John D. Archbold* (1921). During the last war the average size of ships built was 20,000 to 25,000 tons, and

---

THE ENGLISH CHANNEL.

This channel between the North Sea and the Atlantic is 350 miles long and divides the south coast of England from the north coast of France. It is 21 to 150 miles wide and the average depth is 260 feet. Both shores belong to the same chalk formation. The British Isles were once a headland of the European continent, but about 7,000 years ago the surface of the sea rose, covering the rolling grasslands between Dover and Calais, and cut Britain off from the continent. Ever since, the Channel has been a capricious and confusing stretch of water, with tides, currents, and whirlpools which put even the best sailor to the test. Fog appears on the Channel at all times of year. There are few shipping lanes with so many marks and navigational aids: almost 1,000 buoys, 11 lightships, and 32 English and 21 French lighthouses. In spite of all these aids, the greatest danger on the Channel is that of collision. It is estimated that 300,000 ships a year cross the straits between Dover and Calais, the narrowest point of the Channel, and there are always about forty ships in the straits simultaneously.

Ever since the 1830s there have been plans for a tunnel under the Straits of Dover between France and England. The governments of the two countries have agreed about the construction of a railway tunnel of some 32 miles, which should be ready in 1975. There has been a tremendous increase in passenger and vehicular traffic across the Channel in recent years. In 1959–65 the annual number of passengers on all routes rose from 2.5 million to almost 3.5 million. The number of cars in the former year was 226,000 and in the latter 554,000. Over 2 million people and about 65,000 cars were also carried across the Channel by air.

Liberty steamships built during World War II, in the "mothball fleet" somewhere on the US coast. In 1968 the US reserve still included a total of over 6.7 million G.R.T. of these and other wartime merchant craft.

these reached a speed as high as twenty knots.

The trend of shipbuilding technology is toward greater specialization. The most highly standardized type of vessel at the moment is the tanker, and it is this type that shows the most rapid increase in tonnage. Because of the simple handling of cargo, the benefits of large vessel units have been used to full advantage.

Large tankers

There has been a fast rise in the demand for giant-sized tankers in the last few years. The reason is not only the phenomenal upsurge in the use of oil but also the fact that refineries have increasingly started to invest in actual consumption areas instead of oil fields. Competition and prestige questions have played their own part here.

The United States is the first builder of large tankers. Soon after the war the US produced a tanker of 32,000-ton carrying capacity. Europe followed along the same lines. The Greek shipowner Onassis added to his fleet the 47,000-ton *Al-Malik Saud Al-Awal*, built for him in Hamburg in 1954.

The magical 50,000-ton limit was exceeded in 1955, with the completion of the *Sinclair Petrolore* (55,000 tons). Four years later the giant *Universe Apollo* (106,000 tons) appeared on the seas. Japan has built the world's biggest ships, the real mammoths. The tanker *Idemitsu Maru*, completed in November

The world's first ocean-going tanker, the *Glückauf*, used auxiliary sails as well as a steam engine. The vessel was built in Britain in 1885.

1966, was the first ship to exceed the 200,000 d.w.t. limit.

At the moment the biggest ship in the world is the *Universe Ireland*, which was completed in Japan in August 1968, the first of a series of six ships of the same size—326,000 tons. The technical data on this ship are: length 1125 feet, beam 193 feet, draft 98 feet, engine power 37,400 shp, speed 14.6 knots, cost 20 million dollars. Her deck would take 62 tennis courts and her height from the tip of the funnel is over 200 feet, the equivalent of an 18-story building. The *Universe Ireland* and the rest of the American-owned ships in the series, some of which have already been built, have been chartered long-term by the Gulf Oil Corporation for oil shipments from the Persian Gulf to Europe and the Far East. Even larger craft are on the way, as Japan is just building a 372,400 d.w.t. tanker (cost 28 million dollars) and 420,000–450,000 d.w.t. tankers are being planned.

No other specialist branch of shipping has developed so rapidly and become such an important proportion of world shipping as tanker traffic. Oil transportation is, indeed, now the largest of the many areas in which international shipping operates. Tankers form the biggest vessel group (about 69 million G.R.T. in 1968) and now account for well over 35 per cent of the world's merchant marine and about 58 per cent of the tonnage of all motorships. There are at present over 500 tankers of at least 30,000 G.R.T. plying the world's shipping lanes, and well over a hundred ships of at least 50,000 G.R.T.

The biggest tanker fleets (1968) sail under the following countries' flags: Liberia (14.7 million G.R.T.), Norway (10.0 million), Britain (8.4 million), Japan (6.8 million), USA (4.5 million), USSR (2.9 million), France (2.7 million), Panama (2.7 million), Italy (2.4 million), and Greece (1.9 million). The world's biggest privately owned tanker

The *Esso Flame* (1966) is the first liquid gas tanker to be built in Finland. This highly automated ship needs a crew of only thirteen men. Technical data: length 242 feet, beam 36 feet, depth 13 feet, 3 liquid gas tanks tot. 37,000 cu.ft., 8 cargo tanks tot. 23,000 cu.ft.

Giant tankers for Finland: the oil refinery Neste Oy has ordered two 110,750 ton tankers, the first of which was delivered in November 1969. Each ship is 885 feet long, 129 feet wide, and 45 feet in draft.

A bulb in the bows reduces resistance to water. The picture shows the 90,600 ton tanker *Esso Bayer*, built in Hamburg in 1964.

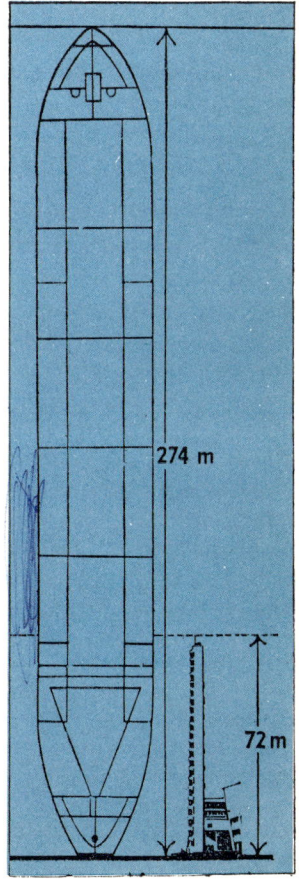

274 m

72 m

line is Standard Oil (N.J.), whose 165 ships accounted for some 5 per cent of international tanker tonnage in 1967.

The structure and cargo of a tanker

The specially built tanker differs greatly in structure from the usual dry cargo ship. The hull is divided into three longitudinal sections with two bulkheads; lateral bulkheads then divide these into several compartments, or tanks. There are usually 24 to 30 of these tanks, depending on the ship's size, and even more in mammoth tankers. There is thus only a small area of unobstructed liquid surface in each tank, not enough to disturb the vessel's equilibrium as it rolls to and fro. The engine room in a tanker is in the stern, where it can most easily be separated from the inflammable and highly explosive cargo by oil-tight and water-tight vacuum tanks running across the ship. As the engines have been transferred to the stern, the propeller shaft and tunnel need not pass through the cargo containers, which would increase the risk factor and reduce the cargo room. With the gradual advance of hull and engine construction techniques, the size of tankers has grown.

Tankers are divided into two main groups on the basis of the oil product quality that they carry: clean tankers and dirty tankers. The former carry light and purified oil products such as petroleum, kerosene, gas oil, and certain fine fuel oils. The dirty tankers, on the other hand, carry the heaviest, unpurified products (crude oil, diesel oil) and thicker fuel oils. When dirty cargo is carried, it is heated during the trip by means of steam-bearing coils to

---

THE LOADLINE. In the name of seaworthiness a ship is not allowed to load up too deep, only up to its loadline. About 20 to 30 per cent of a ship's total load capacity — assuming it to be loaded right up to full immersion — must not be utilized. To prevent overloading, the law prescribes that a line must be painted on the ship's side showing the height of the main deck — the deckline — and under it another line — the loadline — the upper edge of which shows how low the vessel may lie in the water in summer. This loadline is also marked with a freeboard disk. The distance between the deck and loadlines is called a ship's freeboard. The freeboard height varies depending on the season and zone, and is marked in a special way on both sides of the freeboard disk. The loadline is also often called the Plimsoll line in memory of Samuel Plimsoll, the man who put the bill before the British parliament in 1868.

ICEBREAKERS. Icebreaking is a fairly recent specialized branch of the age-old pursuit of seafaring. When sail and oar were replaced by engines in the nineteenth century, and iron, and later steel, began to be used for ships' hulls, it became possible to travel even in icy waters. As early as the 1850s the hulls of certain passenger and mail ships began to be reinforced for this purpose. The wooden-hulled paddle steamer *Norwich* (1836) became widely known as an icebreaker on the Hudson river near New York. However, the honors for building the first ship specifically for this purpose must go to Philadelphia, which constructed a special vessel in 1837 to break up the flood ice which occasionally hampered shipping on the Delaware river. This ship, *City Iceboat No. 1* (length 172 feet, width at the paddle guards 59 feet, engine power over 1,000 horsepower), was used for a good eighty years, though it was not needed every year. The pioneer in this field in Europe seems to have been the little steamship *Pilote*, with which the Russian merchant Britnev tried from 1864 onward to insure regular connections from Kronstadt to the coast in winter and spring. This enterprising merchant redesigned the stem so that the bows could lift up and crush the ice floes.

The first real icebreaker was the *Eisbrecher I*, built in Germany in 1871 (length 200 feet, beam 33 feet, engine power 3,000 horsepower). This ship worked on the Elbe between Hamburg and Cuxhaven. Kristiania (Oslo) built an icebreaker called the *Mjölner* (1877), Gothenburg the *Isbrytaren* (1882), and Denmark the *Staerkodder* (1885). The Danish ship *Bryderen* made a demonstration voyage to Hanko and Helsinki, Finland, in 1889. A year later the Finnish government's first icebreaker, *Murtaja*, built in Sweden, was completed. As well as the Scandinavian countries, the Soviet Union, West Germany, the USA, and Canada have all purchased icebreakers to insure all year round navigation.

keep it liquid and easy to pump during unloading. The ship's own pumps are used for unloading, whereas cargo is loaded by pumps on shore or under the large storage tanks' own pressure.

Specialized tankers

With the increasing diversity of tanker cargoes over the years, specialized tankers have been built as need dictated. A number of other liquids and fluid substances have joined natural oil: whale oil, spirits, wine, molasses, tar, glues, industrial chemicals, etc.

Natural gas and liquid gas continue to account for an increasing amount of international energy and the fast-growing chemical industry's needs. As sea transportation is the cheapest over long distances, shipping companies were prepared to seize the opportunities offered by this specialized traffic well in advance. As early as the late 1940s, specialized ships were classified which were designed to carry liquid gas under pressure. The first vessel of this kind in Europe was the *Rasmus Tholstrop* (1953), which can carry 320 tons of liquid gas. Gas tankers are still at an interesting stage of development, mainly because the raw material must be carried at rather low temperatures (methane at -161 °C., liquid gas at -42 °C., etc.).

One specialized form of tanker is the combination ship. In this the holds in the central section are used for ores, while tanks for oil are built into the sides and bottom. On certain routes this kind of vessel, which the United States was building as long ago as the 1920s and whose maximum capacity nowadays exceeds 70,000 tons, has proved very economical, carrying oil one way, ore the other.

The biggest ship-owning nations, 1969, (mill. B.R.T.): Liberia (29.2), Japan (24.0), Great Britain (23.8), U.S. (19.8), Norway (19.7), Soviet Union (13.7), Greece (8.6), Italy (7.0), Western Germany (7.0), France (6.0), Panama (5.4), The Netherlands (5.3).

The birth of a modern ship

A hundred and fifty years ago, when practically all ships were wooden-hulled sailing craft, shipbuilding was still a relatively straightforward process. The main craftsmen involved in this traditional trade were the actual ship builder (a carpenter), the rigging-maker, and the sail-maker. Today's tremendous steel hulls, complex modern screw mechanisms, and various technical refinements call for knowledge and skill from almost all trades and crafts. Primitive boatbuilding yards have been replaced by huge shipyards, fitted with all the equipment that science and technical invention can offer.

In the past, when ships mainly differed only in size, a shipbuilder could start off building several craft at once without worrying his head about selling them. If he was lucky, a customer turned up as soon as the hull began to take shape. Today things are quite different in this respect. There is such a multitude of different kinds of ships on the world's seas that even in a quiet period no shipbuilder is likely to start building speculatively. In other words, all modern ships are built to order, with exact specifications and delivery dates, and quality requirements are usually very high.

Before considering this stage, however, a review of the factors which provide the impetus for the development of a shipbuilding industry would be useful.

The invention of the steam engine and the consequent adoption of iron, and later steel, as the construction material for ships' hulls displaced the old craft of building wooden ships. This revolutionary change did not take place all at once, however; things developed gradually and there were many intermediate stages, as the account of the triumphal progress of steamships has already shown.

The first iron ships are built

The use of iron for ships' hulls was originally opposed for several reasons. Apart from the fact that the specific gravity of iron was too great, it was thought that the iron in the ship would affect the reliability of the compass. Then there was fear of sinking, as a leak would be difficult to plug, particularly at sea. The "sweating" of an iron-hulled ship would also spoil the cargo, etc. There were many other prejudices, as well as the age-old established status of wood as shipbuilding material, that slowed down the acceptance of iron. It also took time before builders in iron learned the best ways of making joints.

The ribs of a wooden-hulled war reparation schooner for the USSR being finished off at the F. W. Hollming Oy shipyard, Rauma, Finland.

To begin with, iron was allowed to replace only the parts of wooden ships (e.g., the outboard rail) which were difficult to make sufficiently strong out of wood. After craftsmen had learned how to roll iron into sheets in the mid 1780s, it became possible to build iron-hulled vessels. In Britain, particularly, it had already become increasingly difficult and expensive to get timber suitable for shipbuilding, and this fact stimulated ship designers' interest in iron.

By the mid-nineteenth century iron had already made a successful breakthrough. The completion of the first iron ocean-going ship, the *Great Britain* (3,270 G.R.T., length 318 feet) in Bristol, England, was the main factor here. This ship, the brainchild of the well-known shipbuilder Isambard K. Brunel, featured another important innovation—the screw. She was also equipped with six-masted schooner rigging. With 60 passengers and over 300 tons of cargo the *Great Britain* set off on her maiden voyage from Liverpool to New York on July 26, 1845; the Atlantic crossing took 14 days, 21 hours, and her mean speed was 9.3 knots. Her good fortune did not last long, however, as on her third trip she ran aground in Dundrum Bay, off the Irish coast.

Although the first large iron ship met with such bad luck, she still pointed the way for this splendid new shipbuilding material. This period marked the beginning of a great boom in shipbuilding, though in the first flush of enthusiasm the mistake was made of building a really giant ship.

Around 1852 the same engineer, Brunel, proposed to the Eastern Navigation Co. the construction of a steamship five to six times bigger than any previous vessel built, for use on the Indian and Australian route. On long voyages big ships had the advantage: the bigger the ship, the faster she could travel. It was estimated that a vessel of the dimensions proposed for the Leviathan would maintain a speed of fifteen knots with less power per ton than ordinary vessels required at ten knots. The giant craft would have plenty of room for passengers and cargo, and she would carry enough fuel for the whole trip. Brunel also suggested that the ship use both paddle wheel and screw, augmented of course by sails.

The Great Eastern — *a premature giant*

This famous ship was designed in accordance with John Scott Russell's "wave-line theory," and construction of the hull was begun in Millwall in May 1854. Three months after the first attempt, the new ship, named the *Great Eastern*, was finally launched sideways into the Thames on January 31, 1858, after drastic use of highly expensive hydraulic machinery. Her dimensions were indeed impressive for the day: displacement 32,000 tons, 18,915 G.R.T. and 13,344 N.R.T., length overall 686 feet, beam 83 feet. She had six masts with sails, and five funnels.

On her first trial voyage the ship's heater exploded and five men lost their lives. Brunel himself died a few days later after a sudden illness. Before the vessel could be put into service, it proved necessary to renew the wooden decks and reinforce the engines. It was thus not until June 17, 1860, that the *Great Eastern*, contrary to the original plan for using her on long-distance routes, set off on her maiden voyage to New York. On this trip the ship took 800 first-class passengers, 2,000 second-class passengers, and 1,200 third-class passengers between-decks, as well as a crew of 400. She also carried 10,000 tons of coal and 6,000 tons of cargo. Her average speed was about 14 knots, and her coal consumption 12.5 tons an hour.

BUILDING A SHIP is not just a technical feat; it is also an art. Of course a ship is primarily a mechanical creation, but no seaman would be satisfied with this definition alone. It is also an architectural creation which is not produced merely with graphs and calculations. A shipbuilder must also be an artist. The British in fact call their shipbuilders naval architects.

The *Great Eastern* made her second voyage the same year. She then ran into a bad storm and began to roll heavily. Brunel had been so sure that the ship's great size would keep her stable even in a storm that he had left all the furniture and fittings loose, without mooring devices. As the storm raged they began rolling from one side to the other, injuring many passengers. The outer bottom was also torn open about 3 feet wide and 84 feet long, but thanks to its double bottom the ship stayed afloat and managed to make port. Since no dock was large enough, the damage to the ship had to be repaired in New York by divers. Repairs took six months and ran up quite a bill. On the *Great Eastern*'s third voyage in 1861 a storm broke her paddle wheels and snapped off the rudder support; the unlucky ship was driven at will by the storm for three days until it was possible to repair the rudder.

The *Great Eastern* made another five voyages from England to America. However, it proved impossible to get enough cargo, and as passengers were starting to steer clear of the giant, she could not be used purely as a passenger ship either. The owners hoped she could be used as a transport ship as she could have taken a good 10,000 troops. However, the Admiralty did not feel justified in entrusting so many men to a single vessel.

Finally the *Great Eastern* was sold at auction, after which she did her most valuable work in 1863–73, laying the first cables across the Atlantic. She was then put to various special uses and finally served as a warehouse barge. The ship's last owner finally sold her for scrap in 1891 and made a large profit. All her other owners and outfitters had suffered heavy losses. In time the *Great Eastern* cost her builders a good million pounds—a staggering sum in those days.

Economically the *Great Eastern* was a complete failure. Technically, on the other hand, she was magnificent. Her main fault had been in being built several decades too early. In any case she was convincing proof of the validity of iron for ship construction.

SAVING WEIGHT BY WELDING. The riveted steel hull of a 10,000-ton cargo ship weighs roughly 3,300 tons. If it is welded, the saving is as follows: (1) 130 tons for the side and bottom plates and the deck plates; (2) 200 tons for the rib structure, deck balks, and double bottom; (3) 170 tons for various attachment plates and their rivet heads. The total saving is thus 500 tons, over 15 per cent. In a 15,000 ton tanker, the steel of which weighs about 4,000 tons, a good 1,000 tons of steel, or 25 per cent, can be saved by welding.

The training ship of the Finnish Navy, the *Matti Kurki* (displacement 1,580 tons, length 305 feet) leaving Obbnäs naval base for a foreign visit.

The changeover to steel-hulled ships

Steel followed close on the heels of iron. As the tenacity of steel is about 30 per cent greater than that of iron, a ship's hull can be much lighter. This of course suited shipowners perfectly, as a vessel could then carry more cargo or fuel.

The first steel ship is thought to have been built in 1857 by the British shipyard Samuda Brothers J. & G. Rennie. In 1879 a larger sea-going steel ship was built for the Union Steamship Company of New Zealand, and two years later the Allan Line had the first Atlantic steamer built of steel.

A few figures showing the rise in world tonnage in this century and particularly in the postwar period provide a concise yet illuminating survey of the scale of shipbuilding output: 1900, 28.9 million G.R.T.; 1914, 49.1 million G.R.T.; 1925, 64.3 million G.R.T.; 1939, 69.4 million G.R.T.; 1948, 80.2 million G.R.T.; 1955, 100.6 million G.R.T.; 1960, 129.8 million G.R.T.; 1965, 160.4 million G.R.T.; 1968, about 190 million G.R.T.

The modern shipbuilding industry

Modern shipbuilding is a huge, long-range industry with many branches, which needs definite orders for three to five years ahead if it is to operate flexibly and economically. This has not always been the case, however.

The shipbuilding industry shows that fast expansion does not necessarily go hand in hand with high profits. Since the early 1950s deliveries of new vessels have tripled in tonnage. The capacity of the shipbuilding industry has, however, grown even faster; as a result, growing competition has lowered ship prices and weakened profits. The shipyards have tried to cope with their difficulties primarily by cost-cutting rationalization measures. In several cases losses were unavoidable, and government aid in some form was the only possibility if operations were to continue. The danger of unemployment and a drop in exports are the main reasons why governments have been ready to subsidize their shipyards. In some countries such support takes the form of direct state aid, but it is more usual to grant tax reliefs, investment aid, low interest government or semi-government loans, state credit securities, etc. In the USA, France, Italy, and some other countries, direct government aid has been given throughout the postwar period.

In the last ten years the shipyards in most traditional shipbuilding countries have found themselves faced with increasing difficulties. This is mainly because of the disproportion between the international shipbuilding industry and the demand for tonnage, the oversupply on both the freighting and the shipbuilding markets. Competition over prices, delivery terms, etc., has grown constantly keener.

Since World War II a new factor on the shipbuilding market has been the emergence of the developing countries, which have made their own contribution to the already complex scene by setting up their own shipbuilding industry: partly for reasons of employment, but in some cases obviously to satisfy national pride by developing an independent merchant fleet—even though shipping is an industry that demands tremendous capital and is highly sensitive to economic flux.

As little as thirty years ago Britain was still building almost half the whole world's merchant tonnage, and several years after the last war she still held first place. There have since been revolutionary changes in the situation. The sun rises in the east, and the future of shipbuilding in Europe is seriously threatened by the fantastic achievements of the Land of the Rising Sun. As recently as 1948, following her World War II losses, Japan had no shipbuilding industry at all, but her shipyards had been almost untouched by allied bombing. In 1949 Japan started building ships, and West Germany followed suit, though it took

HORSEPOWER AND POWER CONCEPTS. Horsepower (hp) is a unit of measurement which is used to determine the working capacity of engines. One horsepower represents the ability to raise 550 pounds to a height of one foot in one second.

Many power concepts are used when talking of ships' engines, the most important being towing pull, shaft power, indicated power, and braking power. "Towing pull" means the power needed to tow the vessel, and it is thus also the power which is needed for the ship to overcome the resistance of the water (and air) meeting it. "Shaft power" is the power received by the screw shafting, and it is measured somewhere along the shafting, at the forward end. Shaft power is as great as the sum of the friction losses of the bearings and gaskets between the shafting screw and power measurement point, and the towing power and screw losses. The concept "indicated power" is used of piston engines, though usually only when speaking of piston steam engines. Indicated power then means the power which the steam develops on the piston. "Braking power" is a concept most generally used of diesel engines. It is the power received by the shaft clutch and greater than shaft power by the amount of bearing and transmission loss occurring between the engine and the shafting. If there is no loss here, these powers are equally great. In practice, unless precision is specifically needed in this respect, no distinction is usually made between braking power and shaft power.

---

both countries some years to start producing large vessels and an output of any significance.

Japan's phenomenal rise

In 1968 more ships were produced than ever before—2,740 ships with a total capacity of 16.8 million G.R.T. The most important shipbuilding countries were Japan (8.3 million G.R.T.), West Germany (1.2 million), Sweden (1.1 million), Britain (1.1 million), France, Norway, Denmark, and Italy. There are now over sixty shipbuilding companies and concerns with a total annual output of over 100,000 tons. The six biggest are in Japan. Then comes a Swedish shipyard, then two more Japanese, a West German, a Danish, and two more Swedish shipyards.

In 1968 Japan produced the world's biggest dry dock (length 1300 feet,

View of a Japanese shipyard in Tokyo. The tanker *Nissho Maru* (1962, 131,000 tons) is just being launched.

width 234 feet), which can be used to build ships up to 500,000 tons. In future her shipyards will be able to build tankers in the same size class at the old, smaller docks, since the Mitsubishi concern has developed a method of welding two halves of a ship together under water. A ship was already produced this way in 1966. A similar welding method has been studied and tested in Europe, too, in Norway and West Germany.

The success of the Japanese shipbuilding industry was vitally influenced by her advanced level of technology and efficient organization of labor and capital, the location of the steel industry close to the big new shipyards, speed of deliveries, climatic factors, low prices, favorable terms of payment, etc. The Japanese Export–Import Bank, with its great capital, can alone often handle most of the loans needed by the country's shipbuilding industry.

It takes an average of three months to build a ship at a Japanese shipyard, from laying of the keel to launching. An equal time is then needed to complete the ship at the fitting quay. Of course it takes somewhat longer to build a giant tanker, possibly the most important Japanese product.

Payment terms have offered as much as 80 per cent, sometimes even higher, credit. The payment period is ten years and the interest rate quite low. Thus a new ship can in normal conditions pay for itself almost completely during the repayment years.

More than half of Japan's shipbuilding output goes to foreign customers, the rest of the new ships being needed by the country's own shipping industry. Since almost all her raw materials have to be imported and Japan aims to handle at least 60 per cent of her foreign trade with her own ships (mainly because of the balance of payments), shipping has developed into one of the country's central industries.

Amalgamation and collaboration

The tough competition from Japan has provoked many European shipyards into collaboration. The choice is either amalgamation or cooperation. A wave of amalgamation is sweeping over the whole European shipbuilding industry. Shipyards have amalgamated in Britain, Sweden, and other countries at such a rate that within a few years possibly only half of Europe's present couple of hundred shipyards will be operating, shipbuilding circles estimate. If the shipyards are technically high standard, they usually choose cooperation, as they are not likely to gain anything by amalgamation. Various forms of cooperation can be used to handle such fundamental matters as purchasing, storage distribution, technical planning, credit arrangements, possibly even voluntary cuts in output. The most usual solution is still amalgamation, however, as most shipyards seem dogged by some fundamental drawback, maybe several. In Sweden the shipbuilding industry and the shipping companies cooperated to found the Swedish Ship Research Foundation, in 1968.

Shipbuilding is one of the world's most important assembly industries; no other handles such vastly divergent sizes of parts as the shipbuilding industry, which needs parts ranging from rivets weighing a few ounces to steel castings weighing a hundred tons or more. A ship has more parts than any other moving structure. The shipyard is the place where all the parts are assembled, joined together, and installed to form a perfect operational entity—a ship.

The growing importance of subcontractors

Although many large shipyards have themselves started to manufacture main engine parts, equipment, special instruments, and other engineering products, and other engineering products needed in a ship, they still have to order the bulk of their machinery and equipment from subcontractors. Economic feasibility factors have greatly increased specialization within the industry and thus the necessity for subcontracting.

Countries involved in large-scale shipbuilding have also developed an extensive industry to make the special equipment needed, based on the subcontractor system. Its entire output often goes mainly to the shipbuilding industry. Including raw materials, the value of subcontracted supplies often accounts for 60 to 70 per cent of a ship's total cost.

One characteristic of modern shipbuilding that makes its own demands is that most of the vessels being built today are specialized ships: they have been designed for a specific purpose and call for certain properties. The situation was quite different even in the first couple of decades of this century, when the typical "universal ships" carried pretty well anything on all the world's seas.

Specialization

The shipyards themselves have also shown some tendency toward specialization, and some have concentrated on the construction of specialized types. In this way a yard can benefit from past experience to win itself a special status and a recognized reputation. A good example is the Finnish shipbuilding industry's concentration on icebreakers: Finland is now the world's leading producer in this field.

Planning of ordinary tankers and small cargo ships aims at cutting out unnecessary preliminary work. Often the yards have their own standard types which they can build considerably more cheaply than vessels made to the customer's precise specifications. It is quite rare for a large number of ships to be built to exactly the same blueprints, however.

Finally, a factor characteristic of all types of ship is the mechanization of systems and equipments: the next stage will be automation. The aim is to concentrate control and direction of all the ship's functions, together with her navigation, in the wheelhouse. The object is of course to operate the ship rapidly and safely with a smaller crew.

Preparations for ship construction

The first important stage of the actual construction of a ship is building the steel hull. But before that a great deal of work of preparation is needed, based on the customer's statement of his requirements. The technical section of the shipping company draws up a specification of the ship, the degree of detail depending on the type of ship

The 37.5-ton bow section of the icebreaker *Karhu* being lifted into position with cranes in Helsinki, Finland.

The icebreaker *Sampo* (displacement 3,540 tons, 2,730 G.R.T., length 242 feet, beam 21 feet) on its construction base in Helsinki, September 1959.

in question. This is usually followed by a preliminary blueprint of the general design. If the project is a large cargo or passenger ship, the technical section's work may be quite considerable before various shipyards are invited to submit bids. An architect is usually engaged at this early programming stage. Cooperation between the various experts working on the design is extremely important, as all the dimensions in the horizontal and vertical must be compressed to the minimum because of loading and stability factors.

Throughout the ages shipbuilding has aimed at fine design, even though builders' capabilities did not always live up to this goal. Nowadays, however, even more serious attention is given to design, particularly in passenger ships. The part of a ship above the waterline can be compared to the facade of a building, and viewed from the side it must form a harmonious whole. A passenger ship, especially, should be well-disposed and attractively proportioned.

Though esthetic values are difficult to measure and matters of taste are constant bones of contention, there are certain general rules which produce a balanced ship's design. First, the ship must be functional: the design should suit the purpose. It must look and be stable, seaworthy, and fast. It must be streamlined and float well. Its main dimensions must be symmetrical and practical.

Some aspects of ordering a ship

Apart from purpose, type, and engine quality, the most important requirements are usually connected with

---

SHIPS IN LARGE SERIES. In spite of 23.6 million G.R.T. losses during World War II, the world merchant marine had risen to over 70 million G.R.T. in 1945, surpassing 1939's 69.4 million G.R.T. The explanation lies in the astounding amount of shipbuilding done in the USA during the war years. The American tycoon Henry J. Kaiser was asked by President Roosevelt to organize fast and extensive serial production of rather simply constructed transport and cargo ships. In all, Kaiser produced 5,047 steamships, mostly in the 7,000 G.R.T. class. The most famous were the Liberty cargo ships, 2,710 of which were built. Other types included 531 Victory cargo ships, 1,068 C-type vessels, and 594 tankers.

When Kaiser, who had started as a messenger boy at $ 1.50 a week, died at his home in Honolulu in 1967 at 85, he was head of a huge combine worth 200 million dollars. It included sixty companies with factories producing a vast range of goods in fifty different countries.

a ship's deadweight and speed. The shipping companies often have their own requirements about classification, method of construction, ice reinforcements, location and decoration of crew's quarters, navigational equipment and other fittings, and loading gear.

Recently the shipbuilding industry has started to use computers in the practical work of calculation; routine calculations involved in the design of the hull can now be done by computer easily and at moderate cost. Work which used to take months now takes only a few hours, with more exact and accurate results. Computers handle 20 or 30 per cent, in some cases as much as 40 per cent, of the basic calculations.

The shipyards usually take a month or two to complete their bids. When the order is given, it is important for both sides to have the specifications made up in as much detail as possible before the contract is signed to avoid the disputes that only too easily arise as the project proceeds.

Classification and working drawings

When the contract is signed, the shipyard's drawing office first makes the ship's classification drawings, which must be approved (by Lloyd's in Britain, Norske Veritas in Norway, etc.) before construction work starts. This kind of classification is necessary before an insurance policy can be issued. A more exact weight calculation can be made on the basis of these classification diagrams and the final general arrangement drawings, and the displacement checked.

The final engine power is determined with a model of the ship and what are called "model tests." This method permits the hull, particularly, to be planned so as to reduce the vessel's water resistance to the minimum.

It is now time to manufacture and purchase the necessary materials, machinery, equipment, etc. For some time previously, the subsections of the drawing office have been making the numerous working drawings needed. The drawings for a medium-sized (about 6,000 tons) ship take dozens of designers and draughtsmen several months, and their number may reach two thousand or more. At the same time the ship theorists are carrying out all kinds of essential calculations with the aid of computers. However, there are so many factors affecting the correct shape of the ship, for instance, that the practical tests noted above are needed as well as theory.

The stages of the production process

The production process proper begins with what is called "lofting" the lines of the hull. The vessel's lines are drawn life-size and wooden patterns made from the drawings for marking out the sheet metal and profile steel. The marking shows how the sheet is to be cut or bent, where the welds and apertures are to come, etc. An increasing number of shipyards have recently changed over from life-sized line drawings and wooden patterns to what is called "optic lofting." Briefly this fast, work-saving method consists of the production of very exact 1 to 5 or 1 to 10 scale drawings of the various structural parts in surface plating form. These drawings are photographed and projected life-size in negative straight onto the steel plate and the lines marked in. Then the steel goes to the plate workshop for the complex job of cutting, flexing, scoring, etc.

In the last quarter-century, welding, particularly arc welding, has become the main method of joining and seaming in shipyards, although America has gone back to riveting certain seams on the insistence of the classification authorities there.

In a welded ship the plates are not overlapping, but edge to edge. Ribs and balks can be smaller, because with their rims welded they are very strong. Girder irons are also unnecessary, and there are no rivet heads. A welded seam is more easily made waterproof or oilproof than a riveted seam, and properly done it is usually stronger. The hull and decks are smooth and easier to maintain and paint. The travel resistance of a welded hull is lower.

A welded ship's hull is usually about 15 per cent lighter than a riveted one. The saving in weight can be utilized by cutting engine power, for instance, which also means a saving in fuel. If the same engine power is retained, the result is a higher speed, which in turn saves traveling time. If the displacement is increased, there is more cargo space. In naval ships, another alternative is to use the saving in weight to take on heavier and more plentiful armament. A fine example of this was the German navy in the period between the wars.

With the spread of welding, shipyards have started to use the section building method far more widely and effectively. This offers considerable advantages over the traditional method of construction. The various structural elements are welded into larger sections either in the welding shed or on welding planes outside. When the sections thus produced are assembled on the construction base, the ship's steel hull gradually takes shape.

From hull to finished ship

The construction of a ship is begun by setting the high, strong wooden blocks on which the keel will rest in position. Because the keel is no longer important for balance and steering, as it was in the sailing era, it now merely acts as a strong backbone for the ship's "skeleton." In large ships a flat keel made of keel plates is used.

Laying the keel is an important milestone in the construction process. When this has taken place, the sections are assembled and welded together. Work begins with the bottom plates. Then follow the double bottom, the main engine base, the bulkheads, the stems, the shell plating sections with frames, deck balks, the deck plating sections with beams and knees, and finally the deck structures. Once the hull is finished, the construction process is mainly assembly, installation, and decoration.

The point at which the ship is launched depends mainly on the shipyard's employment situation, the number of construction bases available. In a busy period the ship is launched as soon after completion of the hull as possible, because the construction base is needed for the next job. Depending on the ship's size and the equipment at the yard's disposal, the construction

LAUNCHING has been accompanied by various ceremonies since far back in history. An Assyrian clay tablet (c. 2100 B.C.) tells of the launching of a kind of Noah's ark, when two bulls were sacrificed to insure the favor of the gods. The Icelandic sagas tell of the "hlun rod" custom, or the "reddening of the turning logs." In this macabre process people were deliberately forced between the logs turning under the ship as it moved into the water so that the victims' blood would stain the logs and the new ship. In the 1770s the explorer Captain James Cook described a similar custom in the islands of the South Pacific which was thought to bring good luck when war canoes were launched. As recently as the 1840s, when the great war canoes of Thakombau, first king of Fiji, were being launched, his faithful subjects were used as blocks underneath them, and crushed to death.

Giving a ship a name is a relatively recent custom, believed to have started in the thirteenth century. The first time a woman launched a ship was in 1811, in Britain. Water and wine were earlier used for christening ships. The steamship *Lackawanna* was christened with champagne at the Brooklyn shipyard in 1882, and this has now become the general custom.

stage on the base usually takes about three to six months.

Launching, fitting-out, and surrender

The launching of a ship is in fact a complex and often tensely awaited process, usually attended by a large audience. The launching can be considered a ship's moment of birth and christening simultaneously. After the lady chosen to be the ship's "godmother" has shattered a bottle of champagne against the bows from a tower structure set up on the quay, given the ship her name, and wished her success, men on deck remove the covers hiding the name on both sides of the bows. Now the ship is allowed to slide away from

Gentlemen! No apologies! She should have been ready seven minutes ago.

The launching of the Polaris submarine *George Washington Carver* in Newport News, August 1965.

HOW A SHIP FLOATS. The law named after the man who discovered it — Archimedes (287-212 B.C.) — says that when an object is immersed in liquid it apparently loses a weight equal to that of the amount of liquid it displaces. The law also applies to gases. Thus an object which weighs a hundred grams and has a volume of ten cubic centimeters displaces ten cubic centimeters of liquid, weighing ten grams, and when immersed seems to weigh only ninety grams. On the other hand a floating object displaces only the same amount of liquid as it itself weighs: an object placed in liquid will sink until it has displaced its own weight. Thus a cruiser with a displacement of 10,000 tons settles down so far in the water that it eventually displaces that amount of water. The amount of water displaced by a ship can be worked out either from the ship's weight (including all fittings and cargo) or from the volume of the part above water level.

A ship floats even though it is made of materials that are heavier than water (e.g., iron, specific gravity 7.86), as its mean density (the figure for which is the same as the specific gravity) is less than that of water. This is because of the air inside the ship's hull and its various parts. If these parts were filled with water, the ship's mean density would rise and the ship would sink. This is in fact the procedure in submarines; otherwise they would not submerge.

---

her sloping base along carefully lubricated tracks, usually stern first, into her proper element. At some shipyards long ships have to be launched sideways. A large vessel is helped on its way with hydraulic presses.

When the ship has straightened herself after the launching, tugs tow her to the fitting quay. Immediately the hurried process of fitting her out, installing engines and a huge range of equipment, plumbing, etc., begins. The biggest parts that have to be lifted inside the ship are usually her main engines, for which the fitting quay needs a powerful 80 to 100-ton crane.

Even so, it is sometimes essential to dismantle the main engine into manageable sections and reassemble them in the ship's engine room. This stage takes several months.

While the finishing touches are still being added, the ship's delivery tests begin. Usually she is docked again for bottom painting. After these and certain other finishing processes, the main engine is tested at the quayside. It is then time for the yard test run in actual working conditions at sea. In these the new ship, her engines, and all her equipment are put through extremely thorough tests. If she meets all the

A medium-sized five-cylinder B. & W. marine diesel engine made by the Rautpohja Works of Valmet Oy, Finland. Shaft power 2,900 hp/170 rpm. Cylinder diameter nearly 20 inches. Engine length 25 feet, height 27 feet.

various demands made on her with respect to navigation, main engine power, fuel consumption, etc., it is then usual to carry out a brief trial and demonstration of the gleaming new ship, at which representatives of seafaring and other invited guests are present, as well as men from the shipyard and the shipping line. After this trial the vessel's delivery documents are signed and the line's flag is raised at the stern.

If, for instance, a ship has been built in Finland for a foreign shipping company, the flag of the owner's country of registration is raised at the foremast in place of the Finnish flag.

Ship repairs and maintenance

As well as actually building ships, the shipyards have plenty of other work related to seafaring, primarily

The main and auxiliary engine control room of the car-ferry *Finnhansa* (Helsinki 1966, 7,481 G.R.T., 14,000 shp). Closed-circuit television receiver above.

ship repairs and maintenance. Many yards have in fact concentrated on work of this sort. If a ship is to be seaworthy, she must be docked once a year. Most of the running repairs are done at the annual docking. The quality and extent of repairs is of course something which each shipping company solves in its own way. Repair of wrecked ships and the formalities with the insurance companies form a chapter to themselves. In the north the main problem is ice damage. This often happens even to ships built for the winter, a type specially developed in Finland and characterized by thicker plate, more ribs, and considerably higher engine power than ordinary ships of the same size.

There has been a great technological advance in the machinery, equipment and gear needed for shipyard work since the war. One of the latest pieces of equipment is the hydraulic crane developed in Germany by the Krupp concern in 1967, which can raise ships onto dry land for repairs or lower newly completed ships into the water. In theory these cranes, which need little space and investment, can be built for ships of all sizes and weights. However, they are said to work most economically for ships 250 to 300 feet long.

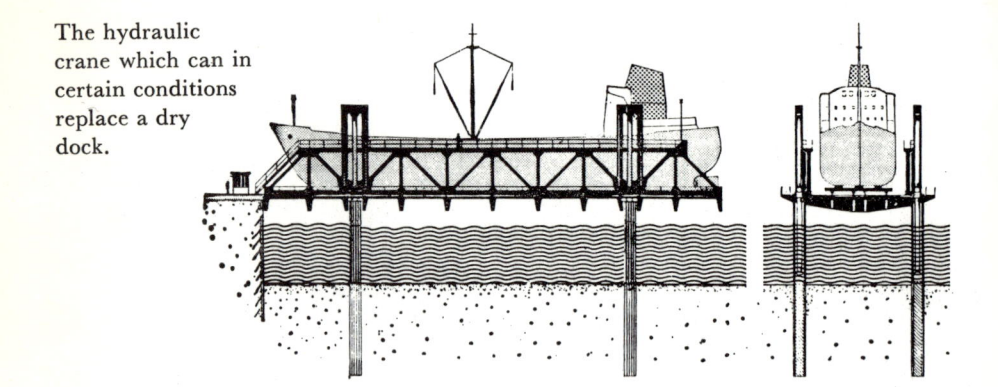

The hydraulic crane which can in certain conditions replace a dry dock.

Harbors: links between land and sea

*The primitive means of water transport used in the distant past were small and rode low in the water. They did not need a deep channel; a foot or two of **water** was enough, and it was fairly easy for them to land almost anywhere, even where there were no quays. The harbor concept came into being only after man learned how to build ships.*

The development of harbors throughout history has closely followed that of shipbuilding. To begin with, sheltered bays which offered safety in stormy weather were used wherever possible. Where nature did not grant suitable protection of this kind, man built a wall, or breakwater, against the sea. The Phoenicians sought out natural harbors as places to stop and trade, and these gradually became the commercial and traffic centers of the Mediterranean.

From time immemorial the Nile delta had been a shipping center where smallish vessels could usually be pulled up into the shelter of the shore. As ships grew in size, this became more difficult and strenuous; there was need for improved harborage.

Harbor building in antiquity and the Middle Ages

Even in antiquity, quite impressive structures were built in the Alexandria, Carthage, and Ostia harbors. As far as is known, the first large-scale harbor was the sheltered anchorage of Pharos island, which was later linked with the mainland by a causeway. The Alexandria harbor area was very impressive by the standards of the day, as it is said to have covered nearly 150 acres. There were two entrance channels, and their breakwaters are said to have been over a mile long; the harbor itself had quays made of great quarried blocks of stone. This may of course all be fable. We do know that around 280 B.C. the Pharos lighthouse was built in the Alexandria harbor.

Carthage built what was for the time a very large harbor, with shipbuilding yards. There was a breakwater on each side of the entrance channel; the naval harbor is said to have had room for 220 galleys, and the merchant harbor covered some 60 acres.

The Romans used several good harbors for their corn, oil, and wine imports. Puteoli, northwest of Naples, lost its lead to Ostia, port of Rome, during the Empire. Apart from being a naval base, Ostia was also an important import harbor. With the decline of Roman power and culture, their advanced

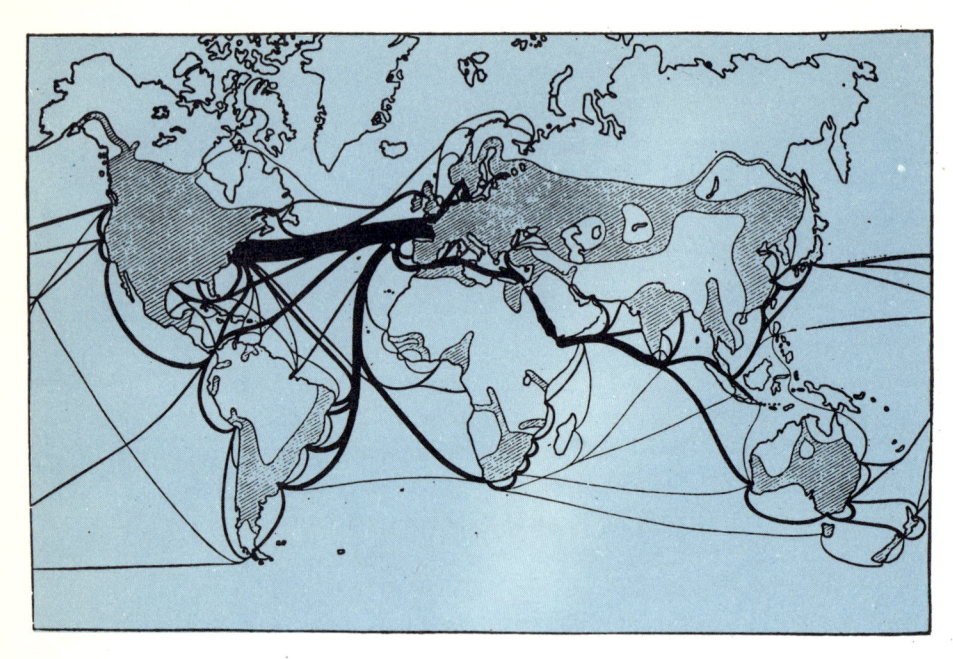

The highways of world trade. The shaded parts of the continents have quite a good railway, river and canal network. The white areas often have large navigable rivers and some railways, but in general economic activity and trade is poorly developed in these areas. Only the most important sea routes are marked.

skill in harbor building, which utilized cement and iron, was also lost.

In the early Middle Ages both harbors and shipbuilding generally deteriorated. With the increase in ship size in the latter half of the medieval period, however, first the Genoans and then the Venetians began to build harbors on the ancient models, and they were followed by other seafaring states. The experience gained in sea harbor construction was also used in inland harbors, although ships had such a slight draft in those days that an ordinary river estuary usually made a good enough harbor. In 1412 regulations limited Hanse merchant vessels to a draft of 9 feet, a maximum length of about 60 feet. Harbors on river estuaries at that time included London, Hamburg, and Lübeck.

Recent developments in world shipping

Harbor development was comparatively slow until, with the discovery of

America, West European seafaring began to expand rapidly. The spread of British rule across continents and seas is inseparably linked with the development of British harbors. British world trade and foreign policy have a close link with Great Britain's ports and docks: London, Liverpool, Bristol, Southampton, Hull, Plymouth, Cardiff, Newcastle.

The North Sea and the English Channel have been a focal point of international trade for a good four hundred years. More shipping is centered on their gray-green waters than on any of the other world seas. The foreign trade of the European Economic Community and Britain totals almost twice that of the USA. Almost three-quarters of the world's entire shipping uses the ports of the North Sea and the English Channel, though the North Sea is not even half as big again as the Baltic, and only about 6.5 per cent of the population of the globe live in the countries surrounding it.

There are several reasons for this busy traffic. First, the North Sea is in a good geographical position, with a direct link to the Atlantic. Its ice conditions are favorable, thanks to the Gulf Stream. Even more vital, huge areas with high production and consumption capacities are grouped round the North Sea. The North Sea countries are among the most highly populated in the world, and are materially and culturally advanced. Several large, navigable, and heavily trafficked rivers flow into this sea (the Rhine, Elbe, Weser, Seine, Thames, etc.), linking it with the interior.

Large harbors develop

Many leading world ports (Rotterdam, London, Antwerp, Hamburg, Le Havre, Bremen, Dunkirk, Amsterdam, etc.) lie on the North Sea, great rivals in merchant traffic and innovative transportation technology.

Harbor development has always been based on the need to load and unload goods between land and sea. Recently, however, another factor has started to come prominently into the picture: the location of industry close to the harbors. Harbor-based industry began with the adoption of large bulk carriers and tankers. These large units

---

PLAN FOR THE PORT OF TOKYO. According to the Japanese Ministry of Transport, Tokyo harbor is going to be extended to make it the world's largest by 1975. The present seven harbors in Tokyo bay will be combined into one mammoth port which will be even bigger than Rotterdam's Europort. The new port would have 374 berths in place of the present 110. A total of nearly eight square miles of sea is being reserved for the plan.

The Royal Yacht *Britannia*, with destroyer escort, on the Mediterranean.

are most profitable when they can be stevedored as rapidly as possible, when their raw material cargoes can be unloaded smoothly into warehouses and tanks on shore.

In the oil industry the simplest method is to set up refineries right next to the crude oil tanks and their pumping equipment. The refined products can then be transported to consumers either by water or overland; pipelines from the oil harbors to the consumer centers of the interior may also be constructed.

Other important bulk goods are ores and cheap coal, transported so cheaply from the developing countries by bulk carriers as to seriously undermine the old mining industries of Europe. But with large quantities of these raw materials coming by sea, it was soon found that steel mills operate most economically if they are built on the coasts near the harbors. The biggest North Sea ports are thus also becoming steel industry centers. It is clear that as the most economic supplies of oil, coal, and ores come from concentrations round the ports, so, too, many other secondary branches of industry will soon follow suit when choosing new sites. Antwerp, for example, is rapidly developing along these lines. Numerous American-owned car, tractor, and other engineering assembly plants have recently been established there.

The Atlantic as main channel of shipping

On the coasts of the Atlantic Ocean and close by lie large, densely populated and exceptionally productive cultural areas whose multifarious needs can be met only through a brisk exchange of goods. This makes the Atlantic the most important ocean in international economics. The world's busiest shipping lanes crisscross it to north and south. Almost half of the world's fifty leading ports lie on North Atlantic routes. From the mid-nineteenth century onward, one can speak of true "giant" ports. In Europe, Rotterdam, London, Antwerp, Hamburg, Bremen, Wilhelmshaven, and Amsterdam are examples. On the east coast of North America by far the most important is New York, but Baltimore, Philadelphia, Boston, and Norfolk on the Atlantic, and New Orleans, Houston, and Galveston on the Gulf of Mexico are also important. The main ports on the east coast of South America are Rio de Janeiro and Buenos Aires.

Compared with the Pacific, twice its size and alone covering about a third of the globe's surface, the Atlantic's advantages are obvious. The formation of its coasts adds greatly to its importance; the Atlantic is long, narrow, and complex in form, with many gulfs and bays, and its fantastically long shores, about 88,000 miles, are of great benefit to the traffic and climate of the countries surrounding it. Another of the Atlantic's advantages is the widespread river network that flows into it. This links the Atlantic to "outside" sea areas twice as large as the Pacific can boast, and through navigable rivers and canals permits shipping to carry goods far into the interiors of the continents.

In the eyes of the general public, at least, great international ports have always had a certain romantic appeal. A modern harbor does not have much

---

MERCHANT SHIPS' FLAGS. The flag of nationality is flown at the stern, or recently, mainly because of changes in rigging, at the head of the jigger mast, while at sea. The line's flag is flown at the top of the main mast. The foremast flies the flag of the country for which the ship is heading. Below this flag, or instead of it, the ship can raise the signal flag P, or the Blue Peter, to announce that she is ready to leave. This flag is lowered as soon as she gets under way. The use of flags and other signaling devices is described in detail in the International Code of Signals.

---

to offer in the way of sea or land romance, however. It is big business, a highly industrialized and mechanized meeting point of national and international traffic. There is work going on all the time, a constant hustle and bustle, day and night, summer and winter.

The starting and finishing point of sea transportation is the harbor where goods are loaded, or delivered to other forms of transport, or stored. The channels, basins, mooring points, quays, loading, unloading, and transportation equipment, the other technical installations, and the warehouses have made human skill, inventiveness, and labor vital to a harbor and its development. A high-performance harbor attracts traffic, which in turn creates the conditions for a properly functioning harbor.

Steamships and railways ushered in a new era in the history of transportation, and thus of harbors and harbor building techniques. If the great harbors of antiquity were the "Stone Age" of harbor building, then the harbors of the Middle Ages and more recent times can with equal justification be called the "Wooden Age." As for modern harbor and marine engineering, it is true to say we are living in a largely "Concrete Age." With iron and steel, cement and concrete and reinforced concrete have brought about a tremendous advance in the techniques of harbor installation construction. Depending on the availability of building materials, the type and amount of traffic, etc., quays are now built of wood, stone, concrete, iron girders, and many other materials.

For the towns on nearby traffic routes and their surroundings, a modern port is a vital economic factor. Directly or indirectly it provides work and a livelihood for large numbers of the population. The significance of harbor traffic for the general public and individual households lies mainly in the fact that it directly and indirectly puts large amounts of money into circulation, invigorating the economic life of the surrounding area. Each ship that arrives sets off a kind of chain reaction from which many inhabitants of the port and its surroundings benefit unawares.

A harbor is a vital link in the chain between the goods' place of origin and the same goods' consumers.

A good port will never develop into an important traffic center merely because of its natural conditions, technical equipment, storage facilities, adequate space, etc., even if it has a fair population. If it is to attract traffic continuously, a harbor must be backed by an economic area with a high production and consumption capacity, an area over which the harbor's influence is felt, to which its roads lead, from which the harbor's export goods

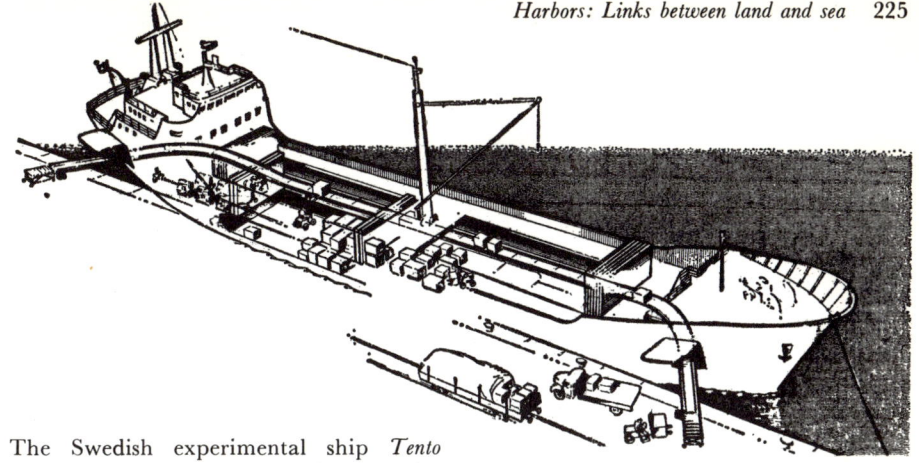

Harbors: Links between land and sea 225

The Swedish experimental ship *Tento* (1966), a "paragraph ship" of under 500 G.R.T., uses a new type of stevedoring system. She is loaded and unloaded simultaneously by conveyor belt, via gates in the bows and stern. The savings are 50 % on time and almost 80 % on labor.

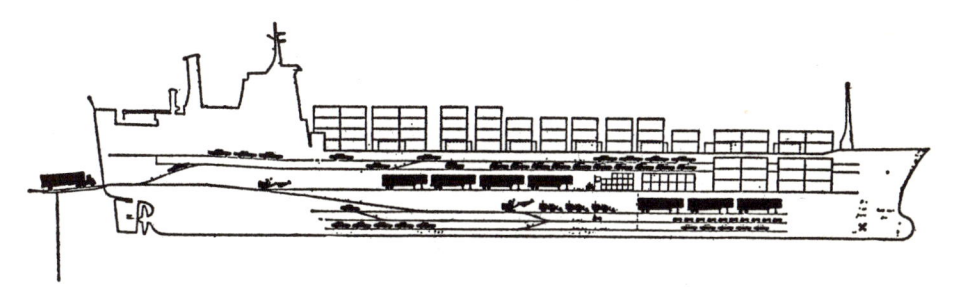

A vessel used for container traffic between Scandinavia and the U.S.A. has five permanent decks from bows to stern and two removable ones. The cargo either enters the ship on wheels or is lifted into and off the ship by harbor container equipment (roll on – roll off).

come and to which its import goods primarily go.

When planning and assessing harbor development, the boundaries of this hinterland, its raw materials, industrial products, energy resources, size of population, consumption level, buying power, and climate must all be taken into account.

Changes in world traffic trends can also have a great effect on a harbor's importance. Busy traffic channels, particularly on long-distance routes, can raise to importance ports whose hinterlands have only a slight, or practically nonexistent, production and consumption capacity, as is true of certain Mediterranean ports. These are im-

15 The sea and man

226 The sea and man

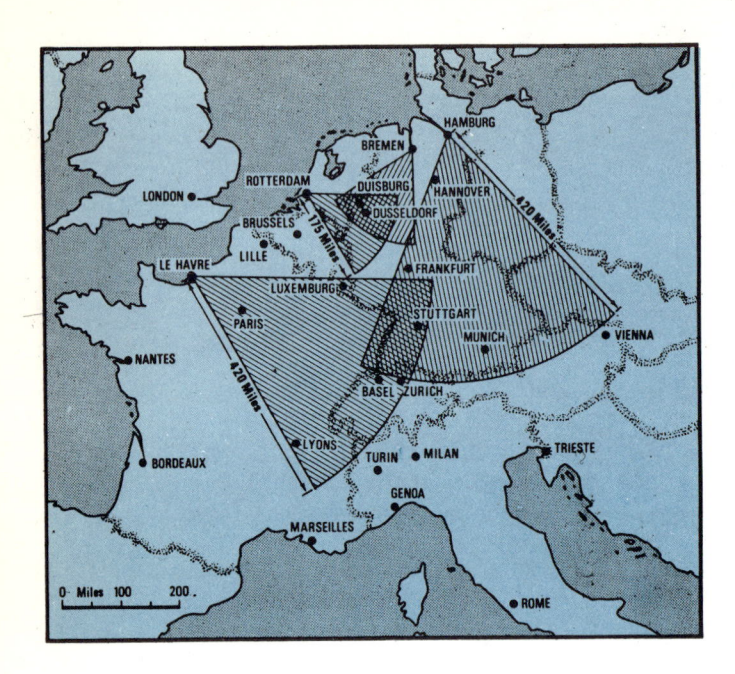

The spheres of influence of some continental ports, according to *Economist* magazine.

The entrance to Rhodes inner harbor with its present figures. In the background the American aircraft carrier *Forrestal* (crew of 2,400). Photograph by the author.

portant ports-of-call where oil, coal, water, and other supplies are stored and which may have ship repair facilities.

Different kinds of harbors

Generally speaking, harbors can be classified as natural or man-made. They can also be grouped by location, purpose, type, general system, and other aspects. Thus there are sea, river, canal, and inland harbors; commercial, passenger, naval, fishing, winter, shelter, and emergency harbors; outer harbors (anchorages); timber, oil, coal, ore, and cement harbors, free[1] and customs harbors; open and closed harbors; long-distance and transoceanic traffic harbors; car-ferry harbors, etc.

Ports and harbors can by no means always be clearly classified by purpose; they are often put to many uses. It should also be pointed out that natural harbors as such are rarely able to meet

[1] A free port is a strictly bounded harbor or part of a harbor consisting of land and sea, kept separate from the normal customs area by means of a customs supervision system. Goods from abroad can be unloaded, stored, packed, refined, etc., there without customs handling, after which they are usually exported. Free warehouses are like free ports, but do not usually include any harbor area proper.

all the demands of today's shipping for safety and comfort.

A harbor is a geographically limited land and water area which, either naturally or by technical development, permits the transfer of goods from water transport to land transport or vice versa, and from one vessel to another, and offers a vessel shelter and maintenance facilities. This definition shows that a modern harbor is expected to offer a wide range of services. A good harbor should have a sheltered, sufficiently large water area and one or more good access channels. It must offer enough anchorage room for vessels waiting to dock. It must have warehouses, quays, and quay installations that meet the needs of all the various kinds of traffic using the port. It must have well-organized connections to the quays and the nearby goods sheds and warehouses, and to the whole of its hinterland. This means not only good motor roads but also railway tracks and goods yards. Complete harbor installations also include floating and dry docks, repair shops, etc.

Expansion and modernization of harbors

The fast rise in the volume of international trade has called for constant harbor expansion and improvement of operating capacity. Unfavorable natural conditions, especially open, unprotected stretches of coast, have in many places (e.g., Italy) made the construction of tremendous breakwaters, harbor basins, etc., essential. In many places all over the world the tide, and in the north, winter conditions, make their own special demands on harbors and their work. Numerous harbors have to be dredged continuously to prevent their silting up.

Vast amounts of money and work have been devoted to the creation and development of harbors and artificial channels. The figures show how important sea traffic trends and economic laws can be, compelling man to imitate nature, however imperfectly, where geography does not grant a natural harbor.

Increasing attention has been paid to quay installations over the years. One type of quay is the pier system adopted widely in North America. The piers, built out at right angles to the shore, are short, intended for only a couple of ships each. The piers are then roofed over their entire length; only a narrow strip of quay is left between shed and ship. A railway and road often run inside these single-story sheds. Loading and unloading (stevedoring) use the ships' own cranes. Goods are carried from the ships straight into the sheds for sorting and customs clearance.

In Europe, on the other hand, harbors are usually built with the warehouses and storage buildings farther away from the quay line; the distance may well be more than 130 feet. Stevedoring is mainly handled by harbor crane. The quays are located along the shore or form harbor basins.

The main factors of harbor operation fall into four main categories. First, the vessels themselves, their size, cargo areas, stevedoring system, etc., must be considered. Second, there is the type and amount of cargo. Third—and here the two former factors vitally influence planning and systems—there is the harbor itself. The fourth basic factor is goods handling in the broad sense of the word.

With growing competition on international freight markets, keener attention has been paid to profit factors, particularly since World War II. Experts have noted that a mere cut in a ship's time at sea, i.e. by increasing its speed, is no longer enough to produce significant savings.

An illuminating example is the Japanese fast cargo ship *Yamashiro Maru* (1964), which has a service speed of twenty knots. According to tests, this ship plies her route Kobe-Hamburg-Kobe, calling at a couple of dozen ports en route, at an overall speed of only ten knots. Increasing speed by two knots on this trip, which normally takes about a hundred days, cuts the overall time by only two days. On the

When Murmansk was founded in 1916 it had 2,500 inhabitants. Three hundred thousand people now live in this, the world's largest Arctic city, which stretches for two miles along the eastern shores of the Kola peninsula. The picture shows the harbor and town.

other hand, if the average forty-eight hours spent in each port could be cut by eight hours, an eighteen-knot ship could do the round trip in the same time as the present twenty-knot ship. The saving in fuel costs would also be about 25 per cent.

Rationalization of docking

Studies made in various parts of the world have shown that a good 30 to 40 per cent of a ship's overall working time consists of various forms of waiting and time-wasting. Cargo handling, which can at the moment account for as much as a third of the total shipping costs, cannot yet put up a very impressive performance: the usual output is only 10 to 25 tons an hour and per working team.

Modern transportation equipment and goods handling methods have brought about a great change in harbor needs. Large quay areas used to be necessary because goods handling methods were slow and a ship could spend days at the quayside. Nowadays goods must move briskly, and a ship must not stay long in port because of the high daily cost. Thanks to efficient new goods handling methods, a modern harbor can accommodate several ships a day per berth. Thus for a particular amount of goods, a modern harbor needs fewer berths and less quay space, but considerably more storage space, goods handling yards, parking areas, and traffic arteries.

With the rising level of harbor efficiency and competition, increasing attention has recently been paid to the purchase of mechanical stevedoring equipment (cranes, trucks, silo installations for grain handling, pumping stations for liquids, etc.). Harbor mechanization has speeded up the loading and unloading of bulk goods, especially—an important achievement, because bulk goods are most conducive to traffic development and a harbor's profitability. Coal, ores, and certain other bulk goods are tipped straight into the ship's hold from specially built railway cars; grain is blown in from a silo or unloaded by suction. The loading and unloading of large oil tankers in some harbors may well take less time than the ship's master needs to attend to the docking and other formalities on shore. Modern giant tankers can load up to 5,000 tons an hour. The loading capacity of efficient bulk-carriers in a well-organized har-

Harmaja lighthouse (1883) is about six miles off Helsinki. Merchant ships heading for Helsinki pick up their pilot nearby. Harmaja's 72,000 candle power light carries for twelve or thirteen miles in clear weather. The lighthouse also has a directional radio beacon and a nautophone type sound signal.

A pilot cutter arriving at the side of a ship in Porkkala, Finland, in winter 1966. Photograph P. Kinnari.

bor is as high as 3,000 tons an hour.

Cargo handling often presents a complex coordination problem, as a large number of enterprises representing many different interests work in a harbor, and these do not usually have any kind of uniform management and organization. Flexible cooperation between the various parties and the intelligent coordination of plans is essential to improvement of efficiency and profitability in a harbor's operations.

The port of Rotterdam

Since World War II the development of certain large ports has been exceptionally fast and prominent. In Europe this is particularly true of Rotterdam, which overtook London in harbor traffic in the mid-fifties. In 1962 Rotterdam crept into first place with close to 97 million tons of goods handled, topping even New York. Rotterdam's total import and export consignments now exceed 150 million tons.

Some 30,000 vessels a year dock in Rotterdam. Of the total tonnage—a round 80 million N.R.T.—about two-thirds are Norwegian, British, West German, Dutch, and Liberian vessels. Rotterdam has almost 300 shipping lines with a close-meshed network all over the globe, and overseas passenger traffic will soon reach 700,000 people a year.

Over the centuries Rotterdam gradually grew from fishing village to great port under the influence of the busy Rhine, but has had to make tremendous efforts to attain its present status. For a long time now the city has been engaged in a relentless and determined struggle to retain its free access to the sea, since the tide (five to six feet) is silting up the river bed and the administration of the Rhine delta has often left much to be desired. The increase in ship size this century, especially in the last twenty-five years, has forced Rotterdam to intensify its dredging work and channel improvement. The harbor area reserved for seagoing vessels in Rotterdam at the moment covers 3,200 acres, with a depth of 20 to 50 feet. There are about 370 acres of harbor area for river craft, some 200,000 of which visit the port each year.

Since 1929, when work first started on the oil harbor, Rotterdam has developed into one of the world's biggest oil harbors. The completion of the Shell Oil refinery in 1938 marked the second important step forward. The completion of the oil harbor two years later confirmed Rotterdam's status as an oil center. The unflagging rise in oil traffic since has made the city Europe's most important oil port.

With an eye to long-term needs, a start was made in June 1958 on the ambitious and tremendously expensive Europort plan, the first construction stage of which consists of the redevelopment of the Rozenburg headland at the mouth of the Nieuwe Waterweg. Of some 3,800 acres in the new harbor section, 2,360 have been reserved for industrial installations, 630 for harbor constructions, and 810 for other purposes. The large-scale construction work of the second stage includes the development of a new harbor area to the west to take supertankers. The Europort plans are geared to the year 2000, and the Dutch estimate that traffic will grow steadily at its present pace up to that date. The gradual execution of the plan continues to endorse Rotterdam's status as the western gateway of Europe's foreign trade.

Rotterdam is a municipal harbor; the city owns and supervises the harbor's water areas and quays. The Nieuwe Maas river section is an exception; it is state-owned. The harbor is administered by an efficiently organized Municipal Harbor Authority.

The port of New York

When the Italian Giovanni da Verrazano sailed along the east coast of the New World in 1542, he became the first European to hit on the narrow channel between what are now Brook-

A partial view of the vast, complex port of Rotterdam, which holds the world goods traffic record, followed by New York and London.

lyn and Staten Island, thus discovering one of the world's best natural harbors. Half a century later Henry Hudson followed his example but he went farther and sailed up the river which was later named after him. In 1626 Governor Peter Minuit of the Dutch East Indies Trading Company negotiated with the Indians for Manhattan Island (22 square miles), which he then bought for 24 dollars' worth of trinkets. This marked the beginning of the New Netherlands colony and its central city New Amsterdam, later called New York.

In 1797, once it recovered from the depression of the War of Independence, New York harbor overtook Boston and Philadelphia and became the country's leading port. The Erie Canal, completed in 1825, linked New York with the Niagara River and Lake Erie through the Hudson River. The opening of the canal meant that a ton of goods could be carried from Lake Erie to New York twenty times cheaper and almost three times faster than before, and the rise in New York's trade and shipping is largely indebted to this canal.

New York is one of the world's biggest natural harbors. It takes in parts of two states, New York and New Jersey, and is sometimes called the New York–New Jersey harbor. The total length of the harbor shoreline is put at nearly 1,000 miles. The water area, too, is vast—about 175 square miles. The main channels are 45 feet deep, and there are some 750 miles of navigable shipping lanes. In fact, New York harbor consists of eight different harbors, which together constitute the world's biggest single harbor area. Newark is mainly a timber harbor; Port Elizabeth handles cotton and colonial goods and recently the fast-growing container traffic; Tomkinsville handles tea and rubber; Brooklyn, tropical goods; etc. There are, of course, no very strict boundary lines. Constable Hooks is New York's biggest oil harbor, and the tankers using it now account for about a quarter of the vessels entering the port of New York.

Each part of the port of New York corresponds to a fairly sizable European harbor. The total harbor area, including the extensive land areas, comprises some 1,470 square miles. There are over 620 miles of quay. The two hundred or more deep-water quays can take about 430 ocean-going ships simultaneously. The harbor is rarely plagued by fog, and the tide is quite slight (four to five feet).

Railways play an extremely important part in this gigantic harbor. There are sixteen railway lines, ten of them trunk lines. Through these and the connecting lines, the harbor is linked with all parts of the U.S., Canada, and Mexico. Rail connections are supplemented by some 10,000 trucks, which handle growing quantities of goods. Forty air routes also serve the harbor, some thirty of them international.

As world trade has increased, so, too, New York's external shipping has risen appreciably, and now exceeds

The departure of the Ambrose lightship from outside New York harbor in autumn 1967 broke a tradition that dated back to 1823. The Ambrose light station has since been built instead. Its light can be seen from 17 miles away in clear weather.

Port Elizabeth, in New York harbor, has in a few years developed into one of the world's leading container ports.

50 million tons. There is also a substantial amount of traffic with American ports, more than doubling the total turnover. In round figures, 25,000 ships a year use the harbor, and over 170 shipping lines offer connections with nearly all the world's ports.

The nineteen-fifties saw the greatest advance in the history of New York harbor, when a gigantic program of building and renovation was carried through with true American zeal, speed, and imagination. The harbor's appearance has experienced a "face-lifting"; it is now cleaner and more attractive. Several of the old piers on both the New York and the New Jersey sides of the Hudson River, which is navigable up to New Baltimore for large craft and up to Troy for small ships, i.e. for about 150 miles, have been replaced with new ones. There has been the same kind of redevelopment in the Brooklyn section. Exten-

A U.S. amphibious helicopter helps recover survivers as tugs and fireboats battle with the raging fire on board the British tanker *Alva Cape* after her collision with the American tanker *Texaco Massachusetts* in New York harbor, June 16, 1966.

sive improvements which will take many years to complete have been started on the east shore of Manhattan, on the East River. All this work calls for hundreds of millions of dollars in investments.

New York harbor, like most other American harbors, is privately-owned. Administration, development, and supervision is entrusted to The Port of New York Authority, a public body based on the similar organization in London. Over the years the Port Authority has expanded into a huge organization mustering tremendous capital and wielding great power; it employs some 5,000 people. About 470,000 others work in various capacities within the harbor, which covers an irregularly shaped area within an almost five-mile radius of the Statue of Liberty.

The port of London

London was a busy harbor long before it became a city and capital of England. Even in the Roman period Londinium was a trading center of importance, naturally enough, because of its fine position on the Thames, the most important river in England. This is 208 miles long and is now quite narrow, over 2000 feet wide in the estuary at Gravesend, but only 950 in London and 320 around Oxford.

Shipping made London the center of world trade in the eighteenth century. The port's importance, in fact, stems primarily from London's status as a great metropolis and its commercial might—that is, from conditions that are partly historical. Even the city's nine-million population is of lesser significance. In this London differs from Hamburg, for example, whose supporting population is greater than that of any other European city.

The London port area at the moment comprises an 80-mile-long area on the Thames from the Nore lightship in the estuary to Teddington inland, the highest point reached by the tide and London's most westerly suburb. This stretch of river is the most busily trafficked waterway in the world. For over 300 years now its mud-colored waves have brought a huge range of the world's riches to the nerve-center of the British Commonwealth, London City. Large ships can sail right into the heart of London and small craft and lighters up to Teddington. It is possible to sail as far as Inglesham through locks.

Five great dock systems situated on a 30-mile-long tidal channel between Tilbury and Tower Bridge play a central part in the Port of London. Docks are vital to the port, as the lower reaches of the Thames are not naturally good harbor waters. The tide is

M/S *Atlantic Span* (1967), the first of ten new container ships ordered by the Atlantic Container Line, in New York's Port Elizabeth terminal.

DISTANCES BETWEEN LONDON AND VARIOUS PORTS
(in nautical miles)

Auckland (via Panama)	11 390	Helsinki	1 041	San Francisco (via Panama)	8 060
		Hongkong	9 688		
Auckland (via Suez)	12 600	Las Palmas	1 695	Shanghai	10 433
		Le Hâvre	199	Singapore	8 248
Bombay	6 273	Marseille	1 998	Sydney (via Suez)	11 534
Buenos Aires	6 291	Melbourne (via Suez)	11 063		
Capetown	6 121			Teneriffe	1 693
Colombo	6 708	Montreal	3 087	Vancouver (via Panama)	8 851
Colon	4 745	New York	3 300		
Gibraltar	1 313	Port Said	3 214	Yokohama	11 150
Halifax	2 736	Rio de Janeiro	5 195		

considerable (about 21 feet in London) and the low-lying shores much too shallow for an open harbor to be possible. The magnificent dock system, which keeps the water level of the harbor basins stable by means of lock gates, permits ships to load and unload unaffected by the tide.

Howland Docks were the first, built on the south shore of the Thames in 1696. They provided the starting point for what are now known as the Surrey Commercial Docks. All the other docks are on the north bank of the Thames. The most easterly, Tilbury Docks, with their four lock chambers, are about 28 miles from the Thames estuary, opposite Gravesend. Large ocean-going ships dock here. The largest lock chamber is 915 feet long and 107 feet wide.

Some 55,000 ships a year visit the port of London, with a total tonnage of 90 million N.R.T. In the last few years goods traffic has been in the 60-million-ton class.

London harbor is managed, administered, and developed by the Port of London Authority, founded in 1908. The Authority employs some 13,000 people, including some 4,500 of the 28,000 regularly employed on the London docks. During the lifetime of the Authority the port has been greatly extended, improved, and modernized. This has been particularly true since World War II. With the vast damage done by bombing repaired by an ambitious reconstruction program, the port of London is again working at full capacity. The expansion program for the near future includes about two miles of deep-harbor berths with extensive land areas, which are essential

About five miles downstream from London and St. Catharine Docks lies the Isle of Dogs. Here are the West India Docks, well known to seamen all over the world.

for today's container and unit cargo traffic.

The port of Antwerp

Though Belgium is not particularly well adapted to seafaring (the country's coastline is short, only 42 miles, and offers no natural harbors), the Schelde estuary is suitable for shipping. Some 10 miles up river, the city of Antwerp has developed into one of the world's biggest and busiest ports. It handles over 80 per cent of Belgium's harbor traffic.

Because Antwerp is almost nine miles from the North Sea, at the heart of a densely populated industrial region and at the crossroads of extremely busy trade routes, its sphere of influence is very great. Apart from Belgium itself, northern France, west and southwest

Germany, and part of Central Europe, it affects even northern Italy and the Balkan countries as far as certain goods traffic is concerned. A dense railway network links Antwerp with a high production and consumption region, its natural hinterland, added to which there are many fine roads carrying busy goods traffic. Here, as in Holland, canals are important, too. They link the water traffic of the interior to the canal system of northwest France and Holland and to the Rhine.

Thanks to its splendid situation, Antwerp began to play a prominent part as a trading center quite early; it is mentioned in the seventh century. Over the centuries, whenever the freedom of the Schelde was unthreatened, Antwerp flourished and grew rich. It became the most important port in Europe in the early sixteenth century, mainly because once the sea routes to America and India had been discovered, the trade of the Mediterranean ports began to flow into Antwerp. It then became the most important distribution center in western and central Europe for spices shipped via the ports of Portugal and Spain.

The abolition of maritime customs dues on the Schelde in 1863, the advance of steamship traffic, Belgium's deliberate program of industrialization, the fast economic development of the New World, and the growing needs of the European countries are the main factors that made Antwerp the focus of a widespread industrial and agricultural hinterland, and thus an international port, toward the end of last century. At that period six new docks were opened. Since then the port has been constantly extended and its equipment modernized to keep it competitive.

The heavy damage Antwerp suffered during the last war has been repaired, and the extended harbor now consists of over 3000 acres of water, about 60 miles of quay, 17 dry docks, over 900 cranes, and a large number of warehouses, railways, etc. In 1966 over 18,000 vessels docked there, with a total tonnage of 57 million G.R.T. The goods passing through the port exceed 65 million tons a year. River and canal barges play an important role; some 60,000 use the port annually.

The docks are reached from the Schelde via seven locks. The Zandvliet lock, 1625 feet long and 60 feet wide, completed in autumn 1967, is the biggest of its type in the world. There is now a great deal of industry in the port area: several oil refineries, two car assembly plants, chemicals industry works, etc.

The port of Hamburg

There are close to thirty ports on the Elbe, Germany's second most important river. Hamburg, the most east-

The Van Cauwelart lock (length 875 feet) and Baudouin lock (length 1170 feet) on the Schelde, Antwerp.

erly member of the chain of great North Sea ports, is by far the biggest and greatest. As early as 1189 Emperor Frederick Barbarossa granted the city extensive privileges to promote its harbor, trade and shipping. In the days of the Hanseatic League, particularly in the fourteenth century, Hamburg enjoyed high prosperity. Its fast development into a real international port began a hundred years ago, when it became impossible to cope with the fast-growing shipping by the primitive goods handling methods of the day. The first modern open harbor basin was then built.

A program of building before World War I created the foundations of the present port of Hamburg, which today stretches more than 9 miles on the shores of both arms of the Elbe and the island area between them. Of the entire harbor area—about 39 square miles—13 square miles is water.

Hamburg, and particularly the harbor, suffered very heavy damage in World War II bombing. Almost 80 per cent of the harbor installations and 44 per cent of its industry was destroyed or put out of action, and some 3,000

16 The sea and man

wrecks—from small river tugs to large ocean-going ships—lay at the bottom of the Elbe. Over the years an extensive program of reconstruction has been carried out, though some considerable expansion and improvement work is still going on.

At the moment Hamburg handles over 40 per cent of the total goods traffic of the West German ports and a good half of the general cargo and sacked goods. Hamburg is also a very important port to Central Europe, as its vast hinterland stretches far beyond the national borders, from the Alps in the south, across Hungary, Australia, Czechoslovakia, and central Germany to Scandinavia in the north and Finland in the northeast.

One of the basic prerequisites for the efficient operation of Hamburg harbor is that the Elbe always remain deep enough. The 36-foot depth of the main channel at the moment ensures fully-laden 45,000-ton ships access to the docks. When the harbor channel is deepened to 40 feet, 60,000-ton ships will be able to make port.

Hamburg's varied goods traffic is at the moment in the 40-million-ton class, over two-thirds of this in imports. Twenty-five thousand ships a year visit the port, with a total tonnage of 35 million N.R.T.

The port can rightly be described as the heart and symbol of Hamburg, and the free port in turn as the nucleus of the port. Hamburg free port (over 6 square miles), founded in 1888, is known throughout the world as an efficiently organized and functional harbor; it has been the model for similar operations in many other ports. Some 60,000 people and over 800 firms work in the free port area.

The harbor's land and water areas belong to the City of Hamburg. The harbor installations and almost all the general cargo sheds, warehouses, etc., are built and maintained by the River and Harbor Construction Authority. These national installations are administered by the Hamburger Hafen- und Lagerhaus-Aktiengesellschaft (HHLA), which is over eighty years old and employs some 4,000 people. A number of private firms also serve harbor traffic.

Other ports

There are many other ports in Europe whose traffic has grown to considerable proportions because of the expansion of international trade and passenger traffic. In the Baltic area, Denmark lies on a number of busy maritime routes, situated as it is between the North Sea and the Baltic, and between the Scandinavian peninsula and Central Europe. Copenhagen's position at this crossroads of trade created the basis for the city's development into an important port and trade center quite early in history. The foun-

Over twenty companies provide regular sailings from Hongkong to Europe, and the same number are run to the North American continent. This picture shows ships tied up alongside the Kowloon docks.

dation of its free port also endorsed the commercial significance of the Danish capital. Copenhagen handles the bulk of Denmark's extensive foreign trade and shipping. It is the biggest port in Scandinavia and at the moment handles some 12 million tons of goods and 22 million N.R.T. of shipping a year.

Once the Suez Canal was completed, the Mediterranean became a sea linking the Atlantic and the Indian Ocean, and it was primarily as a "through road" that it developed so rapidly into one of the most important arteries of world traffic. The significance of the Mediterranean for shipping, surrounded as it is by three continents, is also increased by its position between East and West (the Orient and Europe) and North and South (Europe and the tropics and monsoon lands).

Before it was closed in June 1967 as a result of the six-day Middle East

SOVIET SEAPORTS have been greatly developed in the last few decades, and there are now some 65 of them. In 1928, 25.5 million tons of goods passed through the country's ports. By 1967 the Soviet Union's goods traffic had risen tenfold. Almost half of the country's entire goods traffic uses ports on the Black Sea and the Sea of Azov. Odessa alone handles some 15 million tons of goods a year, added to which it is one of the country's biggest passenger harbors. Counting oil, Novorossiysk harbor, on which the USSR's largest oil harbor was recently built, handled over 23 million tons in 1967. Of the Baltic ports, the largest is Leningrad, with an annual turnover of some 10 million tons. The mechanization level of stevedoring equipment in Leningrad is the highest in the country. Other important Baltic ports are Klaipeda (about 7 million tons), Riga (3 million tons), and Tallinn. Murmansk is the world's busiest port north of the Arctic Circle. There are several ports on the Soviet Union's Pacific coast, the biggest being Vladivostok (over 5.5 million tons), Nahodka, and Vanin. The annual goods traffic handled by the Soviet Union's Far East ports exceeds 30 million tons. By 1970 the Soviet Union hopes to have mechanized goods-handling at all her ports 90 %. Some 15,000 ships a year from forty countries call at Soviet ports, and as traffic is growing all the time, great attention is being given to the improvement and expansion of harbors.

war, the Suez route had become one of the most important in international shipping. It took traffic from European, Atlantic, and Mediterranean ports via the Suez Canal to the Indian Ocean and on to India and the Far East, Australia, and New Zealand, and along the east coast of Africa to the southern tip of the continent. There are a large number of important ports along this route: in the Mediterranean —Marseille, Genoa, Naples, and Piraeus; in India—Bombay and Calcutta; in Ceylon—Columbo; in Indo-China —Singapore; in Indonesia—Djakarta (formerly Batavia); in Chinese waters —Hongkong and Shanghai; in Japan —Kobe, Yokohama, and Osaka; and in Australia—Sydney and Melbourne.

Important traffic channels can sometimes raise to prominence ports whose hinterland has only a slight production and consumption capacity or almost none at all. Port Said at the north end of the Suez Canal is an example of such important stopover harbors.

Age-old Singapore, at the tip of the Malay Peninsula, only 80 miles north of the equator, holds a special place among the great ports of the Far East. The tiny island of Singapore (225 square miles) began to gain in international significance when it passed into British hands in 1819, thanks to the farsighted action of Sir Stamford Raffles. The opening of the Suez Canal gave added stimulus to the growth of Singapore harbor, and it became the leading port of the Far East. The harbor and military installations were built by the British, but the island has been mainly settled by the Chinese.

Since the destruction of war, Singapore harbor has been made more efficient than ever. The total length of its quays is a little over 3 miles, and they will take 25 ocean-going ships and 5 coastal vessels. Over 25,000 ships a year visit Singapore, and its goods traffic is 22 to 23 million tons.

Merchant shipping: its forms and cargoes

It is usual to divide merchant shipping into two main groups: tramp traffic and liner traffic. Each group is characterized by its own special phenomena.

Tramp traffic is the older form of shipping. It is still in extensive use, but since the last war this sector has been shrinking. The constant advance of contract and specialized traffic has done most to effect this decline. Liner traffic has made the present shipping system possible. At present, a good half of the world's merchant shipping is in fact liner traffic. In some seafaring countries the proportion is even higher.

Tramp traffic — the endless round

A shipping company charters a ship to take a cargo of timber, for instance, from Mäntyluoto, Finland, to London. The freighting is done by a broker — a freighting company or agent — who deals in freighting contracts between the freighter and the carrier in tramp traffic and to some extent, too, in specialized traffic. After the cargo ship has unloaded her load of timber into warehouses on the Thames, she often has to travel in ballast, i.e. without cargo proper (her ballast tanks full of sea water), to the bunkering or fuel harbor to take on coal, or, more commonly at the moment, to fill up her fuel oil tanks. She then carries on to Cornwall, still in ballast, and picks up kaoline from Fowey to take across the Atlantic to Montreal. After unloading this, the ship picks up timber from some small port on the east coast of Canada which has to go to Garston, near Liverpool, after which she goes in ballast to the Bristol Channel. On the way she is instructed to pick up a load of coal for Halifax, Nova Scotia, from a channel port. From Nova Scotia the ship brings back a load of timber for Belfast, Northern Ireland. Next, she takes a load of coal from the Bristol Channel to Madeira, and then sails to the west coast of Africa to collect a cargo of ground nuts to go to Nice. And so the eternal round goes on, from one port to the next.

This is a typical example of tramp traffic. Each new stage of such cargo shipping causes numerous negotiations between the shipping company and the dealer regarding the charter party or freighting agreement, the times of loading and unloading, and many other details involved in the charter. The starting point in formulating these complex plans is the final unloading harbor of the last trip. On this basis, the aim is to find the best freights possible and to avoid unprofitable ballast trips. Tramping calls for a lively imagination and the ability to link up the chain of freighting, but above all for a thorough knowledge of the freight market and harbor conditions, good relations with the specialist brokers, and the ability to make quick decisions.

Trip charter and time charter

In tramp traffic the vessel is usually chartered fully laden, and the freighting is done trip by trip, by what is called trip charter. In this the owner hires out his vessel to another shipowner or charterer for a fixed period and an agreed price, or on time charter. The owner shipping company puts the vessel at the charterer's disposal and usually meets all the vessel's normal fixed costs, such as the wages of officers and crew, insurance premiums, interest and amortization, provisions, etc. The charterer then pays the running costs such as fuel, harbor dues and port charges, loading and unloading fees, tug and pilotage fees, crew overtime, etc.

Time chartering often meets only temporary demands for tonnage and may well last only a month or so. It is generally marked by a seasonal character and fluctuations. On the other hand many tramp companies make agreements with the same charterer year after year for the use of one or more vessels on the same routes to carry the same kind of goods.

The main shipments carried in tramping are large bulk cargoes. Because tramp ships often have to travel long distances without cargo after unloading their one-way freight (particularly during periods of general economic depression), the yoften take whatever return cargo they can in the form of various bulk goods, even below cost, to avoid traveling merely in ballast.

Tramp traffic agents

Tramp traffic needs its own professionals, the chartering brokers. Their work includes procuring cargo for ships and keeping in constant contact with

---

ORGANIZATIONS IN SEAFARING. The following trade organizations and central organizations operate in the seafaring activities of Finland alone: the Finnish Shipowners' Association, the Åland Shipowners' Association, the Association of Finnish Small Shipowners, the Association of Passenger Ships, the Finnish Ship Officers' Association, the Finnish Engineers' Association, the Finnish Radio Officers' Federation, the Finnish Seamen's Union, the Association of Finnish Shipping Agents and Shipbrokers, the Federation of Finnish Master Stevedores, the Finnish Forwarding Agents' Association, the Finnish Shipchandlers' Association.

A tug towing a raft of timber bundles through the mile-long Haponlahti canal into Lake Saimaa, Finland. This canal, built 1956–1960 in Sääminki, in the channel from Joensuu to Savonlinna, has cost nearly 1 1/2 million dollars.

company organizations in the various countries in collaboration with importers and exporters. The chartering agent's work in many cases also includes the duties of shipping line representative. Because of the character of bulk goods, chartering agents often have far less direct contact with the goods than the agents of ships of the line.

The central role of liner traffic

Liner traffic is the most highly developed form of merchant shipping, though it has only some 150 years of tradition behind it. In liner traffic, ships sail to an approved timetable on regular services and at specified times between specified ports (usually in both directions), irrespective of their cargo. Mainly for this reason, the freight rates in liner traffic are usually higher than in tramp traffic. In short-distance traffic, of course, liner traffic is very much more regular than on long-distance routes. Liner traffic is also characterized by the fact that anyone can send general cargo according to the fixed tariff.

importers and exporters and their representatives. The chartering brokers have their own widespread international network, through which they receive rapid information about free tonnage and available cargoes. Their work calls for an extensive knowledge of seafaring, languages, and close contacts with the shipping companies and potential customers. They also have to know their way around the various freighting agreements drawn up by the shipping

Liner traffic makes it possible, either directly or through connections, to send even small amounts of goods to all the corners of the globe. It thus simplifies trade considerably. It also plays its part in stabilizing and expanding already established markets. Liner traffic must take questions of national economy into account if it is to operate to exporters' satisfaction and preserve the lead it has gradually won. Regular liner traffic is also of very special significance in transoceanic transportation. By making reloading unnecessary in many cases, direct liner traffic cuts freighting costs considerably, saves time, and reduces the risk of damaged cargoes.

Liner cargo usually consists of consignments from several dispatchers—bale, sack, bundle, box, barrel, and other goods by the ton. The shipping document used is the bill of lading, the receipt given by the ship's master for the goods loaded into his ship for delivery to the destination port. The bill of lading is a kind of goods debenture. In liner traffic the dealers are shippers or consignees, but not charterers.

If there is an exceptionally great demand for tonnage, tramp traffic may benefit because of its greater flexibility, since liner traffic is tied to specific routes and times. On the other hand, liner traffic with its longer-term agreements operates on a more secure basis in depressions and periods when there is little freight. The same shipping company may then engage in both liner and tramp traffic simultaneously.

Liner traffic agents

Each shipping line has its own brokers or agents in its ports-of-call and destination ports. They ensure that goods reach the right vessels at the right time. Their work also includes the entry of goods consignments, or the manifest, and supervision of goods transfer to the harbor warehouses or loading site. The agents also see to the vessel's harbor and other charges, the engaging of pilots and harbor tugs, and various other work on their principal's

---

THE VOLGA–BALTIC WATERWAY. In 1964 an important new 224-mile channel was opened between Leningrad and Yaroslavl. The Volga–Baltic route is intended to take the place of the Marinski waterway, built a century and a half before, which in spite of modernization proved unable to cope with the constantly growing quantities of freight. There are seven locks, a 40-mile excavated canal, and 182 miles of shipping channels along an artificial lake, on this waterway. Vessels take two and a half days to travel between Tcherepovetz and Leningrad, whereas the same journey along the Marinski canal took eighteen days.

---

behalf. Harbor charges include dues and fees for pilotage, light, icebreaking, customs, berthage, guarding, towing, consular services, changing articles, and so on.

It is also the agent's job to negotiate with the ship's master about the stowing of cargo in the ship with an eye to seaworthiness and to the proper location of any goods likely to spoil. When the ship leaves, one of the agent's duties is to inform the shipping company by cable, or nowadays usually by telex, of the ship's departure, the amount of cargo, and the number of passengers.

Liner traffic usually operates by an annual agreement not easily affected by changes in freight rates, although a long depression is of course felt in liner traffic. Liner freight rates lag behind both in a long-term decline and in an upswing, and in the latter the rate of recovery is slow.

Contract traffic and specialized traffic

One intermediate form of tramp and liner traffic is contract traffic. It can be considered an attempt to preserve and stabilize tramp traffic. In this form of shipping a ship is chartered for a fixed period on fixed terms to a particular charterer or shipper. Some tramp traffic companies make agreements year after year with the same charterer about the use of one or more vessels for the transportation of the same goods on the same routes.

Contract traffic plays an important part in efforts to stabilize freight markets. It avoids the kind of violent fluctuations in freight level which were experienced during the Korean War

---

COMPARISON OF TONNAGES. The biggest ship by gross registered tonnage is not necessarily the biggest by displacement. Thus there are, for instance, ore carriers with a displacement of over 100,000 tons which are yet only 72,000 G.R.T. On the other hand the displacement of the largest passenger ships is below 80,000 tons, yet they are over 81,000 G.R.T.

For a rough comparison of deadweight tonnage and gross registered tonnage, the rule for dry cargo ships is 3 d.w.t. = 2 G.R.T. A rough deadweight tonnage is thus attained by adding 50 per cent to the gross tonnage. The gross tonnage is attained by deducting one-third from the deadweight tonnage. The following table gives an approximate idea of the variations in tonnage among various types of cargo ship:

	G.R.T.	N.R.T.	d.w.t.
Dry cargo ship	9,000	5,000	13,000
Tanker	15,000	9,000	24,000
Passenger ship	30,000	16,000	12,000

A phosphate loading depot at Boat Harbor on Nauru island (about 6,000 inhabitants). This lonely coral island, which gained its independence in January 1968, is near Gilbert Island in the Pacific.

and the first Suez crisis, for instance. From the shipping company's point of view such developments are welcome, since it can then operate on a more long-range basis.

The most obvious forms of specialized traffic are transport of oil, ore, fruit, and meat. As they operate on a contract basis, these spheres of shipping, which wrested a great deal of work from tramp traffic, could be considered contract traffic. The large oil companies were among the first "shipless" firms to start carrying their own products in their own ships. This was because they wanted to protect themselves against the fluctuations and losses which their deliveries suffered when countries interfered in the operations of their tonnage during world crises, etc.

Large oil companies are now among the world's biggest tanker companies. Large quantities of ore are also carried in mining companies' own ships. The financial risk in specialized traffic proper is of course much greater than in other forms of shipping because the

The Baltic in summer.
Surf on the coast near Hanko, southwest Finland.

ship is tied to certain products, and its cargo areas can be adapted to other goods only at considerable expense.

Stevedoring and forwarding

The shipping companies engage a stevedoring firm to see to the loading and unloading of goods. Stevedoring costs are usually shared, with the customer paying loading costs from the warehouse, freight car, truck, or quay to the ship's rail — that is, those costs incurred outside the ship — and the shipping company those costs of loading and stowing the cargo in the hold of the ship. At the other end, costs are assessed in reverse.

Efficient stevedoring nowadays calls not only for the necessary labor but also for a large amount of equipment, often expensive: tractor cranes, tractor grabs, lorries, trucks, loading platforms, etc.

As international trade has grown, it has also become very complex, with regulations, licenses, and all kinds of formalities and red tape. It is thus more difficult and expensive for the exporter or importer alone to cope with this maze of paper work. One important cog in the wheel has therefore come to be the forwarding agent, with his extensive international connections. The recipient or sender of the goods gives a forwarding firm the job of seeing to the transportation to its destination of the consignment he is buying or selling. The forwarding agent is provided with the necessary documents, such as the bills of lading, invoices, licenses, etc., which he uses to see the goods through customs and to the ship's side or to the recipient by the agreed form of land, sea or air transport. In brief, the working sphere of an up-to-date forwarding agent is the entire arena of goods transportation from place of production to destination.

Sea freights

Many factors influence the formation of freight markets and fluctuations in them. The main factor here, as in so many other phenomena of economic life, is the law of supply and demand. The general changes that take place on freight markets under this law can be classified as seasonal or economic. Considerable economic fluctuation is, indeed, a leading characteristic of this sensitive field of international activity.

What is called the "normal" freight level is a relative concept. It is possible to call an individual freight market "good" or "bad" only in comparison with other freights simultaneously available. The interests of the two parties involved, the shipping company and the charterer, clash utterly as far as the cost of the freight is concerned.

In liner traffic, freights are normally quoted by the line according to the tariff then in force, and contract freights are also used. Tariffs are usually drawn up on the basis of experience. Each line has its own tariffs, usually endorsed by conference, and these are in no way analogous. Apart from the great differences between harbor charges, each line usually has a relatively limited group of goods that form the bulk of its shipments.

In tramp traffic cargoes circulate on the free market, and this form of shipping takes advantage of whatever freight potential happens to be available. The ship that tenders lowest gets the cargo on international markets.

Sea freight is usually calculated by the weight or volume of the goods, though sometimes by the number of items or by value. It is also influenced

---

THE SHIPPING STATISTICS ISSUED BY VARIOUS COUNTRIES reveal some degree of confusion and disparity in the way they express tonnage and carrying capacity. International statistics (Lloyd's, the League of Nations and its successor the UN, etc.) usually include only vessels of at least 100 G.R.T., leaving out specialized vessels (fishing craft, tugs, icebreakers, etc.). The practice in national shipping registers varies. In Finland the lower limit is 19 N.R.T., in Sweden 20 N.R.T., in Norway 25 G.R.T., and in Denmark 20 G.R.T. To attain the necessary standardization, the Scandinavian maritime law committees have planned to make it compulsory for all ships over 20 G.R.T. to be entered in the shipping register.

MARITIME INSURANCE is the most important form of transport insurance. It is the oldest form of insurance to be practiced as a business. Maritime insurance goes back to the ports of northern Italy in the fourteenth century. It began to rise in significance in eighteenth century London (Lloyd's), and it is there, particularly, that it has developed into a large and complex business.

The purpose of maritime insurance is to simplify the arrangement of credit and financing as well as to cover ships against mishaps during transportation. "Damage by sea" in insurance cases is any mishap that takes place during the period covered by the policy, whatever the cause.

The ship and its cargo, and the freight, can be insured against practically all the dangers and risks that threaten at sea. The policy for the ship, which provides cover for sea, fire, and other damage to the ship in both partial and total loss, is called hull insurance. As well as ordinary marine insurance in which the premiums are rather high, a ship can also take out hull interest insurance. In contrast to civilian damage, ships and cargoes can also be insured against war risk. In time of war, the war risk premiums are very high, particularly if the policy is taken out for only one voyage at a time.

by the relation between volume and weight, the dangerous character of the cargo, harbor and stevedoring charges. By grading freight according to value, the freight rate for cheap goods is on average balanced out against that for expensive ones, so that importing or exporting the former is financially feasible. Even if the freight charge for cheap goods is lower than for expensive ones, it is a higher percentage, since value alone does not decide the freight rate.

Liner conferences

On all the important Atlantic and Pacific Ocean liner routes what are called "conferences" operate, i.e., international conventions between the shipping companies. Their main aim is the regulation of freight rates and in general the stabilization of operating potential in the interests of all parties. The first conference, the United Kingdom/Calcutta Conference, was founded in 1875. The largest and most well-known of these international cartels, the number of which, counting small and relatively insignificant conferences, approaches two hundred, is the Baltic and International Maritime Conference, founded in 1905 and composed of a large number of liner, tramp, and tanker companies, brokers, and individuals. It operates mainly as an international organization for marketing policy and information in the field of navigation without interfering directly in freight rates. Since the last war, conferences for oil transportation, for instance, have been formed, the parties to which are the oil companies and the tanker lines.

To ensure the largest possible basic lading for the tonnage available, the conferences try to make agreements with the shippers. If the latter engage to send all their goods by ships belonging to companies in the conference, they profit by lower tariffs.

There is a fundamental difference between the way the conference system operates in America and Europe. In the United States the government exercises strict control, and the conferences are "open"; i.e., they cannot refuse to accept a shipping company as a member even if it would not normally be considered suitable for liner traffic. In Europe, on the other hand, the conferences are "permanent"; i.e., shipping companies which lack the necessary tonnage, capital, or experience in liner traffic are not allowed into the conference.

The outlook for world shipping

The old saw "necessity is the mother of invention" is by no means a patent truth. Inventions, new ideas, and applications of them in fact occur largely without their being "necessary," but it is undeniable that an emergency—war, crisis, tension, etc.—brings them into the limelight and into use faster than is the case in the normal peaceful round. This proved true on a large scale during World War II; it applied to ships, navigational methods, harbors, and other maritime matters.

In the last fifteen years international merchant shipping has experienced considerable, sometimes even revolutionary, change in its striving to keep costs down and to preserve competitiveness.

International competition, which has become particularly keen in the last few years, has resulted in mergers in the shipbuilding industry especially in Europe, long-term action by governments to improve the operating potential of shipowning, and constantly improved technology to step up the performance of merchant ships and harbors. These are tangible signs that the struggle for existence at sea is going to grow to unprecedented proportions. Experts consider our own age at least as eventful and exciting as the transition from sail to steam and on to the combustion engine.

The trend towards large ships

Literally the most obvious feature of recent developments in shipping has been the increase in average size of ships, and particularly the appearance on the world seas of bigger and bigger tankers. Whereas the average size of merchant ships was about 1,040 G.R.T. at the beginning of this century and 2,227 G.R.T. in 1939, the 4,000 G.R.T. limit has already been exceeded.

Most of the biggest, over 100,000 d.w.t., ships are tankers. Tanker construction has been boosted by the explosive rise in transports of oil, the relocation of oil refineries, and attempts to cut transportation costs. Before the war, oil was mostly refined near the oil fields, and some 80 per cent of transports consisted of refined products, the rest being crude oil. Since the war increasing numbers of refineries have been built near the consumer centers. The ratio of crude oil to refined oil carried has been reversed.

When the route to the oil-producing countries of the Near East via the Suez Canal was closed in June 1967 in consequence of the war between Israel

Two United States Coast Guard icebreakers escorting the Navy tanker *Alatna* through heavily iced McMurdo Sound past the U.S. Antarctic base at Hut Point.

and the Arab states, the oil companies started to work out new ways of cutting their freight costs. This long closure and the similar experience ten years before have accelerated orders for larger and larger tankers. So many giant ships of 100,000 d.w.t. and over have already been built and ordered that in a couple of years some 400 of these mammoths will be sailing the seven seas. As they are so big that they have to take the route around Africa, when the Suez Canal reopens it will probably find itself without the bulk of its previous oil transports.

Large harbors for mammoth tankers

As freights get cheaper, it is becoming increasingly possible to build harbors in Europe large enough for supertankers. Several West European countries are vying for the lead with harbor deepening and extension and even the construction of new harbors to meet the needs of the giant ships of the future. In Bantry Bay on the southwest coast of Ireland a Gulf Oil harbor was completed in autumn 1968 which will take 300,000-ton ships.

Some people believe that before long half-million-ton tankers will be carrying crude oil from the Persian Gulf to the old harbors of western Europe via the Cape of Good Hope. Lloyd's Register of Shipping has drawn up a plan in principle for a tanker of this size. Research indicates that it is possible to build with present materials really large ships which comply with

Three United States Navy icebreakers strain to muscle aside a massive block of ice obstructing the ship channel leading to the United States Research Station at McMurdo Sound, Antarctica.

the regulations of the classification body. To reduce the weight of the steel, a relatively short hull of about 1,360 feet was chosen. On the other hand the beam is 224 feet, because in so large a vessel an increase in width does not disproportionately increase its resistance to water. Calculations put the draft of the mammoth ship at about 83 feet.

Developments press forward relentlessly; there are indications that it is possible to build tankers even of a million tons. (A 372,400 d.w.t. tanker is already under construction in Japan.) The experts seem to think that the technical difficulties involved in the giant ships of the future will be no greater than they are for present vessels. A ship's size is restricted primarily by financial factors: the cost of equipment, storage facilities, waterways, harbor and docking difficulties, etc.

This explosive changeover to giant tonnage has not only left its mark on freight statistics and quotations and caused unemployment among older shipping; it has also produced dangers and unexpected structural faults which it is impossible to foresee.

When the *Torrey Canyon* ran aground in 1967, for instance, the capital losses were tremendous and the compensation the largest ever paid out. But the vast quantity of oil escaping from the wreck also did widespread damage to the coasts of England and France, the total cost of which exceeded the value of ship and cargo.

Serious structural weaknesses have

recently been discovered in the big new tankers. In a rough sea some of the parts reinforcing the hull have twisted and caused splits. On the other hand there have been no actual accidents. The damage is caused by what is called the "panting phenomenon." Whereas a ship's hull normally adapts itself to the movement of the sea longitudinally, the panting phenomenon is caused by the lateral stresses, the rhythm of which is faster than the ship's other movements. The phenomenon is more pronounced in shallow water. It is most economical to add extra reinforcements to prevent panting when the ship is being built. If these are added later, the cost is exorbitant, as many shipowners have discovered.

The half-million to one-million ton jumbo ships will present their builders with new problems. Without experience, it is impossible to say for sure how a ship of this size would behave in a rough sea or in relatively shallow and narrow channels. Mere launching is a problem on which the classification bodies have been working for some time now.

Improving docking

The construction of mammoth ships calls for vastly more efficient shipyards and larger docks. The Japanese shipyards will in future be able to build tankers up to 500,000 tons without having to build new docks.

In the Netherlands a giant shipyard able to build tankers with a carrying capacity of one million tons is being planned near Rotterdam. It is estimated that such vessels will be almost 1,790 feet long, 244 feet wide and 130 feet high. The bows and stern will be built on different bases, the bows in

The Japanese catamaran *Sea Palace* (435 G.R.T.) takes 311 passengers and a crew of 17.

EUROPE'S WATER TRANSPORTS. Because water transportation is so cheap, some freights between European countries go by sea. Certain inland water routes are also of great importance to goods transportation. In normal conditions the Baltic–North Sea–Atlantic–Mediterranean–Black Sea constitute an important lifeline for the European economy. When the cargoes are bulk goods, sea-going ships usually handle transports. The sea route between, for instance, the Baltic and the Black Sea is often more economical than the considerably shorter land route.

a dock 1,495 feet long and 260 feet wide, the stern sections in two 1950-by-275-foot docks. The construction sections will be made in a gigantic assembly hall and transferred to the construction dock with an 800-ton crane 325 feet high.

The Lisnave shipyard near Lisbon, which is owned by Portuguese, Dutch, and Swedish interests, is going to be extended considerably. One of its dry docks is being remodeled to take ships of up to 750,000 tons for repairs.

One special type of ship is the catamaran, the shape of the hull being of Polynesian origin. The Japanese started to build these twin-hulled vessels, which are considered highly seaworthy, in the nineteen-sixties as coastal traffic passenger ships. The *Sea Palace*, a ship of this kind completed in 1966, can take a good 300 passengers and 15 cars. The ship is only about eight feet deep and reaches 14 knots. She plies an open sea route between Hiroshima and Matsuyama. The special advantage of these ships is that there is 30 per cent more cargo space in the hull than in an ordinary ship of the same size. The double hull gives the ship greater stability and good navigability. A catamaran can travel in narrow channels and turns in practically its own space. It is cheap to run because the resistance to water is less because of the shape of the hull and the low draft.

There are also some sea-going catamarans, for instance a 2,800-ton cargo ship in England that carries containers between Tilbury and the North Sea ports. The Soviet Union has catamarans with large deck areas excellent for cargo carrying and speeded-up cargo handling.

New developments in merchant seafaring

The vast distances of the Pacific war arena produced the "landing ship dock" craft on which several revolutionary projects have since been modeled. Some time ago two different plans were put forward for handling sea transports more efficiently.

In one plan the basic idea is a mother ship which travels the great distances between the ocean ports and carries stowed inside her a whole fleet

The sea barge is a new attempt at rationalizing seafaring. Tests with practical applications are being made in at least Britain, the United States, and Japan. Considerable economic advantage is gained by separating engines and cargo areas; the ready-loaded barges are stowed in the ship for the sea passage. Once it reaches its destination the vessel can be raised or lowered to permit barge unloading straight into the sea or out via the stern.

of small carriers. These then distribute goods to smaller nearby harbors.

Another idea is the "sea barge" method. Important advantages are gained by separating the transportation mechanism and the cargo area; ready-loaded barges can be stowed in the ship during open-sea transportation.

A number of barge traffic companies and industrial bodies in the United States are trying to cut the high sea transportation costs by using large towed barges in ocean-going traffic, for example between the ports of the West Coast and Hawaii, across the Pacific. In mid-1968 the first two barges, taking 26,000 tons, were completed, with two 5,000-horsepower tugs to tow them.

Another interesting project is the English "multipacket" or MPT system. This aims at separating the engine and cargo sections by using separate barges for stevedoring. In principle this kind of multi-section ship looks like a line of barges fastened closely together. In an MPT vessel the engines, equipment, crew quarters, etc., are in the stern; the central and forward sections are reserved for freight. The ship is "cut off" fore of the engine room, and the open ends closed off with sealed walls.

So far an MPT model has been tried only in a pool. The system actually has a similar precursor: as early as 1863 a three-section English steamship, the *Connector*, was built. She could deposit her middle section en route and join up her fore and aft sections. A newly loaded middle section could then be picked up at another port. According to contemporary records, the trials

Fast passenger ships like the hydrofoil *Raketa* are used widely on the inland waterways of the Soviet Union.

went satisfactorily but the vessel later proved impossible to sail in a swell and broke up after only one trip.

Hydrofoils

The advances made with forms of transport utilizing the surface effect of land or water have been rapid in recent years, as technology has proved better able to control the progress of craft traveling slightly above the face of land or sea. In water transport, the greatest speed is provided by hydrofoils and hovercraft. The latter certainly hold prime place among new methods of land, sea, and air transport.

A hydrofoil travels in the water on supports like the wings of an aircraft. These produce the lift to raise the vessel by converting the water flow. When the hull is free of the water, it no longer has to fight against the great wave produced at the bows of a normal ship. The Italian professor of technology Enrico Forlanini was the first to put the hydrofoil principle into practice when he fitted metal plates like aircraft wings to a boat on Lake Magiore in 1905. Really fast progress was not made with this new type of craft until World War II. The German shipbuilding engineer Hans von Schertel then experimented with successful hydrofoils which could reach a speed of 50 knots. The structure of the most recent hydrofoils now in use is based on plans produced jointly by v. Schertel and the Swiss company Supramar A.G.

The *Sirena*, which Finland bought from Italy in 1960, was as far as is known the first hydrofoil in international traffic. This passenger ship could carry about a hundred people and was in service for several years between Mariehamn (Åland islands) and Stockholm.

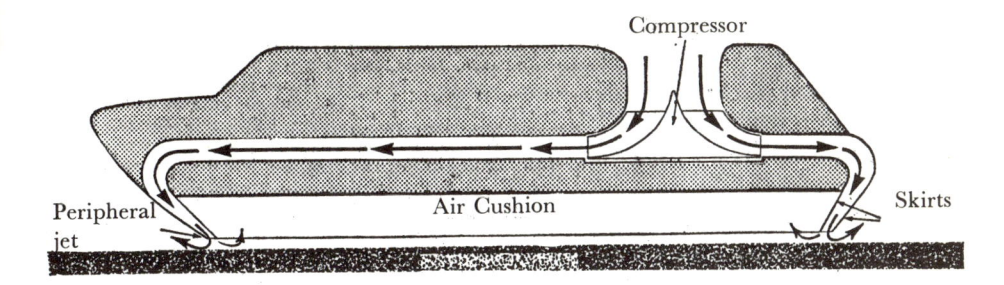

A diagram showing how a hovercraft works. The jet of air sucked in by the compressor is led to the skirts at the sides, where air jets driven downwards under the vessel create the supporting "air cushion." The diagram does not show the screw.

The world's first hydrofoil intended for open sea travel, the *Gromman Dolphin*, was built in Hamburg in 1966. She was sold to a Spanish shipping company and plies between Majorca, Valencia, and Barcelona (88 passengers, crew of 4). She is 75 feet long, carries 59 tons, travels at 50 knots on her hydrofoils, and is powered by a 3,600-horsepower gas turbine. All three hydrofoils can be withdrawn into the hull to permit her to tie up at quays and for docking.

In spite of certain limitations and drawbacks, favorable experiences with hydrofoils in various parts of the world have provided the impetus for research into the construction of hydrofoils of quite a different size and speed class. The hydrofoil is also believed to have a valuable application in naval service. In March 1968 the United States Navy acquired a trial hydrofoil gunboat. This prototype, capable of speeds exceeding 40 knots, has no screw. The gas turbine uses a centrifugal pump to suck water along the rear wing support and eject it very rapidly through a nozzle located under the stern; the water jetting from the stern provides the source of forward movement.

Hovercraft

The latest newcomer to shipping, the hovercraft or cushion-riding ve-

---

THE TIDE AS POWER SOURCE. The first Soviet hydroelectric power station to use the tide as a power source was built in 1968 on Kislaya Bay, Barents Sea, on the Kola Peninsula. The turbines use the rise and fall of the tide, which is 45 feet in this region. Following this pilot plant, there are plans for a 320,000-kilowatt tidal hydroelectric plant on Luboskaya Bay on the east coast of the Barents Sea.

---

hicle, is in fact the first commercially viable application of an idea which has been maturing for several decades now. In Finland the engineer Toivo Kaario was experimenting with a cushion-riding craft of his own design as early as the nineteen-thirties. The principle of the air cushion is that the craft rests on a layer of air formed by a slight over-pressure. It can then travel freely over both water and uneven terrain. A hovercraft can also be used as a floating vessel. In some types the actual air release of the air cushion acts as the propulsion force; in others an air or water screw is used. The actual bearing force is produced by circulation. At speed the hovercraft rides on its skirts three feet above the surface. It is controlled by means of ailerons and exhaust gases in the stern.

Development of a technically and economically competitive hovercraft has been pioneered by Britain. The Soviet Union has also produced craft working on the air-cushion principle for river passenger traffic. The modern hovercraft was invented by aviation engineer Christopher Cockerell, who started the first tests in 1953. Six years later a small four-ton prototype, *SRN 1*, went through the first trials and crossed the English Channel. Since then, the hovercraft has been developed from a scientific plan into a commercial reality, particularly by the British Hovercraft Corporation. In 1961 the *SRN 2* (74 knots), which could take 70 passengers, was completed. In spring 1965 regular services were started across the Channel with the hovercraft *SRN 6*, which takes 38 passengers. A craft like this costs about $ 250,000.

The world's largest hovercraft, the *SRN 4*, the first in the Mountbatten class, was completed in England in

NEW ROUTES TO SOUTH AMERICA. A plan that would affect the whole of South America has aroused interest among the South American authorities, international banking circles, and American experts. The first step involves a relatively cheap method of driving a canal through Choco Valley in Colombia, thus linking the Caribbean and the Pacific and offering an alternative to the Panama Canal. The other two parts of the plan are more difficult: damming the world's largest river, the Amazon (length about 3900 miles), and linking up the network of South America's three great rivers—the Amazon, the Orinoco, and the Paraguay-Parana. This would permit large ships to travel inside the continent between Brazil, Venezuela, Colombia, Peru, Bolivia, Paraguay, and Argentina. The damming of the Amazon alone would produce a sea the size of a unified Germany. The costs of the project would be quite low. According to preliminary calculations, which do not include electric power installations or lock equipment, it would cost 250 to 500 million dollars.

The world's largest hovercraft, *SRN 4*, is in service on the English Channel. It rides above the waves at a height of 10 to 12 feet.

1968 and a few months later put into regular cross-Channel service between Pegwell Bay (north of Dover) and Calais. This craft, which was ordered by Clover-Lloyd Ltd, a company owned by Swedish Lloyd and the Swedish-America Line, can take 250 passengers and 30 cars. The *SRN 4* weighs 165 tons and in calm weather can travel at 70 knots with a 64-ton load. The craft has four 20-foot-diameter screws set on top of four rotary columns and four gas turbine engines.

The fact that the hovercraft is so fast and independent of harbors proper may open up to it a number of applications, particularly if it proves possible to make the craft more economically. The hovercraft's biggest drawback is that it does not operate well in bad weather, in a heavy swell, or on excessively hilly terrain. It also makes a great deal of noise.

Underwater navigation

When the United States started building nuclear-powered submarines in the nineteen-fifties, American civilian financiers, almost simultaneously with Japanese shipping companies and West German nuclear reactor builders, started to work on the use of submarines for certain specialized merchant transportation. Most of these plans are at the moment still only on the drawing-board, but many experts believe that they will very soon become reality; one already has.

The national trade fair held in Lausanne in 1964 included the world's first underwater passenger ship, the *Auguste Piccard*. This took groups of forty tourists on trips some 600 to 1000 feet below Lake Geneva. Since the exhibition, the craft has been used for research. The passenger submarine weighs 160 tons, is 92 feet long and 20 feet wide; its hull is 1 1/2 inches thick. The engine power, from batteries, is 75 horsepower, and the submarine travels at five knots.

Britain has plans for a privately financed 50,000-ton submarine which would be the world's first nuclear-powered underwater cargo craft. It would be able to carry ore safely at all times of year from Diana Bay (Canada) to European ports.

The ships that take shape on the drawing-boards of shipbuilding engineers are stranger than Jules Verne's imaginary craft ever were. Imagine a huge cigar-shaped submarine floating at the quay. At the stern there is a jet engine outlet instead of screws. From the submarine's back a sharp fin rises to a height of 98 feet, and at its tip is a streamlined enclosed gondola which sways like a crow's-nest at the mast; it houses the control room and crew quarters of this incredible-looking vessel. The crew have to reach the gondola by either tower or crane. When the craft gets under way, the horizontal fins press the hull under water; the gondola travels just above the crest of the waves. The vessel's engine, in the enclosed section, takes its air from the surface along the fin in the same way as a submarine fitted with a snorkel.

This submarine combination is primarily experimental. It is a halfway stage toward an atomic submarine suitable for merchant use which in perhaps a decade or so will be carrying liquid fuel in its tank like an ordinary tanker. This method might well make it economic to transport oil from Alaska to Europe. It may have other potential that we cannot even guess at yet.

Why these attempts to make underwater merchant shipping feasible?

Most of the expense of conventional ships stems from their construction, which must be designed to withstand the pressure, stretching, twisting, and flexing of the rolling sea in the worst of storms. But under the surface there are no storms or swell.

At today's relatively modest speeds, surface vessels need what is in fact tremendous power to push their way through the waves. The bows of a submarine push through the water very much more easily. The engineers of one English company estimate that a tanker submarine needs only a third of the power used by a surface vessel

The world's first passenger submarine *Auguste Piccard* being launched on Lake Geneva in 1964. Technical data: length 92 feet, width 18 feet, 40 passengers. The *Auguste Piccard* performed numerous tourist trips during Expo 64, since when she has been used for research.

The portholes of the passenger salon offer a glimpse of marine life.

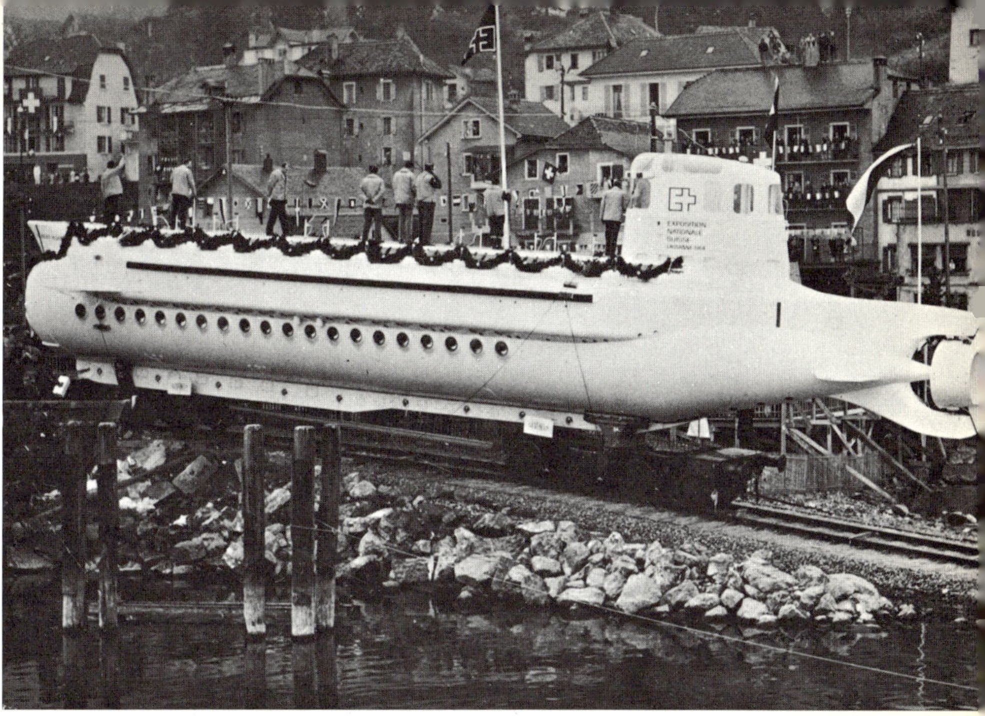

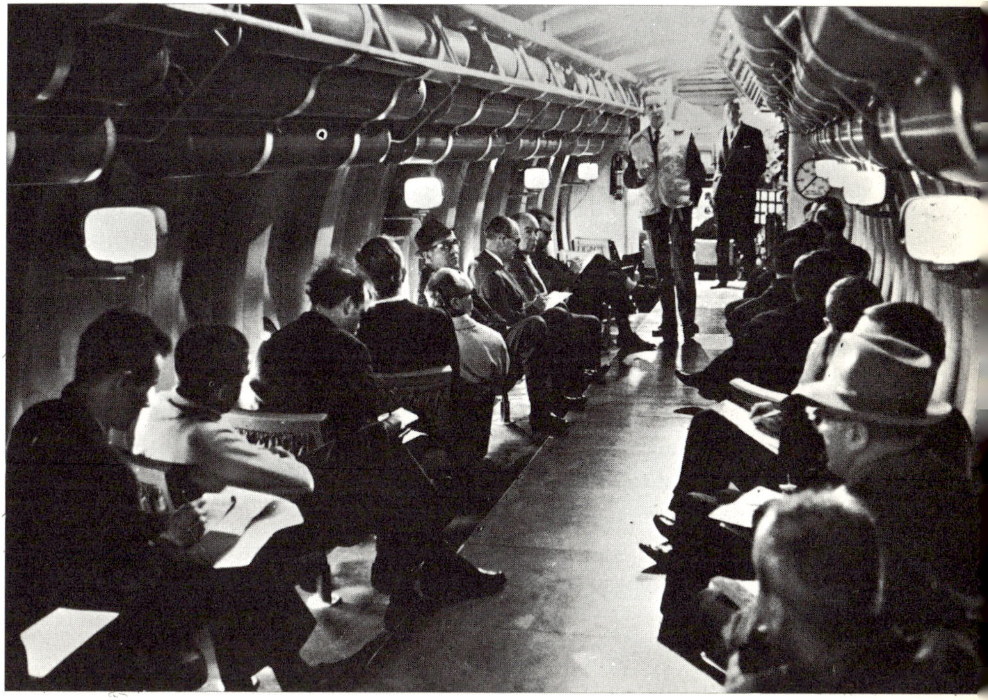

The first highly automated Challenger II class cargo ship s/s *America Racer* (1964, Chester, Pa.) 12,900 d.w.t., length 540 feet, beam 75 feet, speed 21 knots.

to reach a speed of 50 knots. The result will be lower running costs and more cargo moved per unit of time.

Marine automation

Keener competition on the freight markets forces shipping companies to seize on any method of cutting costs. This fact, together with the appearance on the market of gauging and control equipment suitable for marine instrumentation has encouraged a trend toward automation in marine engineering in the last few years.

Great progress has been made in determining a ship's position since the development of a navigation system using radio waves transmitted by satellite. The first satellite built for this purpose was launched by the United States in 1960. Seven years later the system was put at the disposal of American merchant and oceanographic ships. Ships equipped with this highly efficient system's receivers can fix their position anywhere on the globe to within a tenth of a mile. The system consists of three satellites, four land stations (in Hawaii, California, Minnesota, and Maine), and the receiving equipment in the ships. The satellites orbit at a height of nearly 500 miles, passing above both poles.

The expansion of navigation and the diversity of other professions and trades are making it difficult to get properly qualified crews for ships. For this reason, and to reduce costs, great attention is now being given to the development of automation, the control and direction of machines by machines. Marine automation is a fairly new field, but the era of automated ships has begun and is gradually growing in strength. Japan holds the lead here, but the United States and the Soviet Union are gaining experience.

Automation is already quite advanced in the cargo ship *American Racer*, which completed her maiden voyage at the end of 1964. On this ship one man can handle all the machinery and equipment from the bridge. The ship's speed (maximum 21 knots) can be controlled and the boilers and auxiliary engines supervised from one control panel. The Japanese have given themselves a practical immediate goal for automation, a 30% cut in running costs. A substantial reduction like this would of course make their ships much more competitive.

Revolutionary changes like these make completely new demands of seamen and must be reflected in the syllabi of seamen's training schools. In order to cope with adjustment difficulties, mates and engineers, at least, must be trained to handle the control and maintenance work on an automated ship. The future outlook is for a new kind of merchant marine with a new kind of crew.

"Ghost ships" will one day ply the world seas, American shipbuilders predict. They will not need a single man; automatic equipment will handle everything. The only human aid needed will be a pilot when leaving and approaching harbor. The aim of advancing technology is to automate every stage, but this is not likely to happen in this century.

THE CHEAPNESS OF WATER TRANSPORT. In his book *Inland Waterways of Europe*, Roger Calvert uses carefully compiled German technical research findings to show that a horse can drag a load of 330 pounds along a road, 1,100 pounds on rails, and 8,800 pounds kg on water. The book also gives the following figures for a 1,000-ton load using different forms of transport:

	Lorries	Railway cars	Barges
	50	50	1
Men needed	100	3	3
Cost in DM	3 million	750,000	500,000
Life of means of transport	10 yrs	30 yrs	50 yrs

With these calculations the writer tries to show that the cheapest way to transport goods is by water. As counterbalance to the slowness of water transport, he refers to the speed at which land transport wears out and the high price of fuel. Water traffic, though slower, saves on equipment and can carry a much heavier load than land transport per unit of power.

The underwater world and its exploration

Scientists are showing a growing interest in the sea, as well as in outer space. The higher and farther man penetrates into space, the keener, though less publicized, are his efforts to explore the depths of the ocean and to study the sea and the subtle secrets of the underwater world. We have another new name to go with "astronaut"—"aquanaut".

In the dozen years that have passed since the first earth satellite was launched, huge amounts of money and energy have been put into space research. Far less attention has been given to the quiet pioneering work that has been done, on relatively meagre resources, to conquer the "inner space" of our world—the depths of the seas. The direct benefit to mankind that can be expected from study of the seas is probably much greater and of more significance than that which the moon, for instance, can offer.

Ever since the days of Aristotle, the wonderful and multitudinous forms of sea life have fascinated biologists. Throughout the centuries the sea has been the inspiration of poets and an open source of geographical discoveries and scientific observations. It was not until the nineteenth century that there were any really fundamental changes in man's attitude to the sea. The sea has since become the object of intense and comprehensive scientific research and of constantly extending, practical human activities. The prime aim of these activities is the effective utilization of the natural wealth and traffic facilities offered by the oceans.

The growth of world population

The human race is constantly multiplying and needs food, and there are vast stores of raw materials in the sea. The productivity of the seas can be improved as regards both fish and the other fruits of the sea. The natural resources of the great mountain ranges at the bottom of the sea are practically unexplored. It is true that oil is already being drilled, but there may well be precious metals and the uranium needed by our nuclear power industry lurking in the bowels of the sea. Discoveries made on the sea bottom may also throw light on the question of man's origin, and to zoologists the sea is an incomparable treasure trove. The seas's gifts are many, but so are the problems. The list of subjects for oceanographic study is endless. To mention just two, our knowledge of the currents and of wave movements of the deeps.

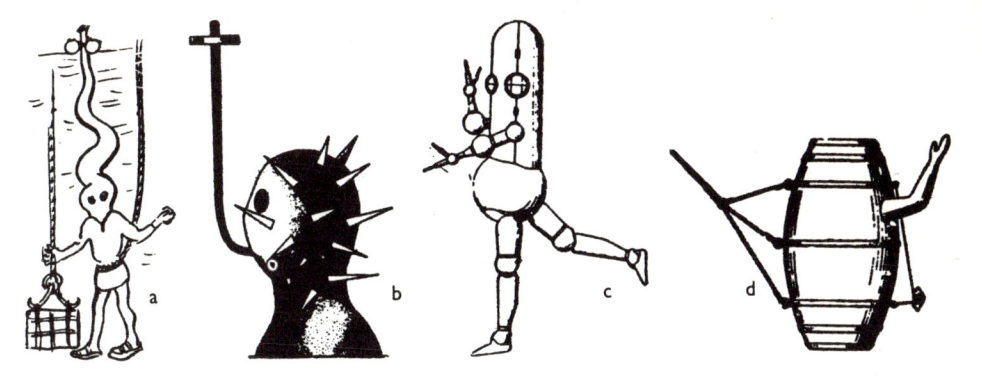

As early as the fourth century B.C. Aristotle was designing the diving suit in picture (a). The air pipe was held on the surface with floats. The all-around genius of the Renaissance, Leonardo da Vinci, also worked on the problem of underwater exploration. Picture (b) shows the diver's helmet he designed, with air tube. Picture (c) depicts the diving suit designed by the Englishman William Barrey in 1802. Picture (d) shows the underwater fishing bell designed by the Frenchman de Batteaux.

At the beginning of the Christian era there were probably about 200 million people on earth, and the figure is estimated to have doubled by 1500 A.D. It took only about 275 years for the population to double again. The invention of the steam engine ushered in the mechanized era, which gave a strong impulse to the fast rise in world population: as human life became easier, more children survived, and the average life span lengthened.

By the beginning of this century the world population had again doubled and stood at 1.6 billion. Since then the rate of growth has accelerated: the 2 billion mark was reached in 1930, 3 billion in 1960. A figure of 4 billion is probable by 1975, and according to UN statistics, around 7.4 billion in the year 2000, though it may of course be subject to unexpected flux. This population explosion is divided very unevenly among the continents. In 1960 the "highly developed" countries had a billion or so people and the rest of the world 2 billion. One prognosis for the year 2000 gives the former countries 1.5 billion and the rest 5 to 5.5 billion.

Hunger has been a fact of life over large areas of the globe for centuries, but the problem threatens to become an emergency with our uncontrolled population growth. An FAO report says that two-thirds of the present world population suffer from hunger. According to estimates, and taking even the most fanciful world economy development plans into account, the globe can support a population of only about six times what it is now—though some experts, particularly in the last few years, have expressed far more optimistic views of the world food situation and production prospects, considering earlier estimates and the claims of largely erroneous and unrealistic panic propaganda.

According to calculations on population growth, output of foodstuffs must rise steeply by the end of the century, e.g., by 300 per cent in Asia, 240 per cent in Latin America, and 160 per cent in Africa. All this means that twice as much wheat, four times as much milk and meat, and eight times as much fish must be produced.

Figures like these, showing a vast mass of humanity spreading inexorably over the surface of the earth, have led pessimists to predict the annihilation of all, or most of, the species through lack of nourishment. Others, however, believe that more advanced agriculture (using irrigation based on automatic equipment and sea water, or artificial rains) and the rational utilization of ocean life will supply enough food for the needs of our growing race.

The history of oceanography

Oceanography proper originated somewhat over a hundred years ago out of the requirements of navigation and fishing; it was a need dictated by purely practical ends. But as oceanography developed, scientists soon recog-

---

UNDERWATER TUNNEL. Japan has decided to build a 22-mile underwater tunnel which will link Honshu' the largest of the archipelago's islands, with the most northerly island. This tunnel, planned for electric trains alone, will be ready in 1975.

---

nized that it is impossible to find reliable solutions to practical questions without clarifying many basic, purely scientific problems.

As recently as the middle of the last century, nothing was known about life in the ocean depths. Even scientists held to the belief that life was possible only in shallow coastal waters and close to the surface in the open sea. Yet strange forms of life had often been cast up on the shore which had come from much greater depths than anyone believed possible. In 1818 John Ross caught live ophiurans (brittle-stars) at a depth of 6,500 feet in Baffin Bay, and the Norwegians raised a number of extremely odd creatures from depths of up to 2,600 feet along their coasts.

Oceanography really got started only when methods, equipment, and devices were developed with which the actual waters of the deepest reaches of the sea could be studied with satisfactory precision. This was roughly around the time that the first ocean cables were laid.

While telegraph cable was being

TRACKING SHIP. The space tracking ship *General H. H. Arnold* is shown at a dock near Cape Kennedy, Florida. The craft is equipped with radar and telemetry instrumentation, and also carries Arcas meteorological rocket launchers and a complete weather station. A sister ship, the *General Hoyt S. Vandenberg*, has similar equipment.

laid at the bottom of the Atlantic in summer 1865, it broke at a depth of 11,700 feet. When the cable-layer *Great Eastern* was laying a new cable between Britain and America a year later, she found the cable that had snapped the previous year. With great difficulty it was successfully raised. It was then found that a great horde of deep-sea creatures previously unknown to science, from protozoans and conchiferous creatures to molluscs and arthropods, had attached themselves to the cable.

Marine research now found adherents among scientists in all the civilized countries. A number of research expeditions were equipped, and a great deal of valuable data was gathered on the chemical composition of sea water, its temperatures at various depths, its fauna, flora, etc. Before this, in the 1850s, the American ship's officer Matthew Maury and the Englishman Edward Forbes had begun some pioneering oceanographic research. Maury can with reason be considered the founder of physical, and Forbes of biological, oceanography.

In 1872 the most famous oceanographic expedition of all time set off on the corvette *Challenger* and spent a good three years on three oceans. The out-

18 The sea and man

An artist's view of the deep sea rescue vessel (DSRV) planned by the United States Navy, which can rescue 24 people at a time. The rescue craft prototype is just being built. It is here seen attached to its mothercraft, a nuclear submarine.

come of this 80,000-mile British expedition was the compilation of more knowledge and specimens than had ever been assembled before. The *Challenger* expedition made hundreds of depth soundings, the record depth being about 26,700 feet, slightly over five miles.

Another important oceanographic project was that carried out by the German *Meteor* expedition in 1925–27. This took in only the central and southern Atlantic, but thanks to its echo-sounder and many other new and reliable devices and methods, oceanography attained a new level of scientific authority. Several other oceano-graphic expeditions have also done valuable research, for instance the Swedes on the *Albatross* in 1947–48, the Danes in the *Galathea* in 1950–52 and the British in *Challenger II* in 1951–52.

From glass bells to deep-sea diving craft

One of the oldest tales about man in the depths is the one telling how Alexander the Great spent several days in a glass bell at the bottom of the sea studying its wonders. According to the story, he saw a sea monster so large that it took three days to pass by. Even in the modern period, the development of practicable diving equipment was hampered by the fact that no-one quite knew how man's respiratory system worked or what air contained.

For exploration of the ocean depths, more efficient equipment than ordinary diving suits or submarines, whose utility ends at six or seven hundred feet, has to be used. Bathyscaphs and other such special craft are suitable for this purpose. Ordinary submarines would shatter like eggshells if they were to penetrate to the ocean depths, where the pressure is a thousand atmospheres and temperatures approach freezing point.

The actual pioneer of deep-sea research must be considered to be the Italian Balsamello, who reached a depth of 535 feet in a steel ball seven feet in diameter in 1889. It was not until the 1930s that more impressive records were set. The American geologist Otis Barton designed a pressure-resistant steel bell with a porthole which could be lowered into the depths on a cable from a surface vessel. In 1934, with his countryman the zoologist William Beebe, he went down to a depth of 3000 feet in this bathysphere off Bermuda. They held this record for the next sixteen years.

In spite of its weaknesses Beebe and Barton's bathysphere marked the beginning of a new era in exploration of the ocean depths. The next great step forward was the bathyscaph (Greek "deep boat") designed in the 1940s by the Swiss scientist Professor Auguste Piccard, which swims freely deep in the sea like a balloon in air. This unusual craft is in fact a tanklike vessel divided into sections, with a spherical research chamber attached to the center point of the base. So far three bathyscaphs have been built. Professor Jacques Piccard (son of Auguste) and Lieutenant Donald Walsh descended to the deepest known point of the ocean on January 23, 1960, in the newest bathyscaph, which is owned by the United States Navy. This craft, called the *Trieste*, descended to a depth of nearly 36,000 feet, the bottom of the Marianas

UNDERWATER EXPERIMENTAL STATIONS. Space technology and deep-sea craft technology have a great deal in common as far as crew accommodation is concerned. In deep-sea exploration and submarines the aim is to allow men to spend long periods at moderate depths. Submerged experimental stations have been built at least in France and the United States. So far the number of people to have spent fairly long periods in them is roughly the same as those who have been in space, though the number of hours is considerably higher.

THE GULF STREAM has been studied by submarine craft for the first time. The Swiss deep-sea researcher Jacques Piccard has designed a unique craft, the *Ben Franklin*, which set off in July, 1969, from Palm Beach, Florida, with six scientists on board to float for six weeks with the Gulf Stream. The 130-ton, 48-foot craft covered 1.444 nautical miles and gave researchers their first opportunity of traveling long distances underwater using the actual motive force of nature.

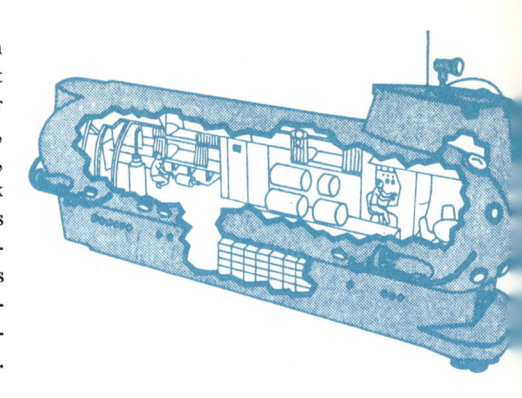

Trench near the island of Guam in the Pacific, in 4 hours, 48 minutes. It is worth recalling that slightly over a year later on April 12, 1961, Major Yuri Gagarin became the first man to orbit the earth in the spacecraft *Vostok*.

In the last few years the nuclear-powered submarine has offered a new and extremely valuable instrument of oceanographic research. One of its first important tasks was in fact the mapping of important areas of the sea bottom. The most precise possible knowledge about the face of the ocean bed will be vital in the future, when submarines travel at all depths.

As the oceans hold no greater depths to which man can penetrate, the breaking of depth records proper has lost its interest. However, deep-sea diving craft continue to be improved, for instance made smaller. There are now some thirty deep-sea diving craft.

The seas are the last unexploited regions of our crowded earth, and thus call for large-scale and purposeful scientific study. Leading experts in many countries are in fact cooperating closely in attempts to explain as fully as possible the secrets of the deeps. They see in the ocean mankind's salvation from the shortage of both raw materials and food that threatens our near future.

In 1958 an international oceanography congress was held at the UN headquarters in which 1,100 scientists from forty-five countries took part. On the international geophysical year model, it was decided to devote the five-year period 1960–64 to basic oceanography; central to this research were extensive projects in the Indian Ocean. Oceanography is also an important branch of UNESCO's activities.

There are at present some six hundred oceanographic research establishments in different parts of the world, many with their own research ships. In

1962 the biggest oceanographic research center in Europe was opened in Bergen, Norway. According to plan, the United States will acquire over a hundred ships serving marine research alone by 1970. The weak state of Soviet agriculture is also forcing the USSR to seek a substitute in fishing, for the development of which proper oceanographic research is absolutely essential.

Since its foundation in 1919, the Finnish Institute of Oceanography has done valuable hydrographic and biological research. The Institute's wide working sphere includes study of the ice conditions in the seas around Finland and the issuing of ice reports for winter shipping, and the study of the physical, chemical, and biological conditions of sea water.

The bottom of the sea

In the last hundred years nearly all the visible surface of the globe has been studied and mapped. The only large and practically unmapped regions left are at the bottom of the sea. In spite of the great progress made recently with research methods and equipment, this part of the globe's surface is still difficult to study and poses a tremendous number of vital scientific problems.

The introduction of echo-sounding in 1923 was a great advance in depth measurement. With this method, which does not need a plumb line or weight, measurement is fast and simple. Briefly, sound waves are transmitted in short sequences by electromagnet from the bottom of the ship, and reflected back from the sea bottom. The depth of the water is found by measuring the time from beginning the transmission sequence to receiving the echo. Since sound travels in water at about 4,800 feet a second, it takes only ten seconds to echo-sound a depth of 24,000 feet, and the vessel can move forward all the time.

Even the greatest depths have been extensively mapped by means of echo-sounding, and yet only some 2 per cent of the whole surface of the bottom of the sea has been covered. Echo-sounding has found the same kind of mountains, valleys, and plains as on dry land.

The average depth of the sea is slightly over 13,000 feet in the Pacific, about 13,000 feet in the India Ocean, and about 12,000 feet in the Atlantic. For some strange reason the sea around Antarctica suddenly becomes very deep, ranging between 13,000 and 26,000 feet, and the continent lacks completely the shallow underwater belt which is to be found in the seas surrounding the other continents. The bottom of the ocean is the thinnest part of the earth's crust.

The average height of dry land is only 2800 feet. The seas are 16,000 feet deep on the average; this is the depth of the normal bed, the "plains" of the deeps. But where the sea covers part of the continental shelf, forming a low shallow coastal sea, the average depth is only 12,000 feet. These figures show that the seas are generally deeper than continents are high. The figure for the extreme heights and depths are the only ones that are analogous: the world's highest mountain Mount Everest is about 29,000 feet above sea level, and the greatest depth so far discovered, in the Pacific, is about 36,000. The deepest point found in the Atlantic, close to 30,000 feet, is in the Puerto Rico Trench northeast of Haiti. Although these may seem great depths, they are as but slight depressions compared with the vastness of the earth's surface.

There is a great deal of volcanic activity in the Pacific area, below as well as above sea level. To their great amazement, yachtsmen may suddenly find themselves in the middle of such a disturbance, with wild rollers and hick clouds of steam rising from the sea around them.

Falcon Island, a volcanic peak rising from the Pacific about 1860 miles east of Australia, suddenly disappeared in 1913. Thirteen years later there was an upheaval nearby, and just as suddenly it appeared above the surface again. It then remained a tiny part of the British Commonwealth until 1949 —when the Ministry for Colonial Affairs reported it had again disappeared.

At the end of May, 1960, there were violent earthquakes on the coast of southern Chile, and the furious, destructive breakers (tsunami) they produced reached as far as the Japanese, Australian, and New Zealand coasts, and the Hawaiian and Polynesian islands. One of the greatest natural disasters of all time, this cost at least 5,000 lives, plus tens of thousands of people injured and hundreds of thousands made homeless.

The landscapes of the bottom of the ocean compete with the great sights of dry land for excitement and splendor. The actual bed of the sea consists of the wide silt-covered plains of the deeps, broken by steep volcanic ranges, flat-topped mountains, deep gullies, and mile-long deep-sea trenches or depressions. This topographical variety is the result of the long and complex geological history of the ocean. A deep-sea plain—some 16,000 feet deep on average—is the actual surface of the globe from which the continents and islands rise.

Probably none of the landscapes of the underwater world has aroused such wonder and curiosity among geologists as the great mountain ridges. The most tremendous of them all, the Atlantic Ridge, is nearly 10,000 miles long, stretching from Iceland to south of Cape Town, turning east to the Indian Ocean and continuing south of

A scientist with a 16-mm camera descending into the depths off the Bahamas.

Australia into the south and east Pacific. This range of mountains, the longest in the world, is 500 miles wide in places, more than twice as wide as the Andes. Though the ridge's average height is 11,400 feet, most of the peaks lie far below the surface of the sea. Here and there, however, they break the waves and form the scattering of Atlantic islands: Ascension, the Azores, St. Paul, etc. The most central point of the Atlantic Ridge, Pico Alto in the Azores, rises to a height of about 29,000 feet above the sea bed, though only a bare third of this is above sea level.

Some valuable work has been done recently in uncovering the secrets of the Arctic sea bed. In 1960 the Soviet Arctic specialist, the late Professor J. J. Gakkel, published his finding that there is a submerged ridge in the North Arctic Ocean, starting from the Atlantic, which links Eurasia and North America. This ridge, named after Gakkel, divides the Nansen Sound into two almost equally large sections. The ridge consists of volcanic mountains, and forms a plunging valley around which mountain peaks soar to heights of 16,000 feet.

The multifarious life of the oceans

The Pacific Ocean covers almost half the face of the seas and a good third of the surface of the globe, but little is known about the sea bed except in the western part. Besides its great deeps, it has other wonders to offer. One of the most fascinating and beautiful is the Great Barrier Reef, the world's largest coral reef, which stretches for over 1,200 miles from the northeast coast of Australia to the coast of New Guinea. The life there, as in tropical waters in general, is exciting, colorful, and kaleidoscopic. The various corals are not the only creators of this brilliant underwater world, for other flora and fauna, such as huge colonies of polyzoans and sponges, have settled there to build among the corals. In the crooks and crannies, between the arms of the corallines, lives a multitudinous community of armored creatures, single-celled slimy organisms, molluscs, crustaceans, and many others. When these animals die their shells disintegrate into the coral and help to form the permanent body of the reef.

The waters of the polar regions are usually thought of as silent and lifeless. In fact, however, they are neither. The millions of ice floes, varying from the size of a man's hat right up to about half a square mile, are in constant motion. Floe grinds against floe, setting up a rumbling sound that can be heard miles away. When one floe rides on top of another, it gives off an ear-shattering screech.

Possibly there is even more life in the northern waters than anywhere but the tropical seas, and here as elsewhere it comprises a kind of pyramid. The base consists of the smallest members of the vegetable kingdom, called plankton. Billions of crustaceans and other similar fauna feed on them. The shell-fish in turn are eaten by walruses, whales, and huge herds of seals. Finally, at the top of the pyramid is the polar bear, which lives mainly on seal and spends most of its life floating around on the ice floes.

Atlantis—fact or fiction?

As the topography of the seas gradually becomes more familiar, the old oft-disputed tales of "lost continents" have taken on new life. This is particularly true of Atlantis, the legendary continent which sank into the ocean and, according to the Greek philosopher Plato, who lived over 2,000 years ago, lay somewhere in the Atlantic beyond the Straits of Gibraltar. A French bibliography published in 1926 contains three thousand works on Atlantis and an infinite number of press articles.

To most people Atlantis is just a myth, the product of some centuries-old storyteller's imagination. However, a substantial number of researchers are convinced of the authenticity of the lost Atlantis tale. New discoveries at the bottom of the sea have made the legend sound highly probable. Most attempts to locate Atlantis have put the

TELENAUT

The Telenaut is a French remote-controlled unmanned submarine. The craft transmits information from the depths through two electric cables. The submarine's TV and film cameras can work at more than half a mile deep. Observers on the surface can operate the cameras when and how they like.

continent in the Atlantic, but the German Jürgen Spanuth, who published a book called *Das enträtzelte Atlantis* in 1953, is sure that Atlantis is in the North Sea west of the Jutland peninsula.

At the international geo-congress held in Helsinki in summer 1960, the director of the Athens Seismological Observatory, Professor G. Galanapoulos, put forward a new theory on the Atlantis legend. He thought it possible that Atlantis was the 30-square-mile island of Thera, in the Aegean Sea some 60 miles north of Crete, one of the remaining fragments of the island of Santorin (Stronghyl), which flourished in antiquity. As a result of a disastrous volcanic eruption around 1450 B.C., the center of Santorin sank to form a gigantic, 1300-foot-deep cauldron. According to Galanapoulos it is still possible to see the remains of a harbor and canals in the depression.

Excavations have continued on Thera, and in summer 1967 a group of American and Greek scientists dug out the first Minoan town ever to have been found untouched. It corresponds to the Roman Empire's Pompeii, which was entombed in ashes when Vesuvius erupted in 79 A.D. The Greeks of the Golden Age never forgot the cataclysm and the lost Minoan culture. These lived on in various legends, and one of these may be the Atlantis story.

The dark world of the sea

If we do not take shallow seas into account, about half of the whole surface of the globe is covered with lightless water miles deep. Daylight never penetrates into these depths, and even in the upper water layers the light is soon dimmed by absorption, which affects the various color components of the light in different ways. In Scandina-

Space communications ship. USNS *Kingsport*, the United States Navy's first satellite communications ship, is being used in the first flight test of the Syncom satellite. Recently converted from a cargo ship, the craft is on station in the Port of Lagos, Nigeria. The Radome on deck houses radar and other communications equipment. Project Syncom is designed to test the feasibility of establishing a 24-hour global communications network using only three relay stations in space orbiting at a speed synchronized with the earth's rotation. The *Kingsport* will also be used in oceanographic surveys, hydrographic research, geodetic surveys and underwater acoustic research programs.

vian coastal waters the strength of light is reduced to half at a depth of about seven feet.

Below the surface, light fades quickly. Red rays stop at 250 to 300 feet, and with them the orange and yellow warmth of the sun. Then the green rays start to fade, and at a depth of 1,000 feet there is only a dark, shimmering blue. In particularly clear water the violet rays manage to penetrate another thousand feet or so. After that there is nothing but the black darkness of the ocean depths.

This dark world guards its secrets well. Its creatures have hardly any sanctuary from their ever-present foes. Below the sunny upper waters, beyond the last point where straggling members of the plant kingdom venture—no plant can live deeper than about 700 feet—the denizens of the deeps live violently and mercilessly off each other. In the end, however, they are completely dependent on the soft rain of dead or dying plants and animals which falls on them from above. Certain small deep-sea fish like dragons, with sabre-toothed jaws, huge mouth, and a body so flexible that they can swallow a creature many times bigger than themselves, are one indication of the fierce battle for food that goes on in the depths of the sea.

No one had ever before seen these greedy predatory fish and other monsters so well and at such close quarters as did the Norwegian adventurer-explorer and ethnologist Thor Heyerdahl and his five colleagues during the brave voyage of the Kon-Tiki across the east Pacific from Peru to Polynesia in summer 1947. In one of his private letters about deep-sea life, Heyerdahl writes: "On dark nights we could see much marine life which we were unable to identify. They seemed to be deep-sea fishes approaching the surface at night. Generally we saw them as vaguely phosphorescent bodies, often the size and shape of a dinner plate, but at least one night in the shape of three immense bodies of irregular and changing shape and dimensions which appeared to exceed those of the raft [Kon-Tiki measured about 45 by 18 feet]."

The earlier belief was that there could be no life in the depths of the sea because eternal darkness reigns there and the water pressure is fantastically high. It is true that there begin to be no fish at a depth of about 22,000 feet, but this does not mean the end of marine life. Even the greatest depths—those where the pressure is 1,000 atmospheres—pulse with life: bivalves, sea anemones, echinoderms, and many others, most of which are very like related creatures in coastal waters.

In the depths of the oceans, under the pressure of great water masses, life often dresses itself in fabulous colors and forms. The researcher's eye is fascinated by the infinite, fantastic spectacle. Many kinds of bacteria have also been found in these depths.

The *Galathea* expedition, including scientists from many countries as well as from its sponsor Denmark, returned in 1952 with some important findings. Ragnar Spärck, Professor of Zoology at Copenhagen University and a member of the group, lectured in Helsinki in 1955 and explained how suitable drag nets were used to study deep-sea life. This threw interesting light on the unexplored Kermadec, Mindanao, Java, and Solomon Trenches. Even at a depth of over 30,000 feet, where the water temperature is usually around 2 to 3 degrees centigrade, about a gram of living organisms was found per square yard of water.

GLASS is expected to prove of great importance in the search for minerals at the bottom of the oceans, as glass is known to withstand high pressure well. Whereas a metal plate has to be made thicker to withstand the pressure at a depth of 10,000 feet, the same pressure on glass merely increases its strength. Glass breaks only under stress, when its molecules are pulled apart.

The United States Navy is at present building a spherical glass craft for underwater use. It opens like a bivalve, allowing the craft's crew of two to get in and out. Scientists hope they will be able to descend to a depth of 14,500 feet in these craft. They will have much better visibility than passengers in metal submarines. Even so, they will feel secure in the knowledge that the transparent walls are not "as fragile as glass," but in fact stronger than steel.

The fruits and treasures of the sea

As the human race continues to grow at breakneck speed, the significance of the sea for human life increases. Scientists and economists are attaching increasing attention to what the sea can offer. As most of our natural resources lie in the sea, the world economy of the future will perhaps be primarily an economy of the oceans. The present marine economy output can be divided into three main groups: (1) the products of the marine animal kingdom; (2) the products of the marine vegetable kingdom; and (3) salts, minerals, and metals.

Marine life comprises a great biological chain, the extremities of which are the world's largest animals at one end, and the minutest of microscopic plants at the other. The seas could be made much more productive of human food, cattle fodder, and fertilizers than dry land. As a whole they receive much more sunlight than the continents, and the plants and animals found there occur throughout a relatively thick water layer.

The wealth of tiny plants and animals, which are given the joint name "plankton," form the basis of the seas' nutritional biology chain. Without them it would be impossible for the world's waters to contain fish. At the moment the flora and particularly the fauna of the seas are their most valuable natural wealth and at an estimate will be so for some time to come.

Johannes Petersen of the Oceanography Laboratory in Copenhagen has estimated that 10 tons of plant or animal nourishment are needed to produce one ton of fish. One ton of predatory fish (e.g., cod) eats 10 tons of plankton-eaters (e.g., small herring), which in turn have consumed 100 tons of plankton. Thus when a trawler brings its catch in to land, each ton of fish in it has consumed about 100 tons of plant cells.

Both warm and cold seas also have "deserts" where there is little life. The decisive factor is the quantity of vegetation. Cold water has a heavier mineral content and contains plenty of nitrogen and phosphorus, which all plants need in large quantities. The life which pulses so richly through tropical waters originates in places from the cold sea currents.

With their vast and diverse elementary wealth, the seas comprise a raw material reserve of still unsuspected potential. As other sources of raw materials gradually run dry and production costs rise, man will begin to utilize this reserve more systematically. In addition to animal, vegetable, and mineral wealth, there is a huge source of energy waiting to be exploited in the tides, wave movements, and currents of the sea. The direct and indirect benefits of the sea could be recounted endlessly. Not least significant is shipping, which continues to expand with the world's growing industrial output. The seas still hold first place as channels of international trade.

The seas as source of food

The half of the world that goes hungry and suffers from deficiency diseases mainly lacks food containing protein, and this is what fish can offer. If we intend to provide everyone with sufficient food—about two-thirds of humanity suffer from constant malnutrition—we will have to resort to the sea on a much wider scale in our search for food, since agricultural output seems unlikely to increase substantially under present conditions. The fact that roughly four-fifths of all known animal species—excluding about half a million types of insects—live in the sea gives some indication of the huge variety of sea life. The seas contain more than 40,000 species of crustacean, about as many molluscs, and some 26,000 types of fish, about 19,000 of them bony fish.

In the light of these figures it seems strange how little man as yet uses and is capable of utilizing the diverse and abundant organic products of the sea. The number of products of the marine animal kingdom marketed in various parts of the world is limited to a few hundred; hardly a hundred species of ocean fish are fished commercially. And yet fish and fish products are of high nutritional value, since they are easy to digest, can be eaten in either a fatty or almost non-fatty form, and contain appreciable amounts of vitamins and minerals as well as vital protein.

At an FAO conference in 1961 on the potential of deep-sea fishing, American scientists expressed their views on the amount of fish in the oceans and how these are utilized: of an assumed 230 million tons, half must be kept for renewal of the fish stock, a quarter is scattered around the world's waters, and only the remaining 58 million tons can be utilized on an industrial scale. Soviet experts, however, have put the ocean fish reserves at 500 million tons or more, in spite of the fact that life in the marine biology chain is a merciless and unrelenting struggle for existence. According to estimates, only one fish in ten million dies a "natural" death, if such a rare event can be considered "natural".

So far, at least, marine animal life constitutes the greatest part of the sea's yield that man puts to his own use: the corals, sponges, worms, echinoderms, molluscs, crustaceans, fish, turtles, whales, and seal. Even in northern latitudes man learned to make use of the fruits of the sea at quite an early date; the remains of Scandinavian Stone Age meals (køkkenmødding) have revealed the bones of cod, haddock, flounder and many other ocean fish, oyster shells, and similar sea products.

Fish the sea's main yield

In 1965 about three-quarters of all that man took from the sea was fishing catch, yet over half of this was herring, cod, salmon, and sea perch alone, which are to be found only in the northern hemisphere. According to FAO statistics, the total yield of food commodities from seas and inland waters throughout the world is now over 50 million tons a year. Fish accounts for about 90 % of this; three-quarters of that figure is ocean fish.

The annual total yield of world sea fishing is rising by about 7 per cent a year, or roughly three times faster than the world's population. The significance of sea fishing for the nourishment of the human race is thus growing. The monetary value of doubling total fishing output would be several billion dollars a year. Some 80 to 90 per cent of the fish catch, in which the six most important countries by quantity are at the moment Peru, Japan, China, the Soviet Union, the United States, and Norway, is marketed as human food. The rest is made into powdered fish

---

THE WORLD RECORD FOR DEEP-SEA DIVING without equipment is still held by the Greek Georghios, the first frogman. In 1913, with only a sponge tied in his mouth, without flippers or diving mask, he dived to the wreck of the Italian battleship *Regina Margherita* at a depth of 200 feet, tied a cloth around the anchor as a mark of his achievement, and returned to the surface.

---

and oil. According to calculations, an average 40 per cent of the gross weight of fresh fish is edible and utilized for human consumption.

Herring and cod

At spawning time cod and herring move in close to the shore in huge shoals. In Norwegian coastal waters, for instance, the millions of herring that work their way up the fjords sometimes crowd together so closely that the water seems to be boiling with fish. Dolphins and other predatory fish circle round the herring shoals, driving the frightened fish closer and closer together, and when they push up into the fjords they are an easy catch for the fisherman.

Herring is the most important domestic fish in the oceans of the northern hemisphere. The North Sea is the most important herring fishing area, its annual catch being estimated at around 6 billion fish, although there are great fluctuations in the herring harvest from year to year and season to season.

Cod is second in world fish production, both in quantity and in value. This deep-water predator lives in an area reaching from the North Atlantic right to the Bay of Biscay and in North America to Cape Hatteras. Only a minute proportion of the cod catch is used fresh; most of it is dried or salted.

Unfortunately, in northern latitudes fishing has become mainly depredation; even so common a fish as the cod is beginning to get rarer off the coasts, and the International Council for the Exploration of the Sea is trying to get regulations accepted specifically to protect the fish of the northern hemisphere.

Ensuring the fish catch

If the catch is to get larger and more reliable, even deliberate and efficient "farming" (e.g., fertilizing), by which the biological output is improved, is not enough: unexploited fish populations must be brought within the reach of fishermen and the marketing potential of fish caught must be improved. Increasing attention has recently been given to the development of fishing techniques. Oceanographic and ecological research, and the study of fish biology and economy, are creating better conditions for the extension and intensification of commercial fishing.

Man is already utilizing the shallow coastal water zones to a depth of 600 to 800 feet. About 90 per cent of all fish and other sea products are caught in these waters. It is now time to utilize the waters of the continental slopes. The surface area of these regions, which go down to about 4,000 feet, is twice that of the shallows, yet at present only 3 or 4 per cent of all ocean catches come from these areas. The seas offer the main catch, and the conquest of deep waters for fish production has already got off to a good start. Soviet fishermen in the Far East, in particular, have had some excellent results.

Most of the species fished are at the end of the sea food chain; they form the final link before certain predatory fish, sea birds, seal, and man. As the "loss percentage" at each link of the chain is high, possibly around 90 per cent, it would be better for man to learn to eat animal plankton, like the whale, instead of fish, or even vegetable plankton and algae, as people do in Japan and Hawaii. Here, however, says the Finnish Professor Ilmo Hela, the outlook does not look promising; both the technical difficulties of catching such food and man's eating habits form serious obstacles.

A net 1930 feet long and 490 feet deep, developed a few years ago, which has usually brought up an eight to ten times bigger catch than other fishing tackle. The net is lowered to form a cylinder with a diameter of about 550 feet. When the bottom is drawn tight, the fish inside the net have no way out. This kind of net has been used in Norway to catch as much as eleven tons of herring at a time. The net costs $ 50,000.

Although it appears that fishing will still be the main branch of marine economy in the year 2000, it is estimated that its relative role will have dropped to about a third. Other material commodities from the sea will have made headway, particularly oil and gas drilled from the bowels of the sea bed.

Whale, seal and vegetation

Whale is also a valuable yield of the sea. Norway, Japan, Britain, the Soviet Union, and Holland are the leading whaling countries. Once the whale have been located and harpooned by the fast whaling ships, they are towed to the factory ship. Here they are cut up, the blubber separated and boiled into oil, the oil clarified and refined and stored in huge tanks — all mechanically and rapidly.

The fast rate at which these valuable sea giants are being hunted down threatens the species with extinction; since 1937 international conventions have attempted to restrict whaling. Many other species are also far too heavily fished. At the moment the annual whale catch comprises some 25,000–30,000 individuals. About 90 per cent of these are silver-bottomed whale and blue whale; the rest are humpbacks, pollack whale, and sperm whale. Blue whale are the largest of all living beasts. They are also the largest animals ever to live on this planet, including the gigantic monsters of some dozen million years ago. The average length of a mature blue whale is about 75 feet, but individuals up to 95 feet long and weighing around 150 tons have been caught.

The International Whaling Commission has a committee studying ways of harpooning whale that will reduce their suffering. In his book *Whales and Whalers*, Professor Budker writes: "Whale are dumb. If they could express their suffering and terror aloud proportionately to their size, there would certainly be few people whose nerves would be strong enough to withstand listening to the death cries of a harpooned whale."

Other economically valuable mammals are also hunted, particularly seal (otary, walrus, and seal proper). The hunting waters are in the Arctic, where rapacious hunting has severely reduced the populations.

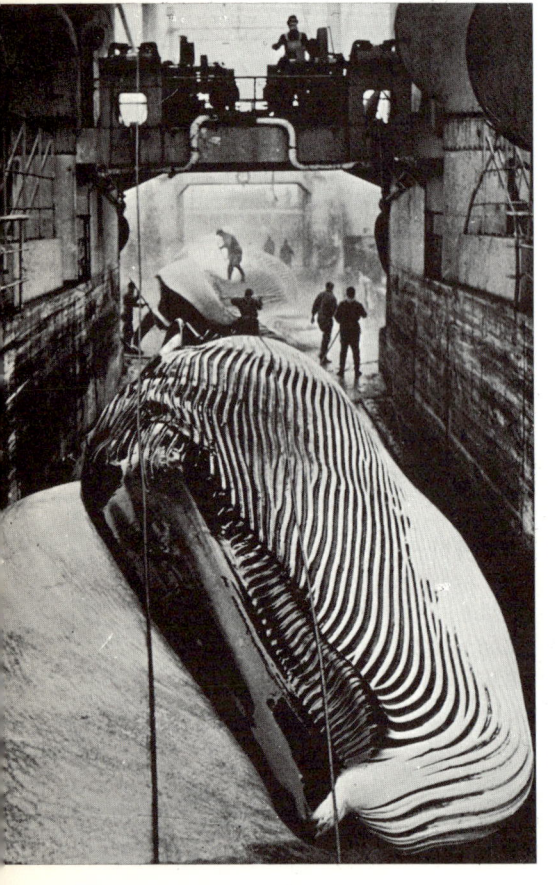

Although animal products hold by far the most important place in water economy output, man has begun to put the profuse vegetation of the seas to use as well. In 1964, this amounted to 560,000 tons, still a mere 1.1 per cent of the total output of our seas and waterways. The utilization of aquatic plants is as yet common only in Japan, which accounted for 65.5 per cent of that figure.

So far no way of utilizing economically the vegetable plankton floating in the surface levels of the seas has been found. Use of the larger seaweeds is also slight compared with the tremendous quantity available. In Japan, however, seaweed is of considerable significance as a food, and it is also an important raw material in certain branches of industry. Extracts made from seaweed include agar-agar jelly, and algines and alginates.

Sea salts, minerals, and metals

The third large group of products from the sea comprises salts, minerals, and metals. Over the ages nature and man have greatly reduced the mineral wealth concentrated in the soil, and through erosion, rivers and floods,

A huge whale meets its end in the factory ship of the whaling fleet.

volcanic eruptions, and even industry, large amounts have made their way into the sea. Marine plants and animals, although skillful chemists, have been able to utilize such minute quantities of these substances that human chemists were until quite recently unable even to demonstrate their existence.

The waters of the seas contain staggering quantities of dissolved components, particularly various nutritive salts. A simple evaporation test will show that a quart of sea water gives up about 1 ¼ ounces of salts and many other substances invisible to the eye.

Because of its salinity, sea water is heavier than fresh water. Since the specific gravity also depends on temperature (warm water is lighter than cold), horizontal bands of water form in the sea, in each of which the salinity and temperature remain almost constant. Thus the salinity of the Baltic is low because of the fresh water flowing into it from rivers. The excess water of the Baltic flows out through the Sound in a slightly saline surface current 10 to 30 feet thick which halts at the Swedish coast of the Kattegat, then spreads out to cover the more saline sea water pushing into the Baltic from the North Sea.

The total amount of the salts dissolved in sea water is so vast that if it were gathered together it would cover the entire surface of the land to a height of nearly 500 feet. By far the most usual of these sea salts is common salt, or sodium chloride. It is mainly found in the dry regions of the warm and subtropical belts where evaporation is so rapid that the water quickly leaves a layer of salt behind. Most sea salt is produced in artificial evaporation basins which are built on the shallow shores of the Mediterranean, India, China, Japan, California, etc.

Common salt is followed in order of prevalence by magnesium sulphate, calcium sulphate, and potassium sul phate. There are also several minerals and metals, even some precious ones. Huge amounts of nodules containing 25 to 30 per cent manganese, with some cobalt, copper, or nickel, have gathered on the bed of the ocean deeps. Hopefully it will soon be possible to mine these valuable natural resources.

The procedures and methods by which the natural wealth hidden away at the bottom of the sea can be raised and utilized present a number of problems. So far only salt, bromine, and magnesium are extracted from sea water—and even these only in small quantities. In future, simple and economically feasible methods of separating many metals directly from sea water must be developed. The separation of salts and minerals from sea water is purely a matter of profitability, and one which will become more practicable as land deposits gradually run dry and production costs shoot up.

An American atomic energy research establishment has invented a way of obtaining uranium in which at high tide huge quantities of water are dammed up in gigantic basins, which then empty during low tide. At the bottom of the basins, absorption layers made of insoluble titanic oxide precipitate the uranium. According to calculations this method will be more feasible than quarrying poor uranium ores. An electric power station and water purification plant could also be combined with this installation.

Another important task for scientists is to discover the processes by which plants and animals concentrate the many components of sea water. It will then in principle be possible to plan similar concentration plants to separate certain components from sea water. Atomic power will be of assistance here. Doctor Amasa Bishop, a scientist in the service of the United States Atomic Energy Commission, believes that the entire world's atomic energy needs could be met by means of the heavy hydrogen in sea water.

It must be remembered that the most important component of sea water, which man needs in increasing quantities every year, is water itself. A method combining the filtering and sweetening of salt water with the separation of elements would permit the simultaneous acquisition of fresh water for urban and agricultural use and various raw materials for the chemicals industry.

Oil — the most precious heritage of the ancient seas

The most precious of all the heritage of the ancient seas is oil, the petroleum that has become an increasingly important economic and strategic factor among the earth's raw materials in the last few decades. It is interesting that all the main deposits are close to ancient or present seas. Presumably remains of the marine animal and vegetable kingdom have floated down to the bottom over dozens or hundreds of millions of years, accumulated there in layer after layer, and under the influence of ever growing pressure and heat gradually turned into oil and gas.

Since it is estimated that world oil consumption will double in the next twenty years, present oil reserves will run dry before long, and new sources must be found. If the organic theory of origin is followed, oil and gas should be sought where there are remains of organic material in precipitated strata. According to another theory, however, oil is to be found where deep cracks have split the earth's crust. These cracks act as channels along which the hydrocarbons try to work their way upwards.

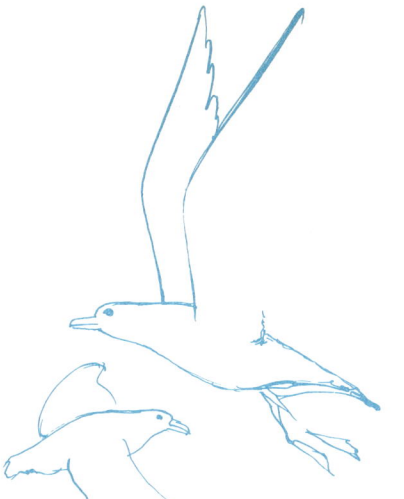

THE SEA FACE AND SPRING. For the sea as a whole, the alternation of day and night, the passage of the seasons, the procession of the years, are lost in its vastness, obliterated in its own changeless eternity. But the surface waters are different. The face of the sea is always changing. Crossed by colors, lights, and moving shadows, sparkling in the sun, mysterious in the twilight, its aspects and its moods vary hour by hour. The surface waters move with the tides, stir to the breath of the winds, and rise and fall to the endless, hurrying forms of the waves. Most of all, they change with the advance of the seasons....

In the sea, as on land, spring is a time for the renewal of life. During the long months of winter in the temperate zones the surface waters have been absorbing the cold. Now the heavy water begins to sink, slipping down and displacing the warmer layers below. Rich stores of minerals have been accumulating on the floor on the continental shelf—some freighted down the rivers from the lands; some derived from sea creatures that have died and whose remains have drifted down to the bottom.... And when in spring the waters are deeply stirred, the warm bottom water brings to the surface a rich supply of minerals, ready for use by new forms of life.

Rachel L. Carson

Oil geologists and the oil companies have recently shown interest in the sea bottom in their search for "black gold." Research and test drilling, calling for large-scale investment, are proceeding in the coastal areas of over sixty countries. Positive findings for oil and gas have already been obtained in the territorial waters of seventeen countries. Man already gets some 16 per cent of his oil and 6 per cent of his gas from strata below the sea.

As early as the 1880s, oil was found below the Pacific bed along the California coast. Drilling was then carried out at an angle from shore quays; a similar drilling method was used in the 1920s and 1930s on Lake Maracaibo, Venezuela, and on the coast of the Gulf of Mexico. Next oil companies learned to build drilling platforms. The first experiments with a floating drilling platform were in 1948, when the ship which formed the base for the drilling equipment was anchored firmly to the bottom. In 1964 the first semi-submersible drilling platform, taking 10,000 tons, was ready for action on the west coast of the United States. It permitted drilling at a depth of 650 feet, even in a 26-foot swell. Since then a more lightly constructed dynamic drilling base that does not need anchors at all has been devised. At the moment there are about fifty floating oil-drilling installations, all of them able to operate far from the shore. These have so far made over a hundred successful oil strikes. The deepest drilling was done at a depth of over 975 feet. Even so, underwater oil research and drilling is still only in its infancy.

Natural gas deposits are usually, though by no means always, found in connection with natural oil deposits. The search for oil in the North Sea was begun as long ago as 1955, but the Dutch discovery in 1959 of an extensive natural gas field at Groningen, right on the North Sea coast, turned the interest there to gas. In March 1967, North Sea gas was for the first time supplied to British homes and factories.

Wrecks and their treasures

It is not only the seas that hide the riches of nature. Man, too, has played a part in caching away ocean treasures; one has only to think of the countless ships that have gone down over the centuries in storms, sea battles, collisions, wrecks, explosions, and fires.

Men have always been fascinated by

SHIP LOSSES. The loss statistics for the world merchant marine in 1967 show the most depressing peacetime figures of all time. A total of 163 ships (at least 500 G.R.T.) with a combined capacity of 747,000 G.R.T. were completely lost. This total loss is some 140,000 G.R.T. above the last five years' average. Of the losses, 64 ran aground (c. 341,000 G.R.T.), the next largest group being destroyed by fire and explosions (32 losses, over 185,000 G.R.T.).

these wrecks, particularly if they are known or believed to contain valuable cargo. From the first wars of conquest on, the victors have always seized their victims' most valuable goods, their gold, silver, and other precious objects, often loading their ships to the brim with these treasures and cheerfully setting sail for home. The victor was not always allowed to enjoy his spoils however. Sometimes the ship fell into pirate hands, sometimes nature took her toll. If the ship was wrecked, she often went to the bottom, cargo and all. It is estimated that at least a quarter of all the gold that man has dug from rocks or washed from rivers has disappeared in this way.

The oldest wrecked ship ever found was lost over 3,000 years ago on the coast of Turkey near what is now the Gelidonia Peninsula. After careful and patient work, a superbly organized in-

The world's largest semi-submersible drilling platform *Sea Quest* (1966, Belfast) being towed into the North Sea for gas explorations. Each side of this triangular platform, ordered by BP, is over 300 feet long, and the top of the drilling tower is some 300 feet above the floats supporting the platform.

ternational expedition has successfully raised the largest single collection of Bronze Age ploughshares, hoes, spades, axes, awls, and knives that has ever been found. The divers even found olive stones and fish bones, the leftovers of meals eaten by seamen long ago.

The Spanish sailing ships that used to carry valuable cargo from the Americas, many of which are known to have sunk, have aroused the greatest ambitions of the treasure hunters. The American William Phips collected what is thought to have been the largest treasure found in a Spanish ship, in a wreck located in 1686 at Cape Cabron, Haiti, at a depth of almost fifty feet. The treasure trove weighed around 27 tons: barrels of gold and silver ingots, various objects in gold and silver, piles of coins and silver plate. The King of England was so satisfied with his tenth that he made the leader of the expedition a knight; thus an illiterate ex-cattlehand became a nobleman addressed as Sir William.

Our own times, too, have produced some adventurous treasure seekers. One of them is the Frenchman Alexandre Korganoff, who has for some time been making preparations for the "expedition of all time" to West Indian waters: he intends to find the valuable cargo carried by the Spanish galleon *Nuestra Señora de la Concepcion*, which sank in 1641. Between Cuba and Florida this treasure ship ran into a hurricane that almost swept her against the shore. Two seamen and a pile of silver ingots disappeared into the sea. The other sailors managed to free the sails trailing along aft of the ship, but the hold was full of water and even after the sea became calm, a broken rudder made it difficult to fix a course. The *Concepcion* was driven around near the Bahama Islands for thirty days; eventually it became impossible to avoid the submerged reefs, and disaster was

The sailing ship *Concepcion* in Havana harbor in 1641, according to an old drawing. The ship had sprung leaks on her way from Mexico to Cuba, and seamen are patching the worst places. Soon after this, the treasure ship, laden with gold and silver, sank on a coral reef off the Bahamas.

inevitable. The *Concepcion* was driven onto the reef and the sea took its toll: when she sank she took 324 men with her. Even so, almost two hundred men managed to make the nearby shore.

Great losses of ships and human life

There have been two disasters at sea in our own time in which the human loss was so great as to overshadow all other cases of shipwreck. When the British luxury liner *Titanic* hit an iceberg on her maiden voyage in the North Atlantic on April 15th, 1912, she took down with her 1,635 men, women, and children of the ship's total complement of 2,229. "The unsinkable ship," then the biggest (45,000 G.R.T.) and most luxurious passenger ship in the world, sank 2 hours and 40 minutes, after the tragic collision.

Though decades have gone by, this disaster and its details are still remembered well. On the other hand, there are probably few that remember the wreck of the American steamer *Eastland* off Chicago in 1915, when 1,810 people lost their lives—probably because it happened during World War I, when reports of shattering losses on the battlefield were an everyday occurrence.

Of the ships lost since the last war, one of the most horrifying collisions was that between two large passenger ships, the Italian vessel *Andrea Doria* and the Swedish vessel *Stockholm*, in fog off the island of Nantucket on the east coast of the United States on July 25, 1956. When she sank the following morning, the *Andrea Doria* took 54 people down with her to a depth of 230 feet. This ship, too, was supposed to be unsinkable: she had eleven watertight sections which were to help her "stay afloat whatever the emergency." There have been many plans for raising this luxurious ship and her valuable cargo (total value about seven million dollars), but so far the sea has kept its own. The deputy director of the Murphy Pacific Marine Salvage company, P.N. Oberle, has said of the *Andrea Doria* (29,083 G.R.T., length 900 feet): "Although so large a ship has never before been raised intact, no-one here thinks this impossible. In marine salvage the question is not of whether a particular job can be done, but of whether it is worth doing."

Increasing numbers of people—thanks to the many improvements made in diving equiment—have recently become interested in studying the treasures of days past hidden beneath the surface of the deep, even those at considerable depths. Discoveries made by chance in the Mediterranean, in particular, have given great impetus to this new branch of science—marine archaeology.

Posterity has been left little written information about ships lost in ancient times, but one example of such rare data relates to a ship from the island of Delos. She set off over 2,200 years ago with a cargo of Greek and Italian wines and ornamental table ware intended for aristocratic Roman families living in southern France. The ship was wrecked off Marseille. She was found in 1952 close to a tiny island, surrounded by coral growths, by the French deep-sea diver Commander Jacques-Yves Costeau. Over more than five years he and his assistants managed, with great pains, to raise 10,000 pieces of table ware and 5,000 wine flasks (amphora).

Ship finds in Scandinavian waters

The raising and renovation of the Swedish warship *Wasa* (displacement 1,400 tons, length 160 feet) is perhaps the most brilliant achievement of marine archaeology. To be able to put his great plans for North Europe into effect, King Gustavus II needed a strong navy and in January 1625 gave an order for the construction of four warships in Stockholm. One of them was the ill-fated *Wasa*. This warship, in her day perhaps intended to be the most mighty in the world, left Stockholm harbor on her maiden voyage on August 10, 1628, but after sailing only a short way fell victim to a sudden gust of wind and sank about a hundred yards south of Blekholmen. The discovery of the ship at a depth of 100 feet caused almost as great a sensation as her original loss. Several attempts were made to raise her over the years. In summer 1959 a serious start was made on the project, which involved numerous technical problems and great expense. It took three years to lift the ship from the mud, but in May 1961 this unique and surprisingly well-preserved piece of history was successfully raised. Thousands of centuries-old weapons, technical instruments, equipment, ornaments, etc., were found inside. This ship, of unique cultural and historical value, provides a complete seventeenth-century milieu and throws reliable detailed light on contemporary shipbuilding and life at sea. As the oldest ship in the world to be preserved in its original condition, the *Wasa* has been made into a museum which attracts vast crowds of visitors. The conservation and restoration of the ship, which is still going on, has called for quite exceptional care, patience, and new technical methods.

The oldest ships' hulks in Finnish waters are up to four hundred years old and well preserved. The Baltic basin is a thousand-year-old trading route, the scene of hundreds of major and thousands of minor sea battles and skirmishes. The trade route to the east has used the islands of the Finnish south coast as shelter for hundreds of years.

The Swedish warship *Wasa* has been raised from the depths and docked for restoration in Stockholm.

Ever since the Viking era men have sailed from Sweden to Tallinn (Reval), to the Turku archipelago via Åland, and along the coast to Porkkala, where the route turned south or continued east. The "shipwreck coast" was so popular because the destructive shipworm or molluscs Teredo and Bankia do not flourish in the only slightly saline waters of the Baltic.

No-one knows how many wrecks lie at the bottom in Finnish waters. Some hundred have been found that are over a century old. More are being found all the time, both on expeditions arranged by the Finnish Association of Sport Divers, and by fishermen's chance. Wrecks are to be found most frequently in the Turku archipelago and along the south coast. So far, the oldest wreck discoveries are late sixteenth century, judging by the objects found, for instance, in the badly deteriorated Crown schooner (discovered in summer 1966 near Medskär) and the wreck of a Swedish warship (autumn 1967 near Jussarö). Under an Act of 1963, the first of its kind in Scandinavia, all ships over a hundred years old found in Finnish territorial waters belong to the Archaeological Commission. Even so, private enterprise in this field—a modern form of piracy—has taken on new life in recent years.

Salvage work on a grounded ship, probably off Porkkala, Finland. Oil painting by Torsten Waenerberg, 1876.

The lack of salt-free water

The globe's stores of salt-free water are rather meagre—only 2.8 per cent of the total amount of water on earth —and territorially unevenly distributed. Even of this amount, some 2 per cent is useless, because it is in the form of icebergs and glaciers. The uneven distribution of salt-free water and the diversity of different countries' economic development level causes great differences in their populations' water utilization. Thus the people of developing countries might well use on an average only one five-thousandth of the amount used per capita in highly developed countries.

The United Nations has devoted serious attention to the shortage of fresh water that already prevails in various parts of the world. What has been called the "desert devil" is threatening to extend its kingdom, partly because of natural changes in climate, but also because man himself promotes dryness and the growing wastes, particularly by excessive forest felling.

The largest though by no means the only scapegoat that can be blamed for the deteriorating water situation is industry, which needs ever growing quantities. What is involved is the artificial alteration of the globe's natural hydrological state, a man-made equilibrium disturbance. River dams, artificial basins, vast waste water networks, poisonous chemicals, plant protectants, general ignorance, and even indifference are among the causes which began to change the natural hydrological cycle decades ago.

Water pollution and its prevention

Perhaps the most amazing example of man's irresponsibility is the pollution of springs, waterways, and seas — a serious universal problem. Water areas are generally, and sea areas traditionally, considered an all-consuming and all-embracing dump for unwanted rubbish.

Although international and national regulations forbid the release of waste oil into the sea, many ships do not observe the rules. The ill effects of such oil can be summarized as follows: (1) oil spoils the beaches and makes the shore unattractive; (2) it kills sea birds, fish, and other marine life; (3) it soils boats, fishing tackle, quays, etc.; (4) it may constitute a fire risk in harbors.

The wreck of the fully laden oil tanker *Torrey Canyon* (118,000 d.w.t.) off the southwest coast of England in 1967 was one of the most costly shipwrecks of all time and a major catastrophe: the foul flow of oil spread far along the Cornish coast and part of France. Later it appeared that the chemicals used to disperse the oil had managed to turn the oil into a harmless emulsion for only a few hours, which meant they added to the sum of damage and in the end caused much greater destruction than the oil itself. Extensive research is now going on to ensure that any similar situation will be handled better next time.

There has recently been more serious recognition of how vital are international collaboration and regulations to prevent excessive pollution. Some experts believe that the problem of water pollution can be solved by worldwide legislation. The most feasible solution, and the one that best suits the present stage of development, might well be a general administration of water reserves that reaches beyond national frontiers.

One of the results of the loss of the *Titanic* was the institution of an international ice patrol service, which has operated with great success. The wreck of the *Torrey Canyon* and all the consequent damage have prompted the IMCO (an intergovernmental consultative maritime organization) to work for an international agreement aimed at suitable procedures to prevent sea pollution caused by oil and other harmful substances.

Our coastal regions must also be made safe from the ill effects of urban and industrial waste, which are in many cases already visible. The sea is of course to some extent able to cope with waste, but research is needed on its "absorption limit," on suitable areas for discharging urban waste, and so on.

The dumping of radioactive wastes has created a new geographical problem since nuclear energy plants began to be built in various countries, mainly at estuaries and near coastal gulfs. Atomic pollution is being dumped in the ocean; sea water is being spoiled by the radioactive materials produced during nuclear tests. Our intellectually highly developed generation, with revolutionary technical devices and methods at its disposal, bears a heavier responsibility for our planet to history and to posterity than any earlier generation.

Bibliography

Audemard, L.: Histoire de la jonque. Rotterdam 1957.
Beck, Stuart E.: The Ship — How She Works. Southampton 1955.
Benson, Richard M.: Steamships and Motorships of the West Coast. Seattle, Wash. 1968.
Bowen, Frank C.: Ships for All. London 1950.
British Passenger Liners of the Five Oceans. London 1963.
Carson, Rachel L.: The Sea Around Us.
Casson, Lionel: Illustrated History of Ships & Boats, Garden City, N. J. 1964.
Chapelle, Howard I.: The Pioneer Steamship Savannah. Washington, D. C. 1961.
Clark, William R.: Explorers of the World. London.
Dodman, Frank E.: The Observer's Book of Ships. London 1961.
Dugan, James: The Great Iron Ship. New York 1953.
Ferguson, Eugene S.: John Ericson and the Age of Caloric, Washington D. C. 1961.
Flexner, James Thomas: Inventors in Action. The Story of the Steamboat. New York, N. Y. 1944.
Gaskell, T. F.: World Beneath Oceans. London 1964.
Gibbs, Jim: West Coast Windjammers. Seattle, Wash. 1968.
Guttmann, Henry: Die Weltwirtschaft und Ihre Rohstoffe. Berlin 1956.
Hambleton, F. C.: Famous Paddle Steamers. London 1948.
Hamlyn, Paul: Ships. London 1963.
Hansa, 100 Jahre Schiffahrt, Schiffbau, Häfen. Hamburg 1964.
Hardy, A. C.: The Book of the Ship. London 1951.
Harnack, Edwin P.: All about Ships & Shipping. London 1964.

Heyerdahl, Thor: Kon-Tiki. 1948.
Humlum, Johannes: Oversøiske transportproblemer. København 1943.
Högbom, Ivar: Världssjöfarten. Stockholm 1934.
Kerchove, René de: International Maritime Dictionary. New York 1948.
Landström, Björn: The Ship. London 1961.
Lane, Carl D.: American Paddle Steam Boats. New York 1943.
Leithäuser, Joachim G.: Weltweite Seefahrt. Würtzburg 1965.
Lloyd's Register of Shipping. Statistical Tables 1969. Crawley 1969.
Martinez-Hidalgo, José Maria: Columbus Ships. Barre, Mass. 1966.
Medawar, P. B.: The Future of Man. London 1959.
Newell, Gordon: Ocean Liners of the 20th Century. Seattle, Wash. 1963.
New York Port Handbook, 10th Anniversary. New York 1968.
Norske Veritas, Det, 1864—1964. Oslo 1964.
Nour, Mohammed Zaki and others: The Cheops Boats. Part I. Cairo 1960.
Obst, Erich: Allgemeine Wirtschafts- und Verkehrsgeographie, Lehrbuch der Allgemeinen Geographie VII, Dritte Auflage. Berlin 1965.
Odell, Carol: A Liner goes to Sea. Sydney 1969.
Ommanney, Francis D. and the Editors of Life: The Fishes. 1963.
Parker, H. — Bowen, F. C.: Mail and Passenger Steamships of the 19th Century. London 1928.
Patrone, Giacomo: Antichi Modelli Navali Italiani. Roma 1961.
Penry-Jones, J.: The Burke Book of Ships and Shipping. London 1965.

Pohjanpalo, Jorma: Finland som sjöfartsnation. Helsingfors 1968.
Preble, G. H.: Origin and Development of Steam Navigation. Philadelphia 1895.
Salonen, Armas: Die Wasserfahrzeuge in Babylonien. Studia Orientalis, Vol. VIII. 4. Helsinki 1939.
Siegfried, André: The Mediterranean. London 1949.
Sjøvolt, Thorseif: The Oseberg Einds and the other Viking Ship Einds. Oslo 1957.
Smith, E. W.: Passenger Ships of the World. Boston 1963.
Spratt, H. P.: Outline History of Transatlantic Steam Navigation. London 1950.
Stewart, Peter: The Beauty of Ships. London 1963.
Suez Canal Report 1965. Ismailia 1966.
Szymanski, Hans: Die alte Dampfschiffahrt in Niedersachsen. Hannover 1958.
Torr, Cecil: Ancient Ships. Chicago 1964.
Wenzel, Heinz: Mare Aeternum. Leipzig 1969.
Wettbewerb in der Seeschiffahrt. Verkehrswissenschaftliche Verhandlungen, Heft 9. Jena 1940.
Villiers, Alan and others: Men, Ships and the Sea. Washington, D. C. 1963.
Woytinsky, Wl.: Die Welt in Zahlen. Fünftes Buch. Handel und Verkehr. Berlin 1927.
Åkerlund, Harald: Fartygsfynden i den forna hamnen i Kalmar. Uppsala 1951.
Nydamskeppen. Göteborg 1963.

Index

The names of the ships have been set in *italics*.

Aegean Sea 42
Air traffic 179, 180
Ambrose light station 234
America, discovery of 78—87
American Charger 184
American Racer 269
Amerigo Vespucci 86
Andrea Doria 297
Antarctica 99
Antilles 169
Antwerp, port of 239
Arab seafaring 59
Atlantic 9, 11, 91, 223
Atlantic Container Line 237
Atlantic Ridge 278
Atlantis 280
Atomic ship 145-154
Auguste Piccard 265
Auris 144
Automation, of ships 268
Autotrophic life 14
Average depth, of sea 277
Average size, of merchant ships 256
Baltic and International Maritime Conference 254
Barbary States 103
Bark craft 31, 32
Bergehus 141, 143
Birka 69
Bjarni Herjulfson 81
Black Ball Line 132, 158, 159
Blue Ribbon of the Atlantic 142, 163, 164, 165, 177

Boat 31, 32, 33
Brandanus 80
Bremen 167
British Queen Steam Navigation Company 160
British seafaring 96
Bulk carrier 183, 185
Canberra 169
Cargo handling 229—231
Cargo ships 181— 198
Carrying capacity 155
Carthage 54, 55, 219
Carvel-built ship 58
Castle 72
Catamaran 26, 259—260
Challenger 273
Chart 75
Charter traffic 250
Chinese seafaring 60, 78
Classification body 211
Clermont 117—120
Clinker-built ship 58
Clipper 129—132
Coastal traffic 42
Cog 72
Columbus 78, 84, 85
Combustion engine 136
Comet 120, 121
Compagnie Générale Transatlantique 168, 173
Compass 75, 175
Composite ship 129
Compound engine 126
Conference 254
Container traffic 185—190
Continental drift theory 13
Cook, James 97

Copenhagen, port of 242
Coracle 26
Cretan seafaring 51—52
Cretans 37
Cunard Line 161, 168
Cutty Sark 132
Deadweight tonnage 155
Deep-sea diving 274, 287
Diesel, Rudolf 139
Diesel engine 139, 140
Discovery, great voyages of 7, 90, 91
Displacement 155
Distances from the port of London 238
Dock 221, 224, 237—238, 241, 242
Drilling platform 295
Dugout 29, 30, 31, 32, 33, 65
Dutch East India Trading Company 92
Dutch seafaring 92
Earth, formation of 11
Echo-sounding 274, 277
Efficiency ratio 141
Egyptian water traffic 43
Emigrants 165, 166
English channel 192
Enterprise 148, 153
Ericson, Leif 82, 86
Erosion 14
Esso Flame 195
Europort plan 232
Figurehead 93
Finlandia 191
Fish 16, 288
Fishing tackle 53
Fitch, John 111, 113, 114

Flag 161
Flags, of merchant ships 223
Floating, of a ship 215
Forwarding agent 252
Fossils 14
France 171
Free-board 196
Freedom of the seas 95
Free port 227
Freight markets 253
Freights and freighting 246, 253—254
Frisians 59, 70
Fulton, Robert 115—120
Galathea expedition 274
Galley 102
Gas turbine ship 144
General cargo ship 182
General H. H. Arnold 273
Glückauf 191, 194
Gokstad ship 66—67
Gondwana continent 13
Gotland 64, 72
Gotland petroglyphs 65
Great Britain 200
Great Eastern 126, 201, 273
Great Republic 131
Great Western 160
Greek seafaring 56
Gromman Dolphin 263
Guffa 26
Gulf Stream 276
Gyrocompass 175
Hamburg, port of 240
Hanseatic League 71
Harbor 219—245
Harmaja lighthouse 231
Henry Ford II 188
Hercules 134
Herzogin Cecilie 135
Heyerdahl, Thor 33, 283
Hide boat 32, 64—65
Hollowed-out craft 29

Homo sapiens 20
Hongkong 244
Horsepower 205
Hovercraft 263, 265
Hydrofoil 262
Ice 19
Ice Age 19
Icebreaker 138, 197
Idemitsu Maru 193
Ilmarinen 123
Imperator 165, 166
Indian Ocean 9, 71, 89
Intelligence ship 145
Iron ship 128, 132, 200
Japanese shipbuilding 205
Kaiser, Henry J. 210
Kayak 33
Keel 65
Kelek 26
Kiel Canal 156
Knot 128
Kon-Tiki 33, 50
Kungsholm 173
Lateen sail 37
Launching 213, 214
Lebanon 47
Lenin 151
Liberty ship 193, 210
Lighthouse 74—75, 170
Liner traffic 113, 157, 249
Liner traffic agents 249
Lizards 16
Load line 196
London, port of 236
Lübeck 72
Magellan, Ferdinand 87
Makurru 48
Malaysian seafaring 50
Mammals 16
Man 7, 17—22
Mare nostrum 58
Maritime canal 154—157
Maritime insurance 254
Mask painting 103

Mast 62
Matti Kurki 203
Mauretania 144, 165, 167
Medieval trade 70—73
Mediterranean 41, 244
Mediterranean seafaring, medieval 60
Merchant crew 182
Merchant marine, of the world 96, 97, 120, 125, 186, 203
Mermaid 43
Metals, of the sea 290
Michelangelo 172, 173
Minerals, of the sea 290
Monsoon winds 89
Monterey 178
Moorsom system 155
Motor ship traffic 141
Multipacket system 261
Nauru island 251
Nautical mile 128
Nautilus 150
Navigation 73
New York, port of 232
Noah's ark 49
Non-saline water 300
Norddeutscher Lloyd 167
Nordenskiöld, A. E. 90, 98
Normandie 168
North Atlantic passenger traffic 179
North Atlantic weather service 136
Northeast channel 90
North Sea traffic 221
Northwest channel 98
Nuclear energy, see atomic power
Oar 28
Obelisk 44
Oceania 97
Oceanographic Research, Finnish Institute of 277

Index

Oceanography 272
Oceans 9—13
Oicoumenē 41
Oil 292
Oil heating 127
Oil, natural 136
Oil transportation 190, 256
Origins of life 13—15
Oseberg ship 66
Ostia 219
Otto Hahn 149, 152
Outrigger 26, 35
Owen, Samuel 120—121
Packet 158
Paddle 28
Paddle steamer 107
Panama canal 156
Panting phenomenon 259
Parsons, Charles 142
Passenger ships 158—180
Passenger traffic 166, 180
Periplus 37, 54
Pharos lighthouse 74
Phoenician seafaring 52
Photosynthesis 14
Pillars of Hercules 56
Piracy 43, 71, 103
Plimsoll mark 196
Poles 280
Pollution, of water 301
Polynesian seafaring 50
Pommern 134
Population, of globe 270
Portolano 37
Portuguese seafaring 77, 88
Power concepts 205
Preussen 132
Primeval man 18
Primitive seafaring 41
Punt, land of 47
Pytheas 57
Quay installations 228

Queen Elizabeth 171, 175, 176
Queen Elizabeth 2 177
Queen Mary 168, 171, 174
Quppu 26
Ra 33
Radar 175
Radio-carbon dating 55
Raffaello 173
Raft 25, 29, 43
Raketa 262
Redoutable, Le 149
Reed vessel 32, also under Ra
Registered ton 155
Rex 168
Rhine 94
Rigging 105
Roman seafaring 58
Rotor ship 135
Rotterdam, port of 231
Rowed craft 102
Royal William 160
Rudder 62
Sail 34, 35, 62
Sailing, main routes 104
Sailing ship 36
Sailing ship, crew 104
Sailing skill 35
Salts, sea 290
Sampo 209
Santa Maria 84, 85
Savannah 152, 158
Scandinavian seafaring 63
Screw 122—124
Sea barge 261
Sea battles 7
Sea chart 75, 86
Seafaring, forms of 246
Seafaring organizations, Finnish 247
Sea fishing 286—289
Sea freights 253
Sea Palace 259

Sea Quest 295
Sea route to India 77
Sea transports, of the world 181, 183
Sea water, transparency of 15
Selandia 141
Shipbuilding, ancient 44, 47, 51, 53, 58, 62, 65, 72, 78, 94
Shipbuilding industry 203
Shipbuilding, modern 127, 199—218, 259
Shipbuilding techniques 106, 193, 199—218
Ship losses 294
Shipping register 250
Shipyard 207
Singapore, port of 244
Sirena 262
Sirius 160
Slave trade 103, 104
Soviet ports 244
Spanish seafaring 88, 89
Specialized traffic 250
Square sail 36
St. Lawrence Seaway 157
Standard displacement 155
Steam as power source 108, 125, 145
Steam engine 109—112, 124, 125
Steam turbine 142, 144
Steel ship 128, 203
Stevedore 252
Stevedoring 228
Stevens, John 115
Stockholmshäxan 121
Subcontractor 207
Submarine seafaring 265
Suez canal 132, 154—156
Suez route 244
Sumerian shipbuilding 48

Suomen Joutsen 137
Tanker 143, 183, 190—198, 258— 259
Tarshish 52
Telenaut 281
Thule 58
Tonnage 155
Tonnage, see merchant marine
Tool 23
Torrey Canyon 258, 301
Trade winds 89
Tramp traffic 246
Turbine ship 142
Turbinia 142, 144
Umiak 31
United States 176
Universe Apollo 193
Universe Ireland 143, 194
Valiant 151

Vandal 140
Vasco da Gama 87—88
Vasco Nunez de Balboa 87
Venetian merchant marine 61
Viking seafaring 68
Viking ships 64, 65—68
Vikings 63— 64, 66— 70, 74
Vinland 82
Visby 72
Volga-Baltic waterway 249
Warship 61, 102
Wasa 299
Water 7, 9, 14, 21, 22, 300—301
Water consumption, Finnish 302

Water, quantity of in Finnish lakes 302, in oceans 9
Water transport, cheapness 269
Water transport, means of 25—33
Water transports, European 260
Watt, James 109
Whaling 289
White Star Line 166
Wind 89
Winter ship type 197, 217
Wooden ship 65
Wrecking 71
Wrecks 294
Yachting 114
Öland 64

Main